CLAUDE SIMON
NEW DIRECTIONS

CLAUDE SIMON
NEW DIRECTIONS
Collected Papers

———◆———

edited by
Alastair B. Duncan

SCOTTISH ACADEMIC PRESS
EDINBURGH

Published by
Scottish Academic Press Ltd,
33 Montgomery Street
Edinburgh EH7 5JX

SBN 7073 0419 9

© 1985 Scottish Academic Press Ltd

Printed in Great Britain by
Lindsay & Co. Ltd., Edinburgh

Contents

Preface

For a novelist who has several times come close to winning the Nobel Prize for Literature, Claude Simon is remarkably little known in the English-speaking world. To give a taste of Simon this book includes, in English translation, a recent interview with him and a hitherto unpublished fragment of the novel on which he is now working. New readers may find it helpful to move next to Stuart Sykes's review of the critical literature which Simon's novels have engendered. Unfortunately, anyone who acquires a taste for Simon by reading this volume will have to satisfy it largely in libraries since few of his novels are in print in English. *Les Géorgiques*, however, will shortly be available; one of our contributors, John Fletcher, has been commissioned to translate it.

This book owes its title in the first place to Claude Simon himself. From *Le Tricheur* in 1945 to *Les Géorgiques* in 1981, each of his thirteen novels has grown out of the one before, both continuing and criticizing his previous work. All Simon's novels are about how human beings try to impose themselves on a world without order or meaning; man is the unwilling victim of what Simon calls History. But though these victims are always versions of Simon and his family, though History repeatedly manifests itself in war and revolution, both victims and History have changed as Simon has written about them. In the forties and early fifties Simon told stories which illustrated that unequal contest: luckless characters struggled in vain to shape their lives or at least glimpse a pattern in chaotic events. By the late 1950's the conflict had moved to another battle-ground. What can we know about others or the past since all knowledge is partial, memories fragmentary? From *Le Vent* in 1957 to *Histoire* in 1967 shadowy narrators reconstruct events which, though vivid in detail, blur and fade into one another at the edges, erasing the contours of plot, character, and chronological time. In the late 1960's the ground shifts again: language itself becomes the issue. Is History anything more than patterns traced fleetingly in language by beings who are themselves moulded by the language they seek to use? *La Bataille de Pharsale, Les Corps conducteurs, Triptyque* and *Leçon de choses* repeatedly break the illusion of reality which fiction, imitating History, traditionally provides. These novels begin from simple descriptions. They develop by elaborating the associations of key words and situations, and thus seem to take shape during the time it takes to read them. Finally, for the moment at least, Simon has come back to story-telling. *Les Géorgiques* is a historical novel which questions the writing of History by telling three parallel, interweaving stories, each of which is retold from elsewhere: Simon's own experiences of Spain and of the Second World War, told in *Le Palace* and *La Route des Flandres*; the adventures of a Revolutionary general, an ancestor of Simon's, garnered from letters and journals; Orwell's account of Spain in *Homage to Catalonia*.

The contributors to this volume were invited to open new perspectives on Simon's work. Their essays were to be exploratory, to raise issues rather than resolve them. In some cases this has involved using critical methods which are themselves relatively new, for example Celia Britton's use of Lacan or Anthony Pugh's blend of historiography with deconstructive theory. Elsewhere, for instance in Jean Duffy's account of textual changes between different published versions of the same material, a traditional method is used to illuminate Simon in a new way. Eclecticism is indeed one of the hallmarks of this collection: the British remain very British, and perhaps nowhere more so than in the French Departments of British universities to which all the contributors are, or have been, attached. Some are students, some teachers, some have moved from one category to the other since this volume was first mooted.

The essays are arranged in broadly chronological order according to the publication dates of the novels with which they deal. The emphasis falls on Simon's more recent work. Three essays, strikingly varied in approach, are devoted to *Les Géorgiques*, and one, by Mary Orr, to Simon's most recent publication, a short text previously published as *Femmes* but reissued in a new format and with a new title in 1983. It follows from this manner of arrangement that varying critical methods lie cheek by jowl, amicably enough for the most part; but the attentive reader — to his delight, I hope — will occasionally catch the hint of a snarl or the gleam of a fang.

I should like to express my thanks: to the Editions de Minuit for permission to quote from Simon's novels; to my wife, to my colleague Bernard Swift, to my father, Eric Duncan, and to a classful of honours students at Stirling University, all of whom helped polish my rough and

PREFACE

ready translations; to the French Department of Stirling University and the Carnegie Trust for the Universities of Scotland for financial assistance which has made publication of this volume possible; and above all to Claude Simon and my academic friends and colleagues for agreeing to contribute to the volume and for waiting so patiently for it to appear.

A<small>LASTAIR</small> B. D<small>UNCAN</small>

Abbreviations

The following abbreviations for Simon's works are used throughout. All references are to the first Minuit or Calmann-Lévy editions.

LT   *Le Tricheur* (1945)

CR   *La Corde raide* (autobiographical fragment, 1947)

G   *Gulliver* (1952)

SP   *Le Sacre du printemps* (1954)

V   *Le Vent* (1957)

L'H   *L'Herbe* (1958)

RF   *La Route des Flandres* (1960)

P   *Le Palace* (1962)

H   *Histoire* (1967)

BP   *La Bataille de Pharsale* (1969)

OA   *Orion aveugle* (text accompanying 20 plates of paintings, sketches and photographs, 1970)

CC   *Les Corps conducteurs* (1971)

T   *Triptyque* (1973)

LC   *Leçon de choses* (1976)

LesG   *Les Géorgiques* (1981)

Fragment

Fragment

Claude Simon

. . . de même que lorsqu'ils commencèrent à croiser les premiers débris des troupes en retraite, avec leurs officiers aux visages sombres, les hommes exténués, poussiéreux, aux regards hébétés, ce fut seulement de ce même air soucieux, attentif mais réservé, sinon sévère, dissimulant avec peine un mépris de professionnels à l'égard d'amateurs, qu'ils écoutèrent les rapports des gradés, cachant de leur mieux leur agacement, leur impatience, jusqu'à ce que le dernier blessé se fût éloigné en traînant la jambe, que les derniers tirailleurs lâchant un dernier coup de feu puis se remettant à courir eurent disparu (la rue du village soudain vide, déserte: pas comme peut être vide ou déserte la rue d'un village un dimanche après-midi ou à l'heure des travaux des champs, mais ce désert, ce vide, cet aspect insolite, menaçant et solennel que présentent une rue, une colline, un pont, un simple boqueteau avant la bataille) et que presque aussitôt, sans clairons ni clameurs, leur arrivât dessus quelque chose qui ne ressemblait ni à une charge ni à rien de ce qu'ils avaient pu apprendre dans les livres ou sur le terrain, que ce fût dans un fortin de pierres sèches, sur les digues des rizières ou sous les remparts de quelque Palais Impérial, c'est-à-dire simplement un mur ou plutôt une muraille de feu qui avançait lentement, paisiblement en quelque sorte, mais inexorablement, avec seulement de brefs arrêts si elle recontrait quelque obstacle, le temps de l'anéantir et de le digérer, puis reprenait sa marche.

Parvenu le 22 août au village de Jamoigne-les-Belles, en Belgique, le régiment perdit dans la seule journée du 24 onze officiers et cinq cent quarante-six hommes sur un effectif total de quarante-quatre officiers et trois mille hommes. Après s'être replié pendant les journées du 25 et du 26, il reçut l'ordre de se déployer à la lisière de la forêt de Jaulnay où, au cours du combat qu'il livra le 27, les pertes s'élevèrent à neuf officiers et cinq cent cinquante-deux hommes. Lorsque quatre semaines plus tard, le corpulent général aux moustaches de jardinier parvint à arrêter et

Fragment

Claude Simon

. . . similarly when they began to meet the first broken remnants of retreating troops, with their sombre-faced officers, the men dead-beat, dusty, vacant-eyed, it was with no more than this same expression, concerned, attentive but reserved, if not severe, disguising with difficulty the scorn of professionals for amateurs, that they listened to the reports of the N.C.O.s, concealing their irritation and impatience as best they could, until the last wounded man had limped off, the last of the sharpshooters had disappeared, firing a last round then breaking into a run again (the village street suddenly empty, deserted: not as a village street can be empty or deserted on a Sunday afternoon or when the fields are being worked, but the abandoned emptiness, the uncanny, threatening, solemn aspect of a street, a hill, a bridge, an ordinary copse before the battle begins), until almost immediately, with neither cry nor bugle-call, something fell upon them which was unlike a charge, unlike anything they had ever learned from books or from experience, whether in a small dry-stone fort, on the dykes of the paddy fields or beneath the battlements of some Imperial Palace, but simply a wall or rather a rampart of fire which moved forward slowly, almost tranquilly, but inexorably, halting briefly if it met some obstacle, just long enough to destroy and digest it, then resumed its advance.

Having reached the village of Jamoigne-les-Belles in Belgium on the twenty-second of August, on the single day of the twenty-fourth the regiment lost eleven officers and five hundred and forty-six men from a total complement of forty-four officers and three thousand men. After falling back throughout the twenty-fifth and twenty-sixth, it was ordered to deploy along the edge of the Forest of Jaulnay where, during the battle fought on the twenty-seventh, losses amounted to nine officers and five hundred and fifty-two men. Four weeks later when the portly general moustached like a gardener successfully halted and even in some places

même, en certains endroits, à faire reculer la muraille de feu (passant la majeure partie de ce temps à dormir, ne se réveillant que pour se faire lire les dépêches, contempler un moment la carte, s'enquérir des réserves, donner ses ordres et se rendormir), il ne restait pratiquement plus un seul, y compris le colonel lui-même, de ceux qui, officiers ou hommes de troupe, avaient par un étouffant après-midi d'août et sous les acclamations de la foule traversé la ville où le régiment tenait garnison pour se rendre à la gare et embarquer dans le train qui devait les conduire vers la frontière, sortant de la citadelle, franchissant entre les quatre colosses de pierre la porte de la muraille construite par Charles-Quint, suivant les étroites ruelles de la ville haute, passant devant les vieux hôtels de briques, la halle médiévale, les cafés aux terrasses fleuries d'hortensias en caisses et décorés de femmes-iris, le balcon du Cercle où les vieux messieurs arrachés pour un moment à leurs tables de bridge et à leurs rocking-chairs applaudissaient de leurs mains parcheminées, leurs faibles voix couvertes par les vivats aigus des cocottes décolletées penchées à leurs côtés, offrant comme dans des corbeilles leurs seins éblouissants, leurs lèvres ouvertes sur les humides grottes roses de leurs bouches aux dents éblouissantes, et jetant des fleurs.

Sur la soie du drapeau préservé à travers les combats (à la faveur d'une contre-attaque, une poignée d'audacieux avait même réussi à s'emparer d'un drapeau ennemi) le Chef de l'Etat ordonna par décret que serait épinglée la plus haute décoration qui pût être attribuée. La cérémonie eut lieu un peu plus tard, comme octobre finissait, à l'arrière du front, sur le plateau de Valmy où devant un ciel gris se découpait en noir la statue du général qui cent-vingt ans auparavant avait mis en déroute au même endroit une armée d'envahisseurs. Il tombait une petite pluie, et le vent d'automne qui balayait en rafales l'esplanade dénudée faisait claquer avec un bruit de soie mouillée les drapeaux des autres régiments du corps d'armée envoyés en délégation, leurs hampes obliques oscillant par à-coups, difficilement maintenues par leurs porteurs au garde-à-vous, la main gauche posée à hauteur de la cuisse sur la coquille du sabre dont le fourreau rigide s'étirait derrière eux, les officiers supérieurs au garde-à-vous également, les lames luisantes de leurs sabres dégainés et verticaux à hauteur de leurs visages, les jugulaires des képis coupant leurs mentons, leurs éperons aux talons des bottes luisantes et noires jetant dans l'herbe détrempée des éclats d'argent, comme des sortes d'échassiers, d'oiseaux bizarres, cambrés, rigides, à la fois rogues, sévères et fragiles. Sur le front des délégations alignées en carré et qui barraient l'horizon de lignes sombres se tenaient

turned back the rampart of fire (spending the greater part of this time
asleep, waking only to have the dispatches read to him, to study the map
for a moment or two, enquire about the reserves, give his orders and go
back to sleep), next to none remained, not even the colonel, of the officers
and other ranks who, on a stifling August afternoon, had been acclaimed
by cheering crowds as the regiment made its way through the town where
it was garrisoned towards the station and the train which was to take it
to the frontier, marching out of the citadel, between the four giant
statues at the gate in the ramparts built by the Emperor Charles the
Fifth, through the narrow wynds at the top of the town, past the old
brick-built town-houses, the medieval market hall, the cafés and their
terraces bright with hydrangeas in flower-boxes and decorated with
painted figures of iris-like women, past the balcony of the Club where
the old gentlemen, torn momentarily from their bridge tables and
rocking-chairs, clapped their shrivelled hands, their thin voices drowned
by the shrill hurrahs of the courtesans leaning forward beside them in
low-cut dresses, offering their dazzling breasts as if in baskets, their open
lips revealing the moist pink grottos of their mouths with dazzling teeth,
and throwing flowers.

On the silk flag carried safely through the fighting (thanks to a
counter-attack a bold handful of men had even managed to capture an
enemy colour) the Head of State directed by decree that the highest
awardable decoration should be pinned. The ceremony took place a short
time later, at the close of October, behind the front-lines, on the plateau
of Valmy, where, etched black against a gray sky, stood the statue of the
general who at the same spot a hundred and twenty years before had put
to flight an army of invaders. A fine rain was falling and the autumn
wind, gusting over the bare esplanade, caught the flags representing the
other regiments in the same army corps and set them flapping with a
slap of wet silk, the slanting flag-staves jerking to and fro, their bearers
standing to attention, straining to hold them aloft, left hands at thigh
level on their sabre guards, scabbards stretched stiffly behind them, the
senior officers also at attention, the gleaming blades of their sabres held
unsheathed and upright at head height, kepi straps cutting their chins,
spurs at the heels of their gleaming black boots glinting silver in the
sodden grass, like varieties of wader, strange, stiff birds, with arched
backs, at once haughty, stern and fragile. The detachments were drawn
up in squares, barring the horizon with dark lines, while in the van,

les généraux de brigades et de divisions, rigides eux aussi, un peu tassés sur leurs chevaux, semblables, avec leurs hauts képis, leurs corps épaissis, le pur-sang arabe à la robe blanche et à la longue crinière que l'un d'eux écrasait sous son poids, leur escorte d'ordonnances en tenue de goumiers, le fusil en bandoulière et montées sur des chevaux de rebut, à quelques seigneurs de la guerre, barbares, sortis tout droit des profondeurs de l'Histoire ou du fond de quelques steppes (eux qui, dans leur jeunesse, avaient parcouru en combattant les continents d'Asie et d'Afrique), moustachus, boudinés dans des uniformes de théâtre et couverts de dorures. Au-dessus du groupe des cavaliers, le soldat de bronze continuait à élever vers le ciel son épée, impassible sous la pluie, la bouche ouverte, poussant son cri de bronze, figé, avec son bicorne et sa redingote de bronze, dans une attitude d'élan, d'enthousiasme et d'immortalité. Le vent qui continuait à faire claquer les drapeaux agitait par saccades un petit arbre bizarrement isolé, poussé là sans raison (ou peut-être récemment planté — ce qui expliquait qu'on ne l'eût pas rasé pour la cérémonie — par quelque comité patriotique), à peine plus haut qu'un homme, comme on en voit dans les pépinières ou bordant les terrains vagues, dépouillé par l'automne, terminé par une maigre fourche, comme dessiné d'un trait de plume tremblotê, pareil à une lézarde, une fissure dans le ciel pluvieux. A côté se découpait la forme massive du général commandant l'armée. Descendu de l'automobile qui l'avait amené, indifférent à la pluie, aux bourrasques qui faisaient flotter sa pèlerine, s'engouffraient dans sa longue houppelande noire, il était debout en avant des porte-étendards. Très droit, une de ses mains gantées de blanc posée sur le pommeau de sa canne et la tête tournée légèrement vers la droite, il regardait au centre de l'immense carré formé par les troupes le porte-drapeau du régiment anéanti.

C'était un sous-officier d'aspect malingre, tout petit et solitaire, à la silhouette bosselée par les cartouchières qui enflaient sa taille, sa capote relevée par derrière en queue-de-pie. Contrairement aux autres drapeaux que le vent continuait à tordre sauvagement, celui qu'il présentait pendait immobile, soit que l'eau de pluie l'eût alourdi (il y avait longtemps, bien avant l'arrivée du général, que son porteur avait pris position), soit qu'il eût été lesté de quelque façon en vue de la cérémonie. Quoiqu'il hurlât à tue-tête, la voix de l'officier qui lisait la citation à l'ordre de l'armée parvenait affaiblie, ténue, à travers les rafales et les claquements mouillés des autres étendards, comme une voix d'enfant, lointaine, un peu irréelle. Lorsqu'elle se fut tue, un clairon sortit du carré que formait la clique en avant des rangs, s'avança de quelques pas. Dans un bref scintillement de cuivre, il fit tournoyer

stockstill as the rest, slightly sunk over their horses, sat the brigadiers and the major generals, reminiscent — with their high kepis, their thickening bodies, the white, long-maned arab thoroughbred which one of them was crushing beneath him, their escort of orderlies in the uniform of African auxiliaries, rifles slung over their shoulders and mounted on cast-offs — of barbarian war-lords, issuing straight from the depths of History or from far-off steppes (men who in their youth had fought their way over the continents of Asia and Africa), moustached, crammed into theatrical uniforms, dripping with gold braid. Above the group of mounted men the bronze soldier still raised his sword to the sky, impassive under the rain, open-mouthed, shouting his bronze shout, fixed, together with his bronze two-pointed hat and his bronze frock coat, in an attitude which combined dash, enthusiasm and immortality. The wind, still keeping the flags flapping, was tugging at an oddly isolated little tree, growing there for no apparent reason (or perhaps recently planted — which explained why it had not been flattened for the ceremony — by some patriotic committee), scarcely taller than a man, such as one finds in nurseries or bordering waste ground, stripped by autumn, tipped by a meagre fork, as if drawn with shaky strokes of a pen, like a crack, a fissure in the rain-filled sky. Next to it loomed the massive silhouette of the general commanding the army. Having stepped out of the car which brought him, indifferent to the rain, to the gusts of wind which sent his cape flying and engulfed themselves in his long, loose-fitting greatcoat, he stood before the standard-bearers. Very erect, one white-gloved hand on the pommel of his cane, head turned slightly to the right, eyes directed to the centre-point of the huge square of troops, he was watching the flag-bearer of the annihilated regiment.

The man in question was an N.C.O., a puny, minute, solitary figure, silhouette bulging where cartridge-pouches swelled his waist, the tails of his greatcoat flapping up behind him. Unlike the other flags which continued to writhe in the wind, the flag he was presenting hung motionless, whether gorged with rain-water (it had been some time, well before the general arrived, since its bearer had taken up position), or else somehow weighted for the ceremony. Although raised to a full-throated shout, the voice of the officer reading the mention in dispatches came faint and thin to the ear through the gusts of wind and the wet slap of the other flags, like the voice of a child, distant, a little unreal. When it fell silent, a bugler emerged from the band massed in a square in front of the line of troops, and advanced a few paces. There was a flash of

son instrument d'un geste adroit, rapide, sauvage lui aussi, et les notes de la sonnerie 'Aux morts' retentirent, comme enrouées, voilées, semblant venir du même irréel au-delà, ensevelies sous la pluie grise d'automne. Puis le porte-drapeau abaissa lentement la hampe, et après avoir replié la proclamation détrempée l'officier d'Etat-Major tira d'un étui la décoration qu'il alla épingler au-dessous de la pique sur la cravate, se reculant ensuite de quatre pas et saluant en même temps que le général portait la main gantée de blanc à son képi et que les officiers aux sabres nus se raidissaient encore. Pendant un moment on n'entendit plus que le bruissement immatériel de la pluie qui continuait à tomber et la protestation furieuse des étendards claquant dans le vent comme des coups de feu jusqu'à ce que brusquement la clique attaquât une marche entraînante, rythmée par des coups de cymbales, presque joyeuse aurait-on dit, tandis que l'un après l'autre, aux commandements, les détachements des régiments rompant leur immobilité s'ébranlèrent. De leur pas cadencé et vif, ils défilèrent devant le drapeau décoré, relevé maintenant, palpitant faiblement, toujours tenu par le petit homme à la silhouette malingre, le vaste carré des uniformes sombres se disloquant peu à peu, les détachements se succédant, la clique n'arrêtant de jouer que lorsque le dernier peloton de la dernière section se fut éloigné. Deux autres sous-officiers s'approchèrent alors du porte-drapeau et avec des gestes de femmes l'aidèrent à rouler l'étendard qu'ils glissèrent dans une gaine d'étoffe noire et huilée cependant que le général commandant l'armée remontait dans son automobile qui s'éloigna en cahotant sur le sol inégal du plateau, et ce fut tout.

Quoiqu'il ne fût pas ménagé (entièrement reformé et recomplété plusieurs fois, engagé rarement il est vrai ou envoyé dans des secteurs calmes comme ces vieilles troupes, vieilles gardes prétoriennes ou ces corps d'élite tenus précisément en réserve pour les actions les plus meurtrières), jamais par la suite, sauf à l'occasion d'une attaque mal préparée qui lui coûta en une matinée près des trois-quarts de ses officiers et un bon millier d'hommes, le régiment n'essuya d'aussi lourdes pertes que pendant ces quatre premières semaines où il laissa sur le terrain plus de morts qu'au cours de chacune des quatre années que dura la guerre. Parmi ceux qui tombèrent dans le combat du 27 août, se trouvait un capitaine de quarante ans dont le corps encore chaud dut être abandonné au pied de l'arbre auquel on l'avait adossé. C'était un homme d'assez grande taille, robuste, aux traits réguliers, à la moustache relevée en crocs, à la barbe carrée et dont les yeux pâles, couleur de faïence, grands ouverts dans le paisible visage ensanglanté

*copper as he twirled his instrument to his lips with a deft, rapid gesture
which had the same suggestion of barbarity to it, and the notes of the
last post rang out, a hoarse, covered sound, it seemed, as if it too issued
from somewhere unreal, out of this world, buried beneath the gray
autumn rain. Then the bearer slowly lowered the pike of the flag, and,
when he had refolded the sodden proclamation, the staff officer drew the
decoration from a case and went forward to pin it to the scarf hanging
below the pike, then stepped back and saluted as, simultaneously, the
general raised a white-gloved hand to his kepi and the officers with
drawn sabres stiffened a little more. For a time there was no sound but
the insubstantial swish of the rain continuing to fall and the outraged
protest of the standards cracking like gunshots in the wind, until
suddenly, to a rhythmic clash of cymbals, the band broke into a rousing,
almost, one might have said, light-hearted march, while, one by one, on
command, the detachments of the various regiments broke from
immobility into movement. In lively quick time they marched past the
decorated flag now raised again, swaying slightly, still held by the same
small, puny figure, the vast square of dark uniforms gradually breaking
up, detachment after detachment, the band playing on until the last
platoon of the last section had moved into the distance. Two other
N.C.O.s then approached the flag-bearer and with womanly care helped
him roll up the standard and slip it into a sheath of oiled black
material, while the general commanding the army climbed back into his
car which bumped and jolted away over the uneven surface of the
plateau, and that was all.*

*Although it was not spared (being several times re-formed and
brought up to full strength, though admittedly seldom committed in
battle, or else sent to quiet sectors, like these old faithfuls, old Praetorian
Guards, crack units which are held in reserve precisely for the bloodiest
engagements), never in what followed, except on the occasion of an ill-
prepared attack which in a single morning cost it nearly three-quarters of
its officers and a good thousand men, never again did the regiment suffer
such heavy losses as during these first four weeks when more dead were
left in the field than in any of the subsequent four years of war. Among
those who fell in the fighting of the twenty-seventh of August was a
forty-year-old captain whose still warm body had to be abandoned at the
foot of the tree against which it had been propped. He was a big, burly
man, with regular features, a moustache curled at the tips and square-
cut beard, and his pale, staring, china-blue eyes, set in a peaceful blood-
stained face, gazed upwards at the bullet-torn foliage in which the*

fixaient au-dessus d'eux les feuillages déchiquetés par les balles dans
lesquels jouait le soleil de l'après-midi d'été. Le sang pâteux faisait sur
la tunique une tache d'un rouge vif dont les bords commençaient à
sécher, déjà brunis, disparaissant presque entièrement sous l'essaim de
mouches aux corselets rayés, aux ailes grises pointillées de noir, se
bousculant et se montant les unes sur les autres, comme celles qui
s'abattent sur les excréments dans les sous-bois. La balle avait emporté
le képi et l'on pouvait encore voir dans les cheveux englués de sang le
sillon laissé par le peigne qui le matin même avait tracé avec soin la raie
médiane encadrée de deux ondulations. A la grande déception du soldat
ennemi qui s'avança prudemment, courbé en deux, le doigt sur la
détente de son arme et qui, attiré par la vue des galons se pencha sur le
corps, écartant les mouches pour le fouiller, les poches de la tunique
étaient vides et il ne trouva ni la montre en or à sonnerie, ni le
portefeuille, ni quelque autre objet de valeur. Avec la bourse, le tout fut
renvoyé plus tard à la veuve ainsi qu'une moitié, de la petite plaque
grisâtre portant le nom du mort et fixée par une chaînette à son poignet,
l'autre moitié de la plaque cassée suivant un pointillé de vides ménagé à
cet effet à l'emboutisseuse ayant été conservé par les bureaux des
effectifs. On n'avait, dans la précipitation, pas eu le temps de faire
glisser l'alliance du doigt qu'elle entourait et sans doute le soldat
exténué, vêtu d'un uniforme verdâtre, aux bottes couvertes de poussière
et de boue, dut-il rapidement couper le doigt du tranchant de sa
baïonnette avant d'être surpris par un camarade ou un gradé. Quant au
nécessaire à fumeur en émail décoré d'oiseaux chinois indigo aux
ventres roses volant au-dessus de nénuphars, il avait été, lui, rangé avant
le combat dans l'étroite cantine réglementaire, peinte en vert foncé et
ceinturée de courroies, transportée dans les fourgons avec les bagages de
la compagnie.

Ainsi venait de prendre fin une aventure commencée vingt-cinq ou
trente ans plus tôt lorsque l'instituteur d'un petit hameau de montagne
(ou plutôt sans doute le principal du collège de la ville voisine) vint
trouver (ou convoqua dans son bureau) le père du jeune boursier encore
dans les basses classes (un paysan, un homme sachant tout juste lire,
écrire et remplir d'additions maladroites les feuilles d'un carnet à la
couverture de moleskine, les chiffres gris inscrits avec lenteur au crayon
— parfois un de ces crayons à encre humectés de salive et dont la trace
mauve pâlissait à mesure que la mine séchait, le papier lui-même
grisâtre, quadrillé, dont la pâte était parsemée de minuscules taches
rousses, comme de la sciure de bois) et le persuada que son fils. . . .

summer afternoon sun was playing. On his tunic the sticky blood made a bright-red stain, already brown at the edges where it was beginning to dry and almost hidden from view by the swarm of striped flies with gray, black-speckled wings which were jostling and clambering over one another, like the flies which settle on excrement in undergrowth. The bullet had shot away his kepi and in his blood-matted hair one could still see the furrow left by the comb which that very morning had carefully traced the centre parting flanked by two waves of hair. To the great disappointment of the enemy soldier who moved forward cautiously, crouching, finger on the trigger of his rifle, and, drawn by the officer's stripes, leant over the body, brushing aside the flies to search it, the pouches of the tunic were empty and he found neither the gold repeater watch, nor the wallet, nor any other valuable. Everything, including the purse, was later returned to the widow, together with half of the small grayish tag which bore the name of the dead man and was secured to his wrist by a slim chain, the other half of the tag, broken along a perforated line machine-stamped on it for just that purpose, having been retained by the records office. There had been no time in the rush to slip the wedding ring from the finger it encircled and no doubt the exhausted soldier in gray-green uniform, boots caked in mud and dust, had hastily to snip the finger off with the blade of his bayonet before being surprised by a fellow private or an N.C.O. As for the enamel smoker's set decorated with indigo, pink-breasted chinese birds flying above water-lilies, it had been stored away before the fighting in the slim regulation tin trunk, painted dark green and bound with straps, and carried in the company's baggage-wagons.

Thus had just ended an adventure begun twenty-five or thirty years before when the schoolmaster of a little mountain hamlet (or no doubt rather the headteacher of the secondary school in the neighbouring town) came to find (or summoned to his office) the father of the young scholarship boy still in the early years of school (a peasant farmer, a man just able to read and write and fill with clumsy addition sums the pages of a notebook bound in imitation leather, the gray figures formed deliberately in pencil — sometimes one of these indelible pencils moistened with saliva, its mauve traces fading progressively as the lead dried, the paper also grayish, squared, pulp flecked with tiny red-brown marks, like sawdust) and persuaded him that his son. . . .

Translated by ALASTAIR B. DUNCAN

Interview with Claude Simon

Alastair B. Duncan

Your text, 'Fragment', describes the circumstances surrounding the death of a man who could be your father. Is it the starting-point of a novel in which this character is to play an important part? How have you set about writing this novel?

I did indeed base this text on what I have been able to learn about my father's death, both from family documents and from the history of his regiment for the First World War. That having been said, and for a host of reasons which we can come back to, the character 'produced' by my writing cannot be my father — any more than in Les Géorgiques *L.S.M. is General Lacombe Saint-Michel or O. is George Orwell.*

As for the second part of your question, I cannot give a satisfactory answer because at this very moment I am working on a number of 'texts' with a view to forming a whole, but as yet (though I have already written some two hundred pages) I have no more than a rough idea of what it will be like, since my initial project keeps changing as I write; this 'Fragment' will be part of it.[1]

In *Les Géorgiques* do you use your family history differently from the way it is used in previous novels? Do you consciously make use of analogies between the nature of the family and the nature of writing?

From L'Herbe *on, all my novels verge on the autobiographical. My family therefore figures in them, among other things; but I do not see any analogy between the family and writing.*

In *La Bataille de Pharsale* the narrator reads a History of Art which criticises German Renaissance painters for 'putting everything on the same plane' — which the narrator describes as an example of 'chronic French stupidity'. To what extent do your novels since *La Bataille de Pharsale* aim to put everything 'on the same plane'? How can this ambition be reconciled with the creation of novels which are, in your words, 'centred wholes'?[2]

Putting everything 'on the same plane' is not strictly speaking one of my 'ambitions'. I would say rather that, unlike what happens in the academic novel (I prefer the word 'academic' to the more frequently and wrongly used 'traditional' for if there is one tradition and one only in art, then it is surely, as Harold Rosenberg has said, 'the tradition of the new') . . . I would say rather that I see man as one thing among other things rather than as a being placed above other things.

The text you mention is by Elie Faure (for whom in other respects I have the greatest admiration). In one passage he seems to reproach the German Renaissance painters for depicting a stone, a blade of grass or a halbard with the same passionate intensity they would devote to the face of a man or a woman. But the German are not alone in this. For example in Bruegel's Procession to Calvary *you have to scour a vast landscape thronged with people to find a tiny Christ-figure carrying his cross; and the same is true of St Paul in* The Conversion of St Paul.

From the Venetians on, painters used effects of composition or lighting (as Rembrandt did, for example) to favour the human figure or figures at the expense of the world around them, which was thrown into shadow, demoted to the role of accessory or complement. It is well known that Rubens concentrated on his human figures while using assistants to paint vast areas of his canvasses and 'specialists' to work on the fruit and flowers. But gradually, influenced by various currents of thought, people came to see that the surrounding world was not just a décor made for man and tailored to fit him. In painting, this evolution culminated in the Impressionists, in whose works light (and consequently the attention of the spectator) is distributed evenly over the whole surface of the painting, so that objects are restored to the same importance as people. Take Cézanne, for instance: before applying a touch of colour at the extreme edge of a painting he would reflect as long (as intensely) as he did when painting the centre of the canvass. Some of his figures (like Harlequin*) do not even have a mouth, while drapery, hangings, a pot of geraniums, or some aspect of dress (Ambroise Vollard's shirt-front, for example) have had attention lavished on them. One could put it this way, that for a long time the world was interpreted solely in terms of man's preeminence. The important literary modes at that time were poetry, in which the poet 'expressed' his moods; drama (tragedy or comedy), where the action was set against particular 'backgrounds'; the philosophical tale or novel, as in the eighteenth century, in which the human body, objects and nature were 'handled' by means of adjectival phrases or stereotyped expressions: 'lily-white complexions', 'rich silks' or 'rags and tatters', 'dewy lawns', etc. It would be interesting to study how, with Balzac, the nineteenth century novel with pretensions to* '*realism*' *(while still functioning as as fable of the socio-psycho-philosophical type) gradually began to introduce description (probably to make things more true to life, to make the story more credible) and how later, with Flaubert (his scenarios, for example, give less space to Emma's moods than to colours, smells and sounds. . .) description became more and more important, to such a degree that the Russian essayist Tynianov was to predict a future form of the novel in which 'the story would be no more than the pretext for an accumulation of descriptions'. Today some writers, of whom I am one, are trying, like the Renaissance artists of Germany or Cézanne, to establish relationships between human figure and surrounding world in which neither dominates — which does not mean, as some reactionary critics have thought it clever to assert, that man is absent from the works of the* nouveau roman, *exclusively concerned, they claim, with the description of objects. They should use a little common sense: how on earth could man be absent from works produced by men?*

It would also perhaps be interesting to try and see whether one of the factors which have contributed to this loss of confidence in classical humanism was not the Second World War and its horrors. The monstrous nature of the First War had already provoked the infuriated rejection of former values that was Dada. As one of my characters rotting in a prison camp writes to his father who is lamenting the bombing of the library at Leipzig: 'If what was said in all the books gathered there could not prevent the library from being bombed, then what was the point of them?'.

Subsequently came the revelation of things much worse than the bombing of a library: the extermination camps — later, the Gulag archipelago — and this was seen by many as signifying the bankruptcy of all these centuries of Humanism so proudly championed by the West. What then was one to cling to? What 'order' could be found in this 'débâcle' to paraphrase the title of Ricardou's article on La Route des Flandres?[3] *Beneath its Parisian sound and fury, existentialism was putting forward no more than a revamped version of 'humanist' marxism (in this case Jdanovism, the enforced practice of Socialist Realism) . . . Hence the attempts (the need) to go back to basics and start afresh. For example, painters like Jean Dubuffet, Tapies the Catalan (or the Italian Novelli, dead alas before his time), simply painting walls or doing doodles or graffiti;, the Americans Robert Rauschenberg or Louise Nevelson making paintings and sculptures from things sometimes picked up from rubbish dumps, bits and pieces, scraps of worn material, etc.; Roland Barthes writing* Le Degré zéro de l'écriture; *Beckett's characters slithering about in the primeval mud or shut up in dustbins; Robbe-Grillet fostering for a while the illusion of 'objective' art, an 'objective' novel; the questioning of our material (language); the interest in anagrams and puns; Lacan; and some experiments and declarations designed to shock. But excesses are always necessary and fruitful.*

As far as the last part of your question is concerned ('how to reconcile this aim with the creation of "centred wholes"'), I do not quite understand what you mean.

The first few pages of *Leçon de choses* and of *Les Géorgiques* give some impression of being 'Directions for Use', instructions for the reader. As you compose your novels, to what extent do you feel that you are shaping, or being called on to shape, a Model Reader?

I have no feeling that I am called on to shape a Model Reader. I have no didactic purpose. As Henri Michaux has said: 'Art has to be earned'. The pages you mention can indeed be seen as brief directions for use but ultimately my over-riding aim was that they should themselves be 'writing'. The first section of Leçon de choses — *'Générique' — was originally a short text written for Maeght, the art dealer, who at that time had had the idea of producing what he called 'Placards' (short texts illustrated by a painter — in this case Alechinsky). But after having written these few pages and sent them off to Maeght, I went on from there, developing the possibilities suggested by the last few lines. . . .*

What is the function of the references to other texts in *Les Géorgiques*? More generally, what is your view of the relationship between tradition and originality in the novel, between the conventional and the new?

I make no attempt to be 'original'. That seems to me a pointless goal. If originality there is, it will appear of its own accord. A few moments ago I recalled Rosenberg's remark that the only valid tradition in art is the tradition of the new. However, if all that is fine or good is new, that proposition cannot be stood on its head: everything that is new is not necessarily good. I suggest we substitute the word 'academic' for the word 'traditional'. There is, alas, an 'academic' tradition, the tradition of the novel which proves a point or demonstrates an idea, in other words of the philosophical tale and the fable, based on some pretence of 'logic' or 'fate' and which sees the novel itself as no more than the locus for a series of causes and effects which are by nature socio-psychological (or even divinely ordained) and therefore external to the text itself. Thus Faulkner, who in other respects is a genius and to whom I am much indebted, could declare in all seriousness in the draft of an introduction to The Sound and the Fury *that 'the children had been sent to the pasture to spend the afternoon to get them away from the house (. . .)* in order that *the three brothers and the nigger children could look up at the muddy seat of Caddy's drawers as she climbed the tree"!*[4] *For me, this kind of statement verges either on madness, or on deception — or perhaps both at once. But then Balzac dedicated the whole of his work 'to the glory of Religion and the Monarchy' while Marx, on the contrary, saw it as an outright condemnation of these two 'values'. Yet at the* textual *level no one before Balzac or Faulkner had ever written as they did.*

Do you make any distinction between novel and autobiography?

Let me repeat that from L'Herbe *on, all my novels are next to autobiographical. Which does not mean that they make up an auto-biography. I do not 'tell all' about myself, and my works are composed pen in hand, in the present of the moment of writing, which presupposes choice, the imposition of order and hence a deformation of 'that* incalculable number *of things which', as Tolstoy observes, 'a healthy man commonly thinks, feels and remembers,* all at the same time'.

In *Les Corps conducteurs* and *Triptyque* you made your metaphors concrete by expanding comparisons into elements of story in their own right, and you often used short, syntactically simple sentences. In *Leçon de choses* and even more in *Les Géorgiques* comparisons reappear, as do seemingly psychological and philosophical reflections, and long sentences interspersed with parentheses. Why these changes?

Because I keep changing, I suppose . . . There has never been anything premeditated about the way I write. I write as best I can. I keep searching. With La Bataille de Pharsale, Les Corps conducteurs, Triptyque *and* Leçon de choses *I had pushed forward in a particular direction and reached a point where it seemed to me no further progress was possible along that road. So with* Les Géorgiques *I tried something different.*

What is the function of humour in your novels?

Sometimes, a 'distancing' function.

Not long ago you took part in a colloquium in New York together with Alain Robbe-Grillet, Nathalie Sarraute and Robert Pinget. Does this mean that after the first 'nouveau roman' with its 'new realism' and the 'nouveau nouveau roman' with its denunciation of realism, there is now a 'nouveau nouveau nouveau roman'? In your novels or in your thinking about the novel do you feel that you have changed in parallel with other novelists?

If I personally have rebelled against the idea of 'realism', it was because I wanted to denounce the nonsensical use of it made by academic painting and the academic novel, past and present. We must agree what words mean: what 'reality' are we talking about? If it is a matter of 'reproducing' or 'representing' the 'real' world (a concept about which scientists themselves are uncertain) then of course there never has been, never can, and never will be 'realism', and the use of the word is pure deception or stupidity. On the other hand, if the word 'realist' were not so devalued, one might use it to describe the efforts of some painters (such as the Impressionists and the Cubists) and of some writers, to render, in *and* through *a particular medium (colours or words), not the 'reality' of the world but the reality of the sensations and* subjective *emotions — partial, fragmentary and questionable — which we receive or experience. No painting, no text duplicates 'reality'; they are in themselves realities and as such part of 'Reality' with a capital R.*

You know (and this is precisely something I had the opportunity to say in New York[5]), there has been a great deal of confusion and many foolish things said (or written) about the nouveau roman. *I think the expression was first used by Emile Henriot,* Le Monde's *literary critic, writing about Nathalie Sarraute and Alain Robbe-Grillet[6]. Thereafter the term became established, partly because both these authors (and later Jean Ricardou) lent it credibility by pronouncements and writings of a more or less theoretical kind, and also because almost all of us were published by the same publisher. As I said to you just now, what united us (and continues to unite us) was that we rejected or rather were violently allergic to the academic novel, stemming from nineteenth century 'naturalism', which at that time held sway in France (and continues to do so. . .).*

One could look for fairly distant ancestors for the nouveau roman, *for example the account of the Battle of Waterloo at the beginning of* La Chartreuse de Parme, *or in Flaubert, or else in Dostoevsky and his monuments of contradictions and unanswerable questionings (some critics rightly spotted that* Le Vent *was simply a remake of* The Idiot. . .*). But ultimately, if there was a decisive break, a decisive moment when the novel was put into question, it came at the beginning of this century (almost at the same time, very interestingly, as just such a radical break took place in painting with Cézanne and, following him, the Cubists), the chief artisans of this break being Proust and Joyce, and, in another register, Roussel. Not to see this — and a certain kind of criticism which never got past Stendhal, Zola and their more or less 'existentialist' imitators did not see it — was to show a curious ignorance of literature. In my own case, it is quite obvious that without Proust, Joyce and Faulkner, I would never have been able to write as I have. Others have had different literary 'fathers'; Robbe-Grillet,* *for example, claims to go back to Gide. . . .*

May I suggest then that for the term nouveau roman *we substitute 'living literature'? (I am deliberately avoiding the word 'modern' which has been used as a cover for too much questionable merchandise.) That having been said (and to convince oneself of the truth of this one has only to turn to the colloquium held at Cerisy in 1971 and read the various statements we made there*[7]*), each one of us has worked in very different directions, and each has developed in his or her own way. You ask me if there is a* nouveau nouveau nouveau roman; *my reply is that we are all still writing and publishing, and just as it would have been very tedious had we all written the same book, it would be equally wearisome were each one of us endlessly to rewrite the same book.*

REFERENCES

1.   This reply was written in Spring 1984. The rest of the interview, consisting of written replies to written questions, dates from February 1983.
2.   'des ensembles centrés': *Nouveau Roman: hier, aujourd' hui,* 2, *Pratiques* (Paris, 1972), p. 92.
3.   'Un Ordre dans la débâcle', *Critique,* no. 163 (décembre 1960), 1011-24.
4.   This draft exists in various versions. One of these is to be found in *A Faulkner Miscellany* edited by J. B. Meriwether (Jackson, Miss., 1972), pp. 156-61.
5.   The text of Simon's paper at the New York colloquium of September 1982, translated by A. C. Pugh, will be found in the Claude Simon number of *The Review of Contemporary Fiction,* forthcoming 1985.
6.   'Le Nouveau Roman. *La Jalousie,* d'Alain Robbe-Grillet. *Tropismes,* de Nathalie Sarraute', *Le Monde,* 22 mai 1957.
7.   *Nouveau Roman: hier, aujourd'hui,* especially vol. 2.

Claude Simon's generation game: the family and the text

Celia Britton

'Generation' is a term frequently used in connection with Simon's writing, in the sense of the generating of the text: the process whereby new textual elements are produced (or 'engendrés',) out of a conjunction of existing ones. But the word has another meaning which is equally relevant at least to one particular aspect of Simon's novels — namely, the fictional process whereby new characters are produced out of a conjunction of existing ones: the reproduction of the family. Taking this pun (and 'engendrer' has the same double sense of textual and sexual procreation) as starting-point, this paper will look at the ways in which the family's generations structure and are structured by the text, and will attempt to explore some of the connections made, in the novels, between writing and family history.

The history/narrative pun of the title *Histoire* indicates that writing is also bound up in various rather complicated and ambiguous ways with the concept of history in the broader sense, which to Simon means the attempt to see the world as order, as *syntax* — an attempt which, as will be discussed later, usually fails. But perhaps the only case of reality not being entirely formless, of having some kind of inherent order, however incomplete, is when that order is based in biology; and so it could be argued that family history is to some extent treated as an exception to the general rule of chaos.

The family represents a nexus of interconnecting relations, in both the human and the abstract sense; in his counterpointing of order and decomposition, Ricardou refers to the 'ordre généalogique' of the de Reixach family.[1] An image of the nexus is provided by the proliferating branches of the acacia tree described in the opening pages of *Histoire*, as it metamorphoses into a family tree: 'cette caricature orléaniste reproduite dans le manuel d'histoire et qui représentait l'arbre généalogique de la famille royale' (p. 10). The same tree, however, (and, of course, the term 'branching tree' has a further and very precisely *generative* linguistic meaning in the context of Chomskean syntax) also serves as a metaphor for the structure of the novel, thus creating from the outset an equivalence between family and text.

The two basic elements involved in building up the family nexus are sexual reproduction and the passage of time; and both of these are repeatedly linked with the basic elements of writing: words, or even simply letters. In *L'Herbe*, for instance, the family initials on the sheets are used to symbolize kinship, sex and time:

> *Ces lourds monogrammes brodés sur les draps . . . que l'on se transmet d'une génération à l'autre: sigles représentant chacun l'alliance d'au moins deux familles . . ., le mécanisme du temps et celui de la reproduction se déroulant donc tous deux sous les symboliques vestiges d'autres temps, d'autres copulations. (p. 204, my underlining)*

Elsewhere in the same novel it is the permanent, monumental quality of writing which serves to link ancestry and the phallus:

> *l'ancêtre, le vénérable grand-père du monde, l'antique et vieux phallus . . . avec sa tête aveugle, son oeil aveugle, sa rigidité de pierre . . .: quelque chose pour être écrit — ou décrit — en latin, à l'aide de ces mots latins non pas crus, impudiques, mais semble-t-il, spécialement conçus et forgés pour . . . les pierres maçonnées . . . (pp. 129-130)*

The repetition of 'pierre' here also, of course, refers to Pierre — the figure in *L'Herbe* and *La Route des Flandres* who is writer and head of the family.

On the more general level it could be argued that the order of generations, of kinship relations, acts as a kind of overall structural *matrix* (and here again, the term has both textual and biological connotations) within which several individual novels fit together; familial and textual relations are superimposed, the family or families overlapping from novel to novel as shown at the top of next page.

This link between writing and the family which can be found in Simon's novels suggests a possible approach via the Lacanian concept of the Symbolic order. What is at issue here is the significance of the Oedipal phase. The structure of the family (the family tree) is maintained by exogamous marriage, which is in turn guaranteed by the

```
                                              grand'mère
                                        ┌─────────┴─────────┐
         paysan illettré                Charles    mère─Henri
      ┌────────┴────────┐                  │
   Pierre─Sabine    Marie    de Reixach─Corinne    narrator─Hélène
      │
Louise─Georges

.........................L'Herbe........................
              ...............La Route des Flandres.................
                           ........................Histoire.......................
```

incest taboo. From the point of view of the individual and his (since most of Simon's protagonists are male) position in the family, the incest taboo is what shapes his relationship to his mother and sisters. Furthermore — and moving as it were from anthropology to psychoanalysis — it shapes his relationship to his father as well, in terms of the Oedipus complex. Lacan formulates this as 'ce que le sujet peut connaître de sa participation inconsciente au mouvement des structures complexes de l'alliance', thereby relating the experience of the individual to the transsubjective functioning of the kinship system; the Oedipal phase is seen here as the moment at which the subject enters into a relational structure which is determined by 'la Loi primordiale . . . celle qui en réglant l'alliance superpose le règne de la culture au règne de la nature . . .': the Law which — and this is the crucial point — is then defined as 'identique à un ordre de langage'.[2] The symbolic order constitutes the domain of this Law, in its double functioning; it brings together family and language as equivalent systems of relations both involved in the positioning of the subject, and so can perhaps illuminate the similar configuration of themes which we find in Simon's novels.

In fact the equation of family and writing is apparent above all in the *transgressions* of the Symbolic order: rejection of the position one has been assigned involves attacking both of these simultaneously. So Georges's hostility to Pierre is both a struggle to escape from his role as heir to the family tradition, as when he complains that his father 'ne s'est jamais demandé si j'aurais pu, si j'avais envie, moi, de faire autre chose, parce que sans doute il n'était même pas concevable dans ou pour Son orgueil que Son fils pût être, pût vouloir être autre chose que ce que lui-même. . . .' (L'H, p. 154), and a rejection of writing: 'Je n'ai surtout pas envie d'aligner encore des mots et des mots et encore des mots. Est-ce qu'à la fin tu n'en as pas assez toi aussi?' (RF, p. 36). The connection is particularly close since the family tradition in his case has been built on the gradual acquisition of writing, from the illiterate peasant grandfather who saw words as a means of power and revolt against the social order, through Marie who was both school-mistress and farmer, and whose intermediate position is indicated by the double ability of her right hand, 'capable alors aussi bien de tracer sur le tableau noir les lettres aux boucles impeccables, aux pleins et aux déliés impeccables, que de tenir le manche d'une bêche et de sarcler un champ de pommes de terre' (L'H, p. 228) — to Pierre, the intellectual, whose hands are covered with 'cette peau blanche et lisse qui n'a jamais — ou alors depuis si longtemps — touché, été au contact d'autre chose que des livres' (p. 147). Georges's revolt is in fact a revolution, in the Simonian sense of a cycle: a return to the position of his grandfather — again marked by the description of his hands being similarly calloused and dirty (p. 146). But here the value attached to writing has been reversed, from rebellion against the existing order to submission to it; and simply by virtue of being a cycle, moreover, it also constitutes a revolt against the idea of history as progress.

Georges, however, is by no means the only threat to the Symbolic order. Simon's novels show both family and textual systems as constantly menaced with disintegration. Ricardou, cited earlier here, goes on to talk about 'la décomposition de l'ordre familial'; the family structure is in fact full of gaps. This is already evident in two early novels, in which the plot is to a considerable extent determined by the absence of a father (Bernard's and Montès's), but in the three 'overlapping' novels — L'Herbe, La Route des Flandres and Histoire — the lacunae are more numerous and more varied, just as the texts themselves manifest increasing 'decomposition' in terms of narrative structure. The gaps in the family occur firstly through deaths: in Histoire, for instance, those of the narrator's grandmother, mother, father, aunt and cousin's husband; and secondly through lack of births, which are the result both of virginity and of adultery. Thus Marie in L'Herbe dies a spinster because her own mother died young and left her to bring up, and dedicate her life to, her younger brother (Pierre): instead of producing a child who would form a subsequent generation, her 'child' in fact belongs to her own generation and any further progress is blocked: the final description of her in the novel refers to 'ce ventre qui n'a jamais enfanté' (p. 257). Corinne, on the other hand, damages the family through her adultery; but although she is in many ways the antithesis of Marie, since she represents the very essence of feminine sexuality, it is significant that she is also, like Marie, described as a woman who has never given birth: 'elle qui n'avait jamais allaité désaltéré été bue par d'autres que des rudes lèvres d'homme' (*RF*, p. 261). Adultery leads to unnatural death (just as Marie's death is the 'monstrous' culmination of a life of unnatural abstinence): de Reixach is presumed to have committed suicide because of Corinne's unfaithfulness. Similarly, in *Histoire*, Charles's wife kills herself because of his adultery; and his consequent state is described as follows:

> *veuf mot boiteux tronqué restant pour ainsi dire en suspens coupé contre nature comme l'anglais half moitié sectionné cut off coupé de quelque chose qui manque soudain dans la bouche les lèvres prononçant VF continuant à faire fff comme un bruit d'air froissé déchiré par le passage rapide étincelant et meurtrier d'une lame. (p. 82)*

The image is clearly one of castration, and it too is seen as an absence, a gap: 'coupé de quelque chose qui *manque* soudain'. (The absence is repeated in the narrator's life: fated to follow in his uncle's footsteps, he also loses his wife). But what is particularly striking is the way in which the point that his wife's suicide has in effect castrated him, is made solely via a play on the material qualities of the signifier 'veuf' and its phonetic associations with other, foreign, words and with the sounds of a 'knife' (to extend the word-play a little). Castration and widowhood — the inability to reproduce — are linked with the idea of the speaking voice which is also 'cut off' — 'quelque chose qui manque soudain *dans la bouche*' — thus underlining the identity of the linguistic and the sexual-familial as forms of the Symbolic order; and according to Lacan the point of insertion into this is, precisely, the Oedipal fear of castration. The thematic level thus does not exist independently of the textual (in fact the text, too, is 'cut off' here — it starts again with a new paragraph).

The existence of lacunae throughout the family matrix, and perhaps especially the absent fathers (or the *disowned* father, in the case of Pierre), seems to be connected with the peculiarly problematic nature of the act of conception in Simon's novels. The individual's existence obviously depends upon this act; and yet it is striking how for many of Simon's characters the fact that they can conceive or be conceived is itself almost inconceivable — Pierre, for instance:

> *contemplant donc . . . celui dont il lui faut probablement admettre qu'il l'a engendré, c'est-à-dire tiré du néant originel, créé à partir de rien . . . projetant donc hors de lui une partie de lui-même . . . une prolongation de lui-même, même si elle en est apparemment la négation, le contraire. (L'H, pp. 144-5)*

Similarly, the Italian in *Le Palace* is described as 'lui qui semblait n'avoir jamais eu de mère, avoir été engendré non par une femme, mais . . . par le désespoir, l'humiliation et la colère' (p. 99). The same kind of ambivalent denial is evident in Bernard's desire not to have been conceived:

> *Si seulement personne n'avait ni père ni mère, et puisqu'on ne va nulle part, ne venir non plus de nulle part, ni surtout de personne: naître de la même façon dont on meurt, de rien, d'un hasard, et non pas, et surtout pas, d'un homme et d'une femme. (SP, p. 15)*

— and in the townspeople's rejection of Montès because he decides to 'exploiter un domaine seulement sien en vertu d'un acte nocturne (cette ténébreuse, obscène, brutale et éphémère saillie, pénétration, fécondation d'une chair par une autre) sans témoins et sans suivants . . . comme si avec sa semence l'étrangère était en même temps venue dérober au mâle, lui extorquer les fertiles terres rouges' (*V*, pp. 19-20).

Conception is thus a paradox and a kind of scandal, because it is on the one hand a purely erotic act — 'brutale et éphémère' — and on the other hand the foundation of the subject's legitimacy, his hereditary entitlement (to land, in Montès's case); it defines his place in the family and society. Since the Oedipus myth is about the enigma of sexual origin and the role played in it by the father, the acceptance of the fact of conception is one aspect of the Oedipal stage.[3] The *denial* of conception is thus rather complex; it is a rejection firstly of the sexuality of the subject's origin, but also of the position which he is, as it were arbitrarily, allocated in the family system of relations and in the Symbolic order generally; and thirdly, it also in some sense constitutes a denial of history, of the succession of generations and the reality of the past, as though it were impossible to accept that at one time one did not exist and had to be, as Pierre says in the passage quoted above, 'tiré du néant, créé à partir de rien'.

The novels facilitate — one might say, collude in — the denial of conception by their suppression of the father of many of the protagonists. It is perhaps as a result of this that the figure of the 'double' recurs in the texts;[4] the progenitor is displaced by a substitute, another older man whose function is to provide a *model* for the subject. (There is also the case of Marie, who is to some extent Louise's double in a female version of the pattern, but there is no link made here with Louise's mother). In Bernard's case, it is his mother's second husband — as Lucien Dällenbach comments: 'Bernard n'échappera pas à la règle. *Répétiteur* malgré lui, il en arrive nécessairement à mettre ses pas dans ceux de son beau-père'.[5] For the student in *Le Palace* it is the American, whom he imitates, 'assis d'une fesse sur le rebord de la table de la réfectoire comme il l'avait vu faire la veille à l'Américain' (p. 202).

But the most prominent examples of the double occur in *La Route des Flandres* and *Histoire*. Georges replaces the father he rejects with de Reixach, and the narrator of *Histoire* replaces the father he has never known with Charles. In both cases the double is imitated primarily in his sexual relationships: Georges is determined to sleep with Corinne, and the narrator is fated to lose his wife in the same way as Charles did. In Georges's case one could almost see his obsession with his double's wife wife as containing an Oedipal element: insofar as the double can be said to function as a substitute father, one of his advantages is that he does not invoke the incest taboo. In both cases, also, the double is a blood relation of the subject's mother. De Reixach is Sabine's cousin, and Charles is the narrator's mother's brother — exactly the maternal uncle of numerous anthropological studies of kinship. The mother is also, interestingly, presented at one point as *Charles's* double: she is 'pour lui pas exactement une femme puisqu'elle était en même temps sa sœur, son double en quelque sorte sous forme de femelle' (*H*, p. 129). It is Charles, too, who adopts the narrator's point of view to express the inherently scandalous idea of his mother's sexuality:

> et toi là-dedans un peu ahuri un peu effaré comme le bon jeune
> homme éperdu de respect et d'amour pour son adorable mère et qui
> l'aurait surprise sur le dos les jambes en l'air dans l'acte même
> auquel il doit la vie. (H, p. 152)

These maternal associations seem to correlate with the double's failure to function within the family structure: both 'lose' their wives, and both participate in the adultery-suicide configuration described above.

It could therefore be argued, to return to Lacan's terminology, that they belong to the pre-Oedipal, maternal order of the *imaginary*, as opposed to the Symbolic; that they are in a precise sense imaginary substitutes for the Oedipal father. As such, they are also involved in the

schema of the mirror-image (which I have discussed elsewhere[6]); the
double, in other words, is another manifestation of the reflection of the
subject's image. It is noticeable that both Charles and de Reixach (in
contrast to Pierre, father figure and writer) are associated with the
visual rather than the textual: with images rather than writing. Charles,
for instance, is shown in the photograph of the painter's studio, the
description of which forms a whole chapter of *Histoire*. De Reixach,
too, appears above all as an instantaneous *vision*:

> *un moment j'ai pu le voir ainsi le bras levé brandissant cette arme
> inutile et dérisoire . . . silhouette obscure dans le contrejour . . . le
> soleil miroitant un instant sur la lame nue puis le tout — homme
> cheval et sabre — s'écroulant d'une pièce. (RF, p. 12)*

As image, the double cuts across the articulations of the Symbolic order
and offers the subject a possibility of immediate identification which
displaces the problem of origin and eliminates the dimension of history,
of time; whole sections of *Histoire* can be read as referring either to
Charles or the narrator: they fuse completely. All this as it were short-
circuits that play of differentiation within an overall symbolic matrix
which language, the family and the text all produce.

The imaginary order, then, abolishes time, arresting it in the instant
of the mirror-image. There is also another form which this denial of
history can take, and which is even more clearly linked to the figure of
the mother: the theme of the return to the womb. This almost always
occurs in conjunction with a reference to reversing or stopping the
passage of time. In *Le Sacre du printemps*, Bernard's reaction against 'la
lente, l'inexorable notion du temps' (p. 222) is to imagine the telephone
cord as

> *une sorte de cordon ombilical menant symboliquement à une
> femme, au sein tiède et noir dont est issue toute vie et après quoi
> soupire la chair nostalgique et gémissante hantée par le désir, et
> plus que le désir le besoin, et plus que le besoin la nécessité d'y
> retourner, d'y mourir à nouveau. (p. 222)*

The evocation of the womb is 'nostalgique', and is furthermore
associated with death, as though the state before birth were also a kind
of non-life. The same configuration of timelessness, birth and death is
apparent in Montès's thoughts as he sits beside Rose's dead body:

> *Comme si, assis là dans le temps aboli à côté de Rose morte, . . .
> il se trouvait ramené à un état en quelque sorte fœtal, lové dans la*

douloureuse et torturante (dit-on) quiétude d'une vie intra-utérine.
(V, p. 186)

In *L'Herbe* there is a further example of this, even more striking in that it arises as a completely non-diegetic metaphor which transposes female into male and death into birth; 'la bossue', already presented as a sort of angel of death, becomes a man waking up after a night in a train:

et lui-même dans cette position passive, fœtale en quelque sorte
. . . le corps affaissé, douloureusement recroquevillé . . . comme
par une nostalgie du sein maternel . . . d'autant plus, donc, que
tout concourt à renforcer cette paisible et illusoire sensation
d'immobilité ou plutôt d'immuabilité cherchée dans le ventre du
sommeil. (p. 111)

The theme of the return to the womb seems in fact to involve a double notion of time: the above extracts stress the idea of a purely static time-lessness, and yet the association of the womb with death — equating the states before and after life — can also be seen as implying that cyclical conception of time which recurs in various forms throughout Simon's novels (with the pun on *revolution,* the themes of decomposition and metamorphosis, etc.). A larger-scale case of this is the entire text of *Histoire,* which starts with the narrator waking up, 'encore vacillant au sortir des ténèbres *maternelles'* (p. 45, my italics), and comparing the cord of his pyjama trousers to a clumsily severed umbilical cord, and ends with him back in the womb:

ce sein qui déjà peut-être me portait dans son ténébreux
tabernacle sorte de têtard gélatineux lové sur lui-même avec ses
deux énormes yeux sa tête de ver à soie sa bouche sans dents son
front cartilagineux d'insecte, moi? . . . (p. 402)

The echo of 'ténèbres/ténébreux' only underlines our recognition that the whole work of the text, in its gradual and precarious constitution of the narrator's identity, has been to produce, at the end, his biological starting-point.

Yet what the two concepts of static and cyclical time have in common is that they both oppose *history* — which for Simon has two main features. Firstly it is linear: it imposes an artificially directional order on reality; it embodies the rationality of progress. Secondly it is man-made, and hence not integrated with the natural cycles of life and death; it is the impossible attempt of human beings to 'organize' the world, as described in the quotation from Rilke which opens *Histoire*.

These two features, however, also belong to writing. History and writing are equally unreal, and for the same reasons. Since it is a product of man's mind, writing does not really exist — it is merely 'griffonnages sans autre existence réelle que celle attribuée à eux par un esprit lui non plus sans existence réelle' (*RF*, p. 244). And the reporting of the Spanish Civil War is merely an endless *line* of words, 'kilomètres de phrases enthousiastes tapées sur ruban à machine par l'enthousiaste armée des correspondants étrangers de la presse libérale' (*P*, p. 17). Writing is meaningless also because it is bound up with a liberal conception of history, as itself one-dimensional progress. In this passage from *Le Palace* the futility of writing and of history is directly connected with the image of the foetus which, as argued above, itself represents a negation of history. But whereas in the above examples it was an expression of nostalgia for the security and stasis of the womb, and the cyclicity of the natural order, this foetus has been unnaturally ejected from the womb: it is the abortion of the revolution, and its death has been caused by writing — the extract just quoted in fact begins: 'une puante momie enveloppée et étranglée par le cordon ombilical de kilomètres de phrases enthousiastes . . .', and on the preceding page it is referred to as 'un fœtus à trop grosse tête langé dans du papier imprimé, rien qu'un petit macrocéphale décédé avant terme . . . et jeté aux égouts dans un linceul de mots . . .' (p. 16). The particular violence — even for Simon — of this image of the aborted foetus, rotting away wrapped in newspaper in the sewers, makes it clear how profoundly antagonistic are writing and the womb: writing can only destroy the foetus, as it encourages a facile and a fallaciously historical view of time.

The initial connection made here between the family and writing thus leads us into a set of oppositions: between maternal and paternal figures, and between two modes of representation and two conceptions of time. On the one hand, the Symbolic order brings together the nexus of family relations based on the Oedipal structure (the 'name of the father'), the nexus of textual relations built up by the linear structure of writing, and the idea of History as structured rational progression. On the other hand, the imaginary order serves to link the pre-Oedipal relation with the mother to the mirror-image, and thus to the double, who is both an equivalent of the mirror-image, and an extension of the mother; it also implies a rejection of History in favour of the 'maternal' time of the cycle of birth and death.

REFERENCES

1. Jean Ricardou, 'Un Ordre dans la débâcle' *Critique*, no. 163 (décembre 1960), 1011-24.

2. Jacques Lacan, *Ecrits* (Paris, 1966), pp. 156-7. Rosalind Coward and John Ellis comment on this passage as follows: 'The idea of the Symbolic order which structures all inter-human relations was introduced by Lévi-Strauss. Human law, sociality, is identified as identical to the order of language, "for without kinship nominations, no power is capable of instituting the order of preferences and taboos which bind and weave the yarn of lineage down through the succeeding generations" (*Language of the Self*)'. Quoted in *Language and Materialism* (London, 1977), p. 114.

3. cf. Lévi-Strauss's analysis of the Oedipus myth, where he states: 'Il exprimerait l'impossibilité où se trouve une société qui professe de croire à l'autochtonie de l'homme . . . de passer, de cette théorie, à la reconnaissance du fait que chacun de nous est réellement né de l'union d'un homme et d'une femme'. In *Anthropologie Structurale* (Paris, 1958), p. 239.

4. cf. A. C. Pugh: 'Claude Simon — the narrator and his double', *20th Century Studies*, no. 6 (December 1971), 30-40.

5. In 'Mise en abyme et redoublement spéculaire chez Claude Simon', *Claude Simon: colloque de Cerisy* (Paris, 1975), p. 153.

6. 'Claude Simon: the imaginary origins of the text', *Degré Second*, no. 5 (July 1981), 115-30.

Authorial correction and *bricolage* in the work of Claude Simon

Jean H. Duffy

Given that the writers of the *nouveau roman* have tended to promote specifically textual and linguistic aspects of the novel, it is hardly surprising that in the corpus of criticism which has been written on Claude Simon his exploitation of phonetic and semantic association has been given more attention than any other aspect of his work. The very perceptive and meticulous work of two critics — Gérard Roubichou and Jean Ricardou[1] — has been the inspiration for a good deal of work on the generative and proliferative tendencies of Simon's novels. Further impetus was given to this approach by Simon's own explicit ratification of Ricardou's emphasis on the generation of a text from the associations of an initial seminal passage.[2]

I do not want to deny the paramount importance of generation in an appreciation of Simon's novels. It is perhaps the most distinctive and fundamental feature of his working method. However, the critical celebrity (or notoriety) of this particular aspect has, in my opinion, resulted in a certain imbalance. Indeed, Roubichou and Ricardou have possibly valorized the notion of generation to the point where other, very important aspects of textual production have been eclipsed or given insufficient weight. There has been a tendency to concentrate on explicitly unconventional aspects of Simon's approach, such as his claim that he has only the vaguest of aims when he starts writing.[3] This depreciation of the notion of authorial intention, combined with the difficulties involved in securing access to the manuscripts of a living author, has probably made critics very wary of adopting more traditional investigatory methods. In particular, the fascination experienced by Roubichou and Ricardou for the linguistic intricacy of the texts finally generated from a relatively restricted seminal vocabulary causes them to ignore the question of pre-publication correction and reorganization.

This negligence may seem to have been endorsed by Simon himself in his regret about the revision to which Flaubert subjected *Madame Bovary*.[4] Simon has explicitly stated his preference for the 'édition intégrale' of Flaubert's novel over the much revised version with which we are familiar, arguing that there are internál monologues in the former which anticipate some of the most radical writing of the following century — in particular James Joyce and Surrealist writers such as André Breton. However, such commentaries on the work of others, although revealing, should not be taken as personal statements of aesthetic standpoint. In this same article, Simon had insisted on the indispensability of a 'mise en forme' to artistic communication and on the impossibility of a 'mise en forme' without sacrifice. Furthermore, in spite of his apparent admiration for automatic writing, at the colloquium on the *nouveau roman* in 1971 he severely qualified any analogy between his own conception of the adventure of writing and that of the Surrealists:

> *si le cheminement dont j'ai parlé s'engageait, chaque fois qu'un mot carrefour se présente, dans n'importe laquelle des perspectives qu'il ouvre, ce serait alors simplement l'aventure décevante et avortée de la fameuse tentative* d'écriture automatique *des surréalistes qui, en dehors de ses rebondissements plus ou moins brillants et des révélations d'ordre psychanalytique qu'elle peut fournir sur son auteur, n'aboutit qu'à une suite sans fin de parenthèses qui s'ouvrent les unes après les autres sans jamais se refermer.*[5]

But probably the most unambiguous evidence of often quite radical retrospective alteration in Simon's work consists of the discrepancies between the short texts published in various journals and the subsequently published novels for which they were intended. Many of these texts display shifts in emphasis indicative of changes in general aim during the course of production. These discrepancies bear out Simon's own insistence on the sheer hard work involved in writing and his rejection of the notion of inspiration:

> *Claude Simon: L'inspiration n'existe pas. Cela ne vient qu'à*

force de travail. . . . Tous les jours je me mets à ma table de
travail, mais si je m'occupe d'autre chose, cela ne vient pas.

Michel de Saint-Pierre: Il arrive cependant que le courant passe.

Claude Simon: Parce qu'on s'est appliqué pendant des heures et
des heures à éliminer toutes les formes qui n'allaient pas, toutes les
formes qui ne collaient pas.[6]

The process of generation does not preclude retrospective alteration and
correction; in fact the unpredictable nature of its results most frequently
renders modification imperative for reasons of balance and aesthetic
unity: 'J'ai refait le début de presque tous mes livres, et notamment celui
d'*Histoire,* parce que mon idée initiale ne collait plus avec ce qui s'était
fait'.[7]

Furthermore, in a little-heeded reference, Claude Simon has himself
supplied an analogy which takes into account not only the generative
but also the revisionary aspects of his work. In 'La Fiction mot à mot',
he compares the artisanal and empirical nature of his method with the
notion of *bricolage* applied metaphorically by Claude Lévi-Strauss in *La
Pensée sauvage* to mythical thought. *Bricolage* is an activity principally
concerned with the exploitation and recombination of pre-existing
material, as opposed to free creation on the basis of inspiration and
originality.

> *[L'] univers instrumental [du bricoleur] est clos, et la règle de son*
> *jeu est de toujours s'arranger avec 'les moyens du bord', c'est-à-dire*
> *un ensemble à chaque instant fini d'outils et de matériaux,*
> *hétéroclites au surplus, parce que la composition de l'ensemble n'est*
> *pas en rapport avec le projet du moment, ni d'ailleurs avec aucun*
> *projet particulier, mais est le résultat contingent de toutes les*
> *occasions qui se sont présentées de renouveler ou d'enrichir le stock,*
> *ou de l'entretenir avec les résidus de constructions antérieures . . .*
> *[les éléments de son répertoire] sont donc à demi particularisés:*
> *suffisamment pour que le bricoleur n'ait pas besoin de l'équipement*
> *et du savoir de tous les corps d'état; mais pas assez pour que*
> *chaque élément soit astreint à un emploi précis et déterminé.*
> *Chaque élément représente un ensemble de relations, à la fois*
> *concrètes et virtuelles; ce sont des opérateurs, mais utilisables en*
> *vue d'opérations quelconques au sein d'un type.*[8]

This description corresponds in many ways to Simon's own view of the

relationship between the writer and language. The writer's medium is one which has evolved over the centuries; it pre-exists him and his immediate intention, and he has to make of it what he will. However, the heterogeneity of its elements, their lack of a definite and exclusive use and their contextual plurivalence make for extremely varied possibilities of recombination, the establishment of associations and relationships between objectively unrelated things and the transformation of those words which are particularly rich in potential semantic operations into 'mots carrefours'. Finally, in both *bricolage* and artistic creation the finished product will have gone beyond any initial intention:

> *Une fois réalisé, celui-ci [le projet] sera donc inévitablement décalé par rapport à l'intention initiale (d'ailleurs, simple schème).*[9]

> *Comme me le disait Raoul Dufy un jour que je le regardais peindre: Il faut savoir abandonner le tableau que l'on voulait faire au profit de celui qui se fait.*[10]

However, the productive capacity of the activity should not eclipse its restrictive side. The notions of assemblage, organization and reorganization are fundamental to the process of *bricolage*. Both Simon and Lévi-Strauss attach considerable importance to the choice exerted by the author or *bricoleur* and to the interdependence of the elements in any one specific recombination. Indeed, it is interesting to note that in his fullest definition of what *bricolage* means for him, Simon describes it firstly in terms of the organization and adaptation of material and only secondly in terms of generation:

> *Je ne connais pas, en effet, de terme qui mette mieux en valeur le caractère tout à fait artisanal et empirique de ce labeur qui consiste à assembler et organiser, dans cette* unité *dont parle Baudelaire et où elles doivent* se répondre *en* échos, *toutes les composantes de ce vaste système de signes qu'est un roman. Cela se fait par tâtonnements successifs: il y a des éléments qu'il faut raboter ou limer pour les intégrer et les ajuster, d'autres auxquels on se voit, au contraire, obligé d'ajouter, d'autres, que l'on avait crus excellents et que l'on est forcé de rejeter, d'autres enfin qu'il faut 'fabriquer' . . . pour remplir un vide . . . Et le plus fascinant . . . c'est que ces nécessités purement formelles . . . se révèlent être* éminemment *productrices et, en elle-mêmes, engendrantes.*[11]

Such a commentary makes it easier to reconcile the evident

alterations and reorganization to which Simon has subjected his short
texts with his much-quoted declarations concerning the 'mot à mot'
production of his novels through phonetic and semantic association.
Over and above the choice exerted by the author in relation to the
associations of a particular 'mot carrefour', there is a process of
adjustment dictated by a concern for the unity and coherence of the
whole. Whether such changes are effected in a continuous manner or in
a retrospective survey of the drafts of the novels is impossible to say
without access to manuscripts. However, the existence of a number of
currently available revised fragments do permit a few tentative
observations about the nature of the 'tâtonnements successifs' which,
according to Simon, are necessary to the production of a unified text.
The rest of this article will be devoted to such a comparison of the short
texts and novels from the late fifties and the sixties.

ELIMINATION

The discrepancies between the short texts and the novels suggest
that, in spite of the anarchic impression left by his proliferative
expansion, his accumulation of near-tautologies and his approximative
style, the most common type of retrospective alteration practised by
Simon during that phase of his evolution is that of elimination.

The nature of this elimination is generally quite comprehensible in
terms of the priorities and dislikes of the *nouveaux romanciers* in general
and of Claude Simon in particular. The suppression of the
philosophical commentary or sociological explanation, for example, is a
frequent occurrence. Between the appearance of 'Le Cheval' and that of
La Route des Flandres a considerable amount of the characters'
deliberation about the nature of the war they are fighting has been
eliminated. The insults directed at Hitler — 'ni Wagner ni son gros
porc de copain d'Hitler' — and the discussion in the café on the
justifiability of fighting — 'Je suis un bon Français, mais ça n'empêche
pas que je me demande qu'est-ce qu'on va faire dans cette guerre pour
des Polonais qu'on a seulement jamais vus'[12] — are completely absent
from *La Route des Flandres*. Similarly, the Jewish question and the
paradox of the ignorant anti-semitic peasant Wack who is fighting
against Nazism are given much less prominence in *La Route des
Flandres* than in 'Le Cheval'. In the earlier text, the acrimony of the
relationship between Wack and Maurice is much more pronounced,
and the bartender in the café is given to making stereotyped racist
remarks about the Jewish control of wealth. In *La Routes des Flandres*

the theme of Blum's Jewishness receives its fullest treatment in his angry account of his own background (pp. 282-7). However, this outburst has little bearing on the Second World War as such — rather it acts as a counterpoint to Georges's obsession with his own family, highlighting the relativity of the narrative which has preoccupied us throughout this novel and suggesting that the formulation of experience into narratives is the privilege of a certain class.

Such an elimination of commentary on specific contemporary issues can be explained largely by reference to Simon's condemnation of any attempt to turn literature into a medium for conveying a certain philosophy of life. Any criterion can serve as a basis of judgement and all moralizing is simply the arbitrary adoption of one point of view among many:

> *On peut baser une philosophie et une conception de la vie sur à peu près n'importe quoi, sur n'importe quelle obsession, sur les crampes d'estomac, l'homosexualité, la volonté de puissance, le calcul différenciel, la folie de la persécution, le spiritisme ou l'épilepsie et en faire découler tout un système logique ou onirique. (CR, p. 95)*

Consistently throughout his interviews Simon has insisted on the amoral nature of art and — quoting Elie Faure — the sentimentally neutral nature of the harmony which the writer seeks to establish between different things.[13] Whenever challenged on his 'omission' of a condemnation of war in *La Route des Flandres*, he argues that such judgements lie exclusively in the domain of the moralist or sociologist.[14] With the increasing fragmentation of knowledge, the writer cannot hope to explain the world and should avoid aligning himself with any ideological position.[15] Such considerations may also determine the omission of some of those passages where the narrator in the short texts seems to feel free to embark on long, generalizing tirades on subjects such as the passing of time and the repetitiveness of seasonal habits ('Le Cheval', p. 188) or the inexorable spread of capitalism and its reduction of the natural world to uniform units of currency ('La Statue', pp. 403-5; contrast *Histoire*, pp. 96-7).

In some cases, Simon's suppression of the commentary found in the earlier texts seems to be dictated not so much by a general opinion about the nature of the novel but by a more immediate concern for the coherence of the fiction and by changes in the conception of specific characters in the course of writing. On page 171 of 'Le Cheval', Georges wistfully assesses the odds on whether the nation which is trying to subjugate Europe will return to the cultural pursuits which permitted the creation of the sixth Brandenburg Concerto.[16] Such a deliberation would be out of keeping with the Georges of *La Route des Flandres*. There, despite the erudite references which pepper his narrative, Georges expressess his resentment of the way in which his father focuses his repugnance for the war on the loss of culture caused by the bombing of the Leipzig library (pp. 223-4). If, after an examination of the drafts of the novel, one were to conclude that narrative coherence is one reason for this and other instances of elimination, one would be faced with a disturbing paradox, the possibility of which does not seem to have occurred to most readers of Simon's revised and published novels. It remains possible that a novelist who is largely known for his disruption of traditional concepts of plot and character has, nevertheless, in the final versions of his novels introduced retrospective corrections dictated by conventional criteria relating to coherence and plausibility of characterisation.

However, in spite of this potential inconsistency, it is fair to say that the elimination of a characteristic is more likely to have been determined by a desire to discourage the facile naturalization of the text in purely psychological terms. Thus, while 'La Statue' includes the reflections of the narrator on the desirability of having more money (p. 394), in *Histoire* the reader has to deduce the narrator's precarious financial situation from the various encounters of his day. Whereas the evocation in the short text of the narrator's envy of those who have money facilitates in advance the readerly tendency to try to organize the textual data into nameable proairetic sequences,[17] in *Histoire* the proliferation of the associations activated in the course of the day prevails to the point of making the reader forget for most of the time the motive behind the narrator's actions (the need to borrow money).

The elimination in *Histoire* of a psychological commentary on Uncle Charles which is present in 'Matériaux de construction' may have been determined by the desire to reinforce the powerful but simplified image which the narrator retains of his uncle. In *Histoire* the Charles with whom the narrator is familiar is a recluse living in a twilight world and constantly engaged in a distracted way in apparently pointless distillation experiments. In 'Matériaux de construction' the narrator had ventured quite a subtle hypothesis about the possible reason for this behaviour:

> *je soupçonnais même sa distraction ou sa négligence de faire partie de cet ensemble de précautions pour ainsi dire dont il s'entourait*

comme pour se protéger se ménager en quelque sorte des alibis
contre l'inaction ou l'ennui . . . s'efforçant donc ainsi de vaincre
(ou de s'accommoder de ou de se concilier ou de signer un armistice
avec) le temps, l'une de ses armes . . . étant sans doute cette
persévérante distraction ou étourderie qui lui permettait de justifier
en quelque sorte la répétition des mêmes gestes. (p. 119)

The suppression of this analysis in *Histoire* deniès the reader access to Charles's motives, contributes to the levelling of any psychological 'roundness' that the character might have and strengthens the effect of the narrator's schematization of his uncle into two irreconcilable images — that of a recluse and that of an artistic bohemian (*H*, p. 86).

The differences between 'Comme du sang délayé' and pages 336-7 of *Histoire* reveal a considerable shift in emphasis between 1960 and 1967 from psychological analysis to linguistic play. The initial stimulus for both analysis and punning is the same — the confusion of the associations of the words 'Frascati', 'Fiaschanti' and 'fiasque'. However, the short text gives considerable space to a description of the contingent circumstances and psychological causes for such a confusion, whereas the later version illustrates the indissociable nature of the relationship between memory and linguistic code, and suggests a possible reading of biographical experience in terms of the play of associations between and around those words which have caught the narrator's imagination (pp. 335-6). The earlier passage constitutes a fairly sustained and continuous examination of the process of associative sedimentation and of the way in which, under certain circumstances, a name can take on a quasi-mythical status. The greater concentration of the corresponding passages in *Histoire* and their alternation with passages based on the associative play between Champagne and Champenois give more prominence to the phonetic factor in association and testify to a significant change in Simon's priorities.

The differences between 'Sous le kimono' and the corresponding passage in *La Bataille de Pharsale* (pp. 47-51) are equally striking. The analysis of his former self by the narrator of *La Bataille de Pharsale* stops short at the association which he feels between his adult guilt over illicit sexual desire and his childish guilt over forbidden trips to the fair. However, 'Sous le kimono' provides additional insights into his defiant behaviour in the form of references to his desire to stay out later than those class-mates whom he could not beat in other respects and to his

irritation at his mother's feebleness and chagrin (p. 51). The evocation
of his mother's physical appearance and expressions is itself altered in
an interesting way from one text to the other. Simon eliminates in *La
Bataille de Pharsale* the long, rather digressive comparisons with the
chickens in a farmyard found in 'Sous le kimono' and substitutes for it a
comparison with the expressions of saints in Baroque paintings which is
in fact a recurrent motif in Simon's fiction. This particular substitution
reinforces intertextual relationships between this and other novels and
makes the reader more aware of the principle of recombination on
which the text of *La Bataille de Pharsale* is largely based.

Psychological analysis is not the only feature to be sacrificed to
linguistic play and recombinatory principles. 'Le Cheval' contains a
good deal of sustained dialogue which is compressed, fragmented and
dispersed throughout the text in *La Route des Flandres*. The various
dialogues among the soldiers in 'Le Cheval' about the adulterous and
incestuous intrigues of the locals convey a substantial amount of
unambiguous information to the reader and are punctuated by a
sufficient number of 'dis-je', 'dit Maurice' and 'dit Wack' to prevent
great confusion on the reader's part:

> — *Le champion du tir au fusil était cocu, dit-il.*
>
> — *Pas possible? dis-je. Avec cette tête de Casanova et ce joli nom
> italien, comment est-ce déjà: Ruspoli, Ranavalo, Ri. . . .*
>
> — *Parlez pas si fort! dit l'homme.*
>
> *Il regarda craintivement dans la direction de la cuisine.*
>
> — *Mais tu ne devineras jamais par qui, dit Maurice.*
>
> — *Sans blague, dis-je. Ce n'est pas le Roméo au parapluie?*
>
> — *Si, bien sûr, dit Maurice. C'était l'adjoint. Mais la femme
> c'était la propre sœur de l'adjoint.*
>
> — *Que veux-tu, dis-je. C'est sans doute un type qui a le sentiment
> de la famille. Alors ce bol de lait. . . .*
>
> — *Tu mélanges tout, dit Maurice. Celle-là, c'est celle du frère qui
> est mobilisé. (p. 189)*

Any mystification that there is in 'Le Cheval' is experienced by the
characters rather than the reader and is largely restricted to the attempts
by the 'je' and Maurice to exclude the rather obtuse Wack from their

conversations while preying on his curiosity (p. 181). In *La Route des Flandres* most of the conventional signs by which statements are attributed to specific characters and which permitted the readers to consider them in terms of a play of personalities have been eliminated and the responses made considerably more elliptical and metaphorical. The information which would deflate the myth being built up by the soldiers around this community is never fully revealed. Indeed, the basic facts are obfuscated in favour of quite startling linguistic combinations:

> *et Blum disant: 'Si j'ai bien compris ce boiteux champion de tir au fusil a des peines de cœur?', Georges se taisant maintenant, les mains dans ses poches, occupé à ne pas glisser dans la boue invisible, et Blum: 'Cet adjoint avec son parapluie et ses bottes à rustines! Le Roméo du village! Qui aurait cru ça? Lui et ce bol de lait . . .', et Georges: 'Tu mélanges tout: pas avec elle: avec sa sœur', et Blum: 'Sa s . . .'. . .*
>
> *Mais répète encore ça Il (je veux dire l'adjoint . . .) couchait avec sa propre sœur qui était la femme de ce boiteux c'est bien ça?*
>
> *oui*
>
> *ces gens de la campagne tout de même hein?*
>
> *oui*
>
> *leurs sœurs et les chèvres hein? Paraît qu'à défaut de sœur ils font ça avec la chèvre . . .*
>
> *alors il a transformé sa chèvre en fille ou sa sœur en chèvre et Vulcain je veux dire ce boiteux épousa la chèvre-pied et ce bouc de frère venait la saillir dans sa maison . . .*
>
> *c'est ce qu'il a dit*
>
> *alors c'était du lait de chèvre?*
>
> *qui?*
>
> *celle qui était dans l'écurie ce matin celle qui se cache derrière ce paon mythologique . . .*
>
> *bon Dieu tu es décidément plus bête que Wack on t'a dit dix fois que c'était la femme de son frère . . .*
>
> *merde Quel frère? merde à la fin Qu'est-ce que c'est que cette*

histoire Alors ils sont tous frères et sœurs Je veux dire frères et
chèvres Je veux dire boucs et chèvres Alors un bouc et sa chèvre et
ce boiteux de diable qui a épousé la chèvre qui s'accouplait avec
son bouc de frère qui (pp. 126-9)[18]

The dialogue of 'Le Cheval' never really goes beyond the level of gossip
and idle banter, whereas the verbal exchange in *La Route des Flandres*
quoted above could be seen to demonstrate the way in which a word
('chèvre') becomes a prominent element in the cultural code of a given
community.

The elimination of tool-phrases (such as 'dis-je') also extends to
temporal, causal and concessive conjunctions. Simon seems
increasingly reluctant to establish explicit logical or chronological
relationships between the events of his narrative. Thus, the temporal
connnections which, in 'Le Cheval', structure the account of the
argument between the 'boiteux' and the 'adjoint' ('A ce moment'
'Quand je descendis', 'mais tandis que') are by and large eliminated in
La Route des Flandres which tries to recreate the fragmentary
impression of the images left in Georges's memory. Similarly, the
connective summary of the farm-girl's attitude while the soldiers were
unsaddling in 'Le Cheval' — 'Quand elle vit que nous étions installés et
commencions à dessangler les chevaux, elle sortit' (p. 174) — disappears
in *La Route des Flandres* and is replaced by formulations which stress
the apparent suddenness of her appearance and disappearance and
suggest the discontinuity of Georges's impressions: 'Puis ils furent dans
la grange, avec cette fille tenant la lampe au bout de son bras levé,
semblable à une apparition' (p. 38); '(la jeune fille avait maintenant
disparu)' (p. 40). Simon has on several occasions expressed his tendency
to retain static, isolated images as opposed to more synthetic memories
of a period of time.[19] In both 'Le Cheval' and *La Route des Flandres* he
explicitly endows the 'je'/Georges with such a trait (p. 174, p. 41), but
reinforces the point in the later texts by a reorganization of the temporal
relationships between different moments.

REDISTRIBUTION OF NARRATIVE DATA

The often quite radical redistribution of the data of the early texts is
in fact another common feature of Simon's *bricolage*. Once again he
occasionally contradicts some of the principles and priorities voiced in
his interviews. A notable instance occurs in the modification of 'Sous le
kimono' in *La Bataille de Pharsale*. Here, despite his declared dislike of

dialogue, Simon transforms what amounted to a summary of the usual course of the narrator's Latin tuition with Uncle Charles into a dialogue:

> *Oncle Charles . . . essayant . . . de me faire traduire la première phrase puis de guerre lasse renonçant et se résignant enfin à me dicter rapidement la traduction du texte de Tacite ou de Suétone que je recopierais après dîner avant d'aller me coucher.* ('Sous le kimono')
>
> > *dextrum cornu ejus rivus quidam impeditis ripis muniebat Je m'arrêtais*
> > *alors?*
> > *rivus: une rivière*
> > *impeditis ripis: aux bords obstacles*
> > *des bords obstacles qu'est-ce que ça veut dire explique-moi*
> > *je me taisais*
> > *tu pourrais peut-être te donner la peine de chercher plus loin que le premier mot que tu trouves dans le dictionnaire combien de temps as-tu passé à préparer cette version?*
> > *je me taisais*
> > *bon très bien impeditis ripis: aux rives escarpées ça ne te semble pas mieux?* (BP, pp. 51-52)

The economical communication of information which is the traditional function of the summary interests Simon much less than the opportunity to explore the medium with which he is working — language. The dialogue with which he replaces the summary fails to fulfil its traditional function as an emphatic narrative mode heralding a turning point in the plot or a crucial behavioural revelation. Its interests lies in the implicit contrast between the poverty of the narrator's childish attempt to translate Latin through word-for-word substitution and the productiveness of the older narrator's sensitivity to the polyvalence and flexibility of language.

One of the main effects that the redistribution of data in the published novels has is to fragment the initial text and to disperse its constituent parts over a chapter or even a more substantial part of the book. No doubt for reasons associated with the publication conditions and lay comprehensibility, the 'content' of the short texts is treated with much greater continuity.[20] Thus the description of the narrator's visit to the bank is presented as an uninterrupted narrative in 'La Statue', whereas in *Histoire* it is a situation-catalyst stimulating, in the narrator's mind, innumerable memories and reflections which constantly interrupt the focal narrative.

Even more than in the case of 'La Statue' and *Histoire,* the content of 'Le Cheval' is dispersed throughout much of *La Route des Flandres.* A comparison of page 175 of 'Le Cheval' and page 42 of *La Route des Flandres* illustrates quite clearly the way in which this dispersal is effected. The notation of a sensory impression in 'Le Cheval' — the sight of a shaving-mirror in the barn — becomes, in *La Route des Flanders,* the hinge for a shift forward in time to the hotel scene between Corinne and Georges with its references to the reflection from the wardrobe mirror. Such promotion of a detail of content and its transformation into a structural articulation which re-orients temporarily the narrative bears out Simon's remarks on the gradual and retrospective nature of the organization of the material:

> There are certain articulations, intersections or exchanges from one series, or set, to another that occur to me at the moment of my initial notes, and others that occur to me during the course of my work.[21]

Alterations of this nature must also severely qualify the impression of continuous and accumulative generation which Ricardou's analyses conjure up in the reader's mind.

Considerably more radical than the pursuit of the associations of a sensory impression or word, however, is the relativization of the narrative perspective which also takes place in *La Route des Flandres.* 'Le Cheval' is recounted entirely in the first person, whereas in *La Route des Flandres* there is a constant vacillation between the first and third persons. Indeed, much of the content of 'Le Cheval' is narrated in the third person in *La Route des Flandres.* Furthermore, in *La Route des Flandres* Georges's role as narrator and/or principal point of reference is challenged by Blum's contribution to the evocation of the various narrative motifs. Thus, the account in the first person in 'Le Cheval' of the visit of the 'je' and Maurice to the café becomes, in *La Route des Flandres,* a retrospective debate between Georges and Blum about the accuracy of their memory of the occasion. The detail of something which was presented as a straightforward fact in 'Le Cheval' is suddenly called into question in *La Route des Flandres,* a novel which is considerably more concerned with the problems of representation than with the furtherance of any one narrative thread. The self-relativizing nature of the narratorial framework in *La Route des Flandres,* based on alternation, collaboration and dispute, subverts the authority of the teller and results in a plurivalent text where various voices co-exist and interact with one another.

EXPANSION

The desire to suggest the problematical nature of representation may also be the source of the third and final type of alteration which I am going to consider in this article — expansion. Thus, in the account of the argument between the farmer and the 'adjoint', Simon introduces in *La Route des Flandres* an explicit commentary — absent from 'Le Cheval' — on the perfidious nature of language:

> *les voix se mêlant en une sorte de chœur incohérent . . . une*
> *parodie de ce langage, qui, avec l'inflexible perfidie des choses*
> *créées ou asservies par l'homme, se retournent contre lui et se*
> *vengent*[22] *avec d'autant plus de traîtrise et d'efficacité qu'elles*
> *semblent apparemment remplir doucement leur fonction: obstacle*
> *majeur, donc, à toute communication. (RF, pp. 59-60)*

The capacity of language to turn against those who would try to impose on it their own meaning is a favourite topic in Simon's interviews.[23] Its significance in his thought is evident from the fact that he comments so explicitly on it in a novel from which he has excised a great number of explicit psychological and quasi-philosophical observations. Simon is obviously much more ready to pronounce on the medium with which he is working than on any other topic.

Sometimes the suppression of psychological interpretation would seem to be dictated by a desire to pursue and expand on the associations of a particular word or sound. Thus, the rather laboured comparison in 'Le Cheval' between the woman's sexual parts and a fountain and the fairly coventional equation of the womb with a promise of security and oblivion give way in *La Route des Flandres* to an extensive and proliferative play on the phonetic and rememorative associations of the word 'moule':

'Le Cheval':

> *sommairement façonnée avec le pouce dans la tendre pâte, la douce*
> *chair de femme, deux cuisses un ventre, deux seins, la ronde*
> *colonne du cou, et au creux de tout cela, comme au centre de ces*
> *statues nègres à la précise, tranquille et glorieuse impudeur, l'antre*

*humide et noir, cette bouche herbue aux âcres senteurs de terre,
d'humus, de coquillage, semblable à une source sous les
broussailles, sable humide aux lèvres altérées du voyageur, du
pèlerin, du soldat perdu, abandonné aux effrayantes ténèbres de la
nuit et de la mort: le doux, l'apaisant refuge, le sein profond de la
nuit. (p. 175)*

La Route des Flandres:
*sommairement façonnés dans la tendre argile deux cuisses un
ventre deux seins la ronde colonne du cou et au creux des replis
comme au centre de ces statues primitives et précises cette bouche
herbue cette chose au nom de bête, de terme d'histoire naturelle —
moule poulpe pulpe vulve — faisant penser à ces organismes
marins et carnivores aveugles mais pourvus de lèvres, de cils:
l'orifice de cette matrice le creuset originel qu'il lui semblait voir
dans les entrailles du monde, semblable à ces moules dans lesquels
enfant il avait appris à estamper soldats et cavaliers, rien qu'un
peu de pâte pressée du pouce.* (RF, *pp. 41-2*)

The digressive expansion is also one of the means by which Simon
effects the transitions between the various temporal levels of the novel.
This is the source of the long narratorial commentary on pages 68-70 of
La Route des Flandres triggered off by the argument between Wack and
Blum. This highly involved and parenthesis-ridden paragraph on the
economic laws governing wars leads up to a startling punning
reactivation of the cliché 'ils ont numeroté mes abattis' which operates
the shift from the barn scene to the sequence in the packed railway
truck. In the context of such cramped conditions, Georges is made
acutely aware of both the articulations of his body and the peculiar
aptness of the old expression:

*'. . . Une histoire d'os comptés, dénombrés . . .', pensant: '. . . ils
ont numeroté mes abattis . . .'*

*Il essaya de dégager sa jambe du corps qui pesait dessus . . . Une
suite d'os s'accrochant et s'emboîtant bizarrement les uns dans les
autres . . . voilà ce qu'était un squelette, pensa-t-il. (p. 70)*

Whereas in the previous example the expansion seemed to develop
fairly naturally out of the context, in this latter case Simon has
obviously had to create an intermediary passage in order to be able to
use a particularly vivid pun. The economy and compactness of the pun

in the final version is shown to be based on a quite substantial addition to an earlier version.

The reactivation of a cliché is a common Simonian practice. Another notable instance from *La Route des Flandres* involves the expression 'avoir des fourmis dans les jambes'. The brief and rather clumsy metaphor on page 173 of 'Le Cheval' describing the mental state of the 'je' — 'tandis qu'à travers ma tête une interminable armée de fourmis chaussées de godillots à clous défilait interminablement' — disappears completely in the corresponding passage in *La Route des Flandres*. However, I would suggest that it gives rise to the evocation on pages 258-9 of *La Route des Flandres* of the sensation of tingling numbness in terms which suggest that real ants are crawling over Georges's body. By teasing out a cliché before us, Simon makes us aware of the metaphoric suggestiveness of the phrases which we take for granted and which have, because of habit, lost much of their initial force. The initial metaphor was simply an isolated, expressive vehicle in a quite conventionally subordinate relationship to the sensation which it was trying to evoke. In *La Route des Flandres*, it takes its place in a passage spanning several pages with a particularly high concentration of puns and metaphors. The expedient and economical expression of the short text has in the later text been incorporated into a highly imaginative associative chain. Simon's promotion of the generative procedures involved in literary production depends, in fact, on a retrospective authorial correction.

Finally, I should like to make a rather more tentative connection between another brief reference in 'Le Cheval' and a much more substantial section towards the end of *La Route des Flandres*. On page 186 of 'Le Cheval' in the scene where the 'je' and the feverish Maurice visit a local café, Maurice makes the following witticism: 'Le soldat français fonctionne au gros rouge . . . Ça l'habitue à la vue du sang. C'est dans le manuel du gradé'. This remark, along with much of the dialogue, is absent from the corresponding scene in *La Route des Flandres* (pp. 124-5). However, although a detailed manuscript reading might reveal otherwise, I would hazard the provisional suggestion that this may be the source of the lengthy passage at the end of *La Route des Flandres* which summarizes the experience of Georges in the style and register of an army manual. In the final version of *La Route des Flandres*, the isolated sarcastic remarks directed by the characters against authority are replaced by a much more devastatingly radical exposition of the gap between representation and reality in the form of an emphatic counterpoint between the turmoil and amorphousness of Georges's experience and the ruthless clarity and calculation of the manual.

CONCLUSION

This article was intended to rescue some of Simon's short texts from relative obscurity. I have tried to do this through illustrating the type of information which can be deduced from the discrepancies between these short texts and the definitive versions included in the published novels. My analysis of three specific forms of alteration — elimination, reorganisation and expansion — despite the obviously arbitrary restrictions of such an enterprise, nevertheless indicates that the short texts cannot easily be dismissed as intimatory excerpts from forthcoming books. In particular, I have argued that the earlier short pieces of writing are important documents for an understanding of the largely language-orientated directions taken by Simon in the writing of his novels.

I should further like to suggest that a serious re-evaluation of the short texts opens up a significant area in Simon studies. A number of the short texts have been deliberately neglected here because the discrepancies between them and the novels — although less striking than the ones which I have analysed here — are of such a detailed nature that they merit a full-length article in themselves. Such is the case of 'Correspondance' and 'Propriétés des rectangles'. These texts are by and large taken up in *Histoire* and *Les Corps conducteurs* respectively. However, there are changes in the order of narration and distribution of material which are quite far-reaching in implication.[24] These variations raise questions once again about the use of the concept of generation. If material is reshuffled in this way in the draft stages, the generative relationships between the different sections, paragraphs and sentences become problematic and the reader can no longer assume that the novel is faithful to the original order of generation and association. Considered in this perspective, no judgement about departure-point and digression, source and variation could be final without reference to the other drafts of the novels.

The potential lines of inquiry which might be pursued if one had access to the publisher's proofs and manuscripts of the novels are numerous and varied. A comparison of the original drafts, proofs, short texts and the novels would undoubtedly shed light on the criteria by which Simon considers that the possibilities of generation, recombination and alteration are exhausted and that the novel is complete. Furthermore, variations in the number of versions required for each novel and discrepancies in the nature of the retrospective alterations carried out by Simon at different periods would undoubtedly produce a more subtle analysis of his evolution than has yet been carried out.

Finally, I should like to repeat that this article was intended to complement rather than to challenge the approaches of Ricardou and Roubichou. Indeed, I think that a Ricardolian analysis of the short texts themselves remains possible and highly desirable. An assessment of the relative suitability of Ricardou's models in dealing with the various stages of Simon's novels would allow one to gauge more precisely the extent to which Simon's anti-representational stand is a natural inclination or self-imposed purgative exercise involving the elimination of psychological and fictional 'scories':

> *Anthony Pugh: Je veux insister sur le fait que dans* La Bataille de Pharsale *il n'y a pour ainsi dire plus de narrateur. A ce moment précis, toute une série d'intérêts psychologiques qui disparaissent par rapport à certains de vos précédents romans . . .*
>
> *Claude Simon: Il y a des scories que je me suis efforcé de supprimer peu à peu. C'est effectivement à ce moment-là que j'ai entrevu quelque chose d'autre.*[25]

Ultimately, I would argue that the analysis of linguistic association in the plurivalent text and the more traditional investigatory attempts to define authorial priorities are not mutually exclusive and that their combination would almost certainly yield revealing results.

REFERENCES

1.   See G. Roubichou, *Lecture de 'l'Herbe'* (Lausanne, 1976), and the relevant chapters of J. Ricardou, *Problèmes du nouveau roman* (Paris, 1967); *Pour une théorie du nouveau roman* (Paris, 1971); *Nouveaux Problèmes du roman* (Paris, 1978).

2.   See 'L'Opinion des nouveaux romanciers sur *Pour une théorie du nouveau roman*', *La Quinzaine littéraire*, 1-15 juillet 1971, p. 9 and G. Dörr, 'Biographie oder Bildersprache? Claude Simon über sein neustes Werk *Les Corps conducteurs*', *Die Neueren Sprachen*, 21 (1972), 294-6.

3.   See the preface to *Orion aveugle* (Geneva, 1970).

4.   G. d'Aubarède, 'Claude Simon: Instantanés', *Les Nouvelles littéraires*, 7 novembre 1957, p. 7.

5.   Claude Simon, 'La Fiction mot à mot', *Nouveau Roman: hier, aujourd'hui*, edited by J. Ricardou (Paris, 1972), vol. 2, p. 84.

6.   A. Bourin, 'Cinq romanciers jugent le roman', *Les Nouvelles littéraires*, 29 juin 1961, p. 8.

7.   Claude Simon, 'Rendre la perception confuse, multiple et simultanée du monde', *Le Monde (des livres)*, 26 avril 1967, p. v.

8.   *La Pensée sauvage* (Paris, 1962), p. 27.

9.   *La Pensée sauvage*, p. 32.

10.   'Réponses de Claude Simon à quelques questions écrites de Ludovic Janvier', *Entretiens: Claude Simon*, no. 31 (1972), p. 27.

11.   'La Fiction mot à mot', pp. 96-7.

12.   'Le Cheval', *Les Lettres nouvelles*, no. 57 (février 1958), 169-89 (pp. 171 and 187). Page references to Simon's short texts are hereafter incorporated in my text. Full publication details are given in the Bibliography at the end of this volume, pp. 157-8. I have corrected a number of inaccuracies in Roubichou's bibliography in *Lecture de 'l'Herbe'* which may have been partly responsible for the initial neglect of the short texts.

13.   For example, Claude Simon, 'Je ne peux parler que de moi', *Les Nouvelles littéraires*, 3 mai 1962, p. 2.

14.   A. Bourin, 'Techniciens du roman: Claude Simon', *Les Nouvelles littéraires*, 29 décembre 1960, p. 4.

15.   M. Joguet, 'Dialogue avec Claude Simon: le poids des mots', *Le Figaro littéraire*, 3 avril 1976, pp. 13-14.

16.   A related allusion does occur, however, on page 195 of *La Route des Flandres* in a remark made by Blum about the nature of history: 'Bien, bien: travaillons nous aussi à l'Histoire, écrivons nous aussi notre quotidienne petite page d'Histoire! Après tout je suppose qu'il n'y rien de plus déshonorant ou stupide à pelleter une montagne de charbon qu'à mourir gratis pour le roi de Prusse, alors donnons-en pour son argent à ce Mozart brandebourgeois'. The subversion of the concept of history as a sequence of major events and prominent names and the demonstration of its real banality is an important motif in Simon. Blum's remarks here are in line with the immoderate and cynical outbursts which he makes elsewhere in the novel.

17.   See R. Barthes, *S/Z* (Paris, 1970), p. 26.

18.   Note too the reversal in roles between the 'je' and Blum/Maurice.

19.   'Rendre la perception confuse, multiple et simultanée du monde'.

20.   Neither author nor publisher can afford to expose the readers of rather general literary journals to a 'sample' of writing which is so unfamiliar as to be rebarbative. It would no doubt be an illuminating exercise to try to establish the extent to which the priorities and critical approaches of the individual journals concerned may have affected the type of extracts contributed by Simon.

21.   C. Duverlie, 'Interview with Claude Simon', *Sub-stance*, no. 8 (1974), 3-20 (p. 10).

22.   This combination of a singular subject and plural verbs is apparently an uncorrected grammatical slip which has survived until the final version.

23.   See A. Poirson, 'Un homme traversé par le travail', *La Nouvelle Critique*, juin-

juillet 1977, 32-46, and Y. Berger and Claude Simon, 'Deux Ecrivains répondent à Jean-Paul Sartre', *L'Express*, 28 mai 1964, p. 303.

24. Andrea Cali devotes a chapter of her book *Pratiques de lecture et d'écriture* (Paris, 1980) to 'Propriétés des rectangles'. However, her interest lies principally in the non-recuperability of the short text and not in an analysis of the nature of the differences between 'Propriétés des rectangles' and *Les Corps conducteurs.*

25. *Nouveau Roman: hier, aujourd'hui,* vol. 2, p. 107.

La Route des Flandres: the rout(e) of the reader?

Pat O'Kane

> They teach us to read as children, and for
> the rest of our lives we remain the slaves of
> all the written stuff they fling in front of us.
>
> Italo Calvino

If in the past the focus of much literary criticism was directed almost exclusively on the author and his work, the last decade has witnessed an unprecedented growth of interest in the activity of the reader. Indeed an indication of this major shift in perspective lies in the fact that it is no longer possible to talk simply of 'the activity of the reader' since the nature of the process of reading and the very status of the subject engaged in this process, far from being unproblematic and obvious, now constitute a fertile area of investigation that students of literary criticism can no longer afford to ignore. However, reader-oriented criticism is by no means a conceptually unified school or movement and the plethora of divergent critical terms coined with each new publication can in some cases lead to confusion.[1] Nowhere is this confusion more apparent than in the numerous attempts at defining the 'reader'. Faced with studies of implied readers, real readers, mock readers, virtual readers, and numerous other readers of various kinds, the critical reader, or rather the reader of criticism, may perhaps be forgiven for throwing up his hands in despair and resorting to a more traditional approach to the literary process.[2]

It may be advisable to begin then by attempting to define, as far as this is possible, the reader (or readers) to be studied in this article. In many respects the definition of the reader proposed is simpler, if more limited, than most, in that what we intend to examine is the effect of a literary device whereby the major character of a book (or one or more of the major characters) is revealed to be a reader of books, and where the activity of reading itself constitutes an important thematic element. Obviously all significant literary characters are in some way 'readers of signs' in the sense that Deleuze applies to this activity in Proust.[3] Indeed it is now commonplace to consider the character as a sort of double or 'simulacre' of the reader himself, for, as Dubois points out, the character is 'à chaque fois, celui qui, à la faveur de son attente ou de sa marche, porte un regard et contemple, c'est-à-dire *lit* un paysage, un décor'.[4] However for the purposes of this article our investigations will be limited solely to a study of the reading of books or texts. Our reader then is entirely fictional in the sense that all literary characters are fictional. Our overriding concern however will be to evaluate how the portrayal of reading *in* the fiction can influence and maybe even direct our reading *of* the fiction.

In an extremely interesting analysis of children's first reading manuals in France, Pierre-Alban Delannoy points out that the texts offered seem to have a dual purpose, 'un aspect didactique' in that the books promote the acquisition of basic reading skills, but more importantly (for us at least) 'un aspect *initiatique*' in that they aim to foster as well the child's recognition of the power of the *Book*. In a detailed examination of the function of the illustrations in a variety of reading manuals Delannoy writes: 'l'image semble bien fonctionner comme figure privilégiée de l'album qui constitue l'objet culturel sacrifié, sacrifice qui rend possible l'investissement dans le texte, et au-delà dans le code scolaire et social'.[5] The child is encouraged to sacrifice his reading of pictures in return for a knowledge of the world through the Book: the apprenticeship of reading then functions almost as 'une procédure de passage', a symbolic death and rebirth as reader.[6] The child's accession to the status of reader then is marked not only by the acquisition of new language skills, but also by a symbolic act of faith in the ultimate value of the Book, an act of faith which is dependent upon and continually reinforced by the institutions of school and society.

Many critics have commented on the themes of 'initiation' and 'apprentissage' in the work of Claude Simon. Time and again the unbridgeable gap between 'innocence' and 'experience' is explored with the themes of sex and violence dominating. The coming to terms with reality through the experience of war is perceived by the protagonists as 'quelque chose, en somme, comme la perte des illusions. La perte d'une

virginité rêveuse et romantique, au profit d'une connaissance
substantielle, dans le même moment désenchantée et éblouie' (*CR*, p.
117). Despite the complexity of this initiation, as seen in the somewhat
paradoxical collocation of 'désenchantée' and 'éblouie', a recurring
complaint in many of Simon's novels is the failure of the written word
to inform or prepare the reader for real-life experiences: in *La Corde
raide* we read 'c'est seulement dans les livres, à l'aide de mots, que la
mort prend une grandeur et une majesté solennelle. En réalité, elle peut
être horrible, effrayante ou ridicule, mais pas tragique' (p. 47). The 'je
ne savais pas encore' of *La Bataille de Pharsale* can be seen as a leit-
motif of the narrator making this discovery. Very often then the theme
of initiation (sexual or otherwise) is closely linked to that of literature.
Certainly this sustained questioning of the efficacy of language results
in a crisis of representation, an apparent disillusionment with the Book.
But can we link it in any way to Delannoy's comments on the initiatory
aspect of learning to read, and to what extent is the 'reader' a figure
worthy of study in Simon's work?

Although the fictional figure of the writer/hero is by now a familiar,
not to say hackneyed, novelistic device, outstanding literary characters
whose major preoccupation or distinguishing feature is their dedication
to reading are more thin on the ground by far. It is not without
significance then that in his first novel, *Le Tricheur*, Simon makes an
explicit reference to one of the best known books 'about reading',
namely *Le Rouge et le Noir* which Ephraïm the Jewish watch salesman is
reading (p. 176). The purely thematic parallel between the two texts is
immediately obvious. The Black and the Red represent two ways of
advancement open to Julien Sorel, the church and the army. In the
Simon text the church and the army are represented by two fathers,
Louis's own father who was killed in battle (p.27), and the priest that
Louis himself eventually murders (p. 248). In both cases the father
figure personifies a way of life open to Louis, a model for existence: he
notes of his mother: 'prêtre. Voilà donc ce dont elle rêvait, ou soldat.
Un héritier ou un conquérant' (p. 32). Ultimately, however, the
acceptance of the authority of the father symbolizes an admission of
faith in the power of the Book, a belief in the efficacy of the Book as a
manual or guide through life. Both fathers personify an allegiance to
what Delannoy calls 'le livre sacré' (p. 198), the priest to the Bible
('saint Paul et Sa Parole'), and Louis's father to 'le "Code"'. Lacan sees
the father as the stabilizing influence in symbolization — c'est dans le
nom du père qu'il nous faut reconnaître le support de la fonction

symbolique'[7] — while Delannoy suggests that accession to the status of reader implies the acceptance of the father as 'moniteur-père' (p. 220). Clearly then, Louis's violent repudiation of both father figures can be interpreted as a questioning of the traditional status of the Book, and implicitly therefore as a potential challenge to the accepted role of the reader in literature. This questioning or lack of confidence in literature is apparent in Louis's remark: 'l'espoir n'est que l'aveu de l'impossibilité à supporter le présent. J'ai lu ça quelque part. J'ai d'ailleurs beaucoup trop lu' (p. 218).

But if the fictional reader is encoded largely symbolically or implicitly by intertextual reference in *Le Tricheur,* his presence is much more obvious, thematically, in Simon's later works where the initial ideas on literature and reading are echoed and extended. This is particularly true of *La Route des Flandres* which can be seen in many ways as a 'mise en scène' of the disappointed reader. Initially again it is the 'father' who incarnates the credulous or naïve reader, in this case Georges's father (Pierre) and the ancestor of de Reixach whose portrait hangs in Georges's parents' house. Pierre, endowed with a 'superstitieuse crédulité — ou plutôt croyance — en l'absolue prééminence du savoir appris par procuration, de ce qui est écrit' (p. 36), is entirely convinced 'qu'il n'y a pas de problème, et en particulier celui du bonheur de l'humanité, qui ne puisse être résolu par la lecture des bons auteurs' (p. 222). De Reixach's ancestor too was an equally avid reader: Georges imagines him 'en train de lire consciencieusement l'un après l'autre chacun des vingt-trois volumes de prose larmoyante, idyllique et fumeuse . . . qui, à la fin, lui ferait, appliquer contre sa tempe la bouche sinistre et glacée de ce . . .' (p. 83). In both cases, however, this view of reading as the acquisition of knowledge is ridiculed and ultimately devalued. On numerous occasions it is suggested that the ancestor's suicide (or rather hypothetical suicide) is in fact a direct result of his reading (pp. 83, 84, 194, 202), while Pierre's faith in the value of reading is continually disparaged and eventually shattered by Georges's decision to spend his life working on the land (p. 233). Georges's repudiation of his father and through him of the Book precisely mirrors that of Louis in *Le Tricheur.*

However, as we shall see, a tendency towards reading is by no means restricted solely to the father figure in *La Route des Flandres.* In *L'Herbe* Georges declares:

je voudrais n'avoir jamais lu un livre, jamais touché un livre de

> *ma vie . . . et même, si possible, ne même pas savoir, c'est-à-dire*
> *avoir appris, c'est-à-dire m'être laissé apprendre, avoir été assez*
> *idiot pour croire ceux qui m'ont appris que des caractères alignés*
> *sur du papier blanc pouvaient signifier quelque chose d'autre que*
> *des caractères sur papier blanc. (p. 152)*

Yet *La Route des Flandres* shows that George's refusal to submit to the power of the Book is not quite as categorical as it may appear. Although he claims that since the books in the library at Leipzig were incapable of preventing the war which destroyed them, they are 'manifestement dépourvus de la moindre utilité' (p. 224), he himself constantly has recourse to the books he has read (pp. 31, 45, 72, 100, 259, 287). Not surprisingly this habit provokes the ironic rebukes of Blum: 'mais tu parles comme un livre!' (p. 222), 'tu as trop lu de livres' (p. 131). Georges excuses himself by stating that this is 'une tare héréditaire' (p. 222), an affliction passed on from father to son, from generation to generation.

In actual fact Georges is constantly cast in the role of reader by a complex and sustained metaphorical 'rapprochement' of sexual activity and the activity of reading. 'Lire un texte, c'est faire l'amour avec les mots', writes Jean Verrier.[8] In *La Route des Flandres* this maxim can be interpreted 'au pied de la lettre'. The correlation between sex and reading is suggested in a variety of ways. In *Le Plaisir du texte*, Roland Barthes writes: 'le texte a une forme humaine, c'est une figure, un anagramme du corps'.[9] The Simon text reverses this analogy somewhat in that the body, and in particular the female body, is frequently presented as a text, a body of language or signs to be deciphered. This is perceptible initially in the trivial sense that words used to describe the various females often have decidedly literary connotations as well; 'la chair des femmes', we read, is 'comme des plumes, de l'herbe, des feuilles' (p. 243); the young girl in the barn is described not simply as a woman, but as 'l'idée même, le symbole de toute femme' (p. 41); the woman in the miniature portrait is dressed in 'une simple chemise . . . ses tendres seins offerts soulignés par un ruban . . . avec cette tranquille opulence des sens' (p. 281); while the ladies at the racecourse are dressed 'en robes de couleurs imprimées' (p. 19).

In addition to this, Corinne complains on numerous occasions that in Georges's mind she is nothing more than a sign, 'quelque chose comme ce qu'on voit dessiné à la craie ou avec un clou sur les murs des casernes' (p. 276). Georges, remembering this accusation, thinks:

'comme ce qu'on voit dessiné sur les murs avait-elle dit les deux hiéro-glyphes, les deux principes: féminin et masculin, quelquefois celui-ci n'est plus qu'un signe' (p. 290). This image of Corinne as a hieroglyph or language to be read is further suggested by a striking intertextual reference: 'il me semble qu'il n'est pas très difficile de se figurer à quoi peuvent penser pendant cinq ans un tas d'homme privés de femmes, à peu près quelque chose dans le genre de ce qu'on voit dessiné sur les murs des cabines téléphoniques' (p. 96). These words of Corinne can be linked directly to a section in *Le Sacre du printemps* where the graffiti in a telephone booth are described as 'un graphisme en quelque sorte rupestre . . . comme un ichtyographie de modernes catacombes' (p. 129). This image in turn is echoed in *La Route des Flandres* where we read: 'on disait qu'ils se reconnaissaient en traçant sur les murs des villes et des catacombes le signe du poisson' (p. 290). The introduction of the religious symbolism accentuates the link between reading and sex since the fish is the sign of Christ and Georges describes his penis as 'renflé comme un fuseau un poisson' (p. 290).

The theme of religion brings about a rapprochement between reading and sex in another way. On page 139 we read of Corinne: 'elle avait à peu près l'air et la taille d'une hostie (c'est-à-dire quelque chose d'iréel, de fondant, qui ne peut être goûté, connu et possédé que par la langue, la bouche, la déglutition) au centre d'un de ces énormes et riches ostensoirs'. This obviously refers initially to the oral sexual activity between Georges and Corinne. However, the fact that Corinne is something to be known and possessed 'par la langue' would also seem to point to a link between sexual activity and the activity of reading, and Georges's phrase 'mes mains ma langue pouvant la toucher la connaître' (p. 257) seems to reinforce this. The suggested relationship is further strengthened by a subtle play on the meanings of *consommation,* as consumption and consummation. The ancestor's reading is described as 'indigeste' (p. 194), and Georges imagines him 'ingurgitant pêle-mêle les filandreuses et genevoises leçons d'harmonie, de solfège' (p. 83). In addition to this, Corinne's skin is compared to 'une feuille de papier à cigarette' (p. 238) and this again can be linked to the 'prose larmoyante, idyllique et fumeuse' (p. 83) that the ancestor reads. Georges also drinks or consumes 'le lait de l'oubli' (p. 261) offered by Corinne's body, this 'milk' calling to mind the 'encre blanchie' of the family documents Sabine has amassed (p. 54). The metaphorical association of lait/encre, milk/knowledge with sex and reading is made clear in a striking passage in *L'Herbe* where a group of schoolboys are described as

C

cancres aux doigts tachés d'encre, cherchant, le feu aux joues (dans
les dictionnaires tachés d'encre . . . sorte de Bibles de la
connaissance . . .) cherchant les vieux, les indestructibles mots
latins (matrone, mentule, menstrues), les lèvres tachées de violet
mordillant le porte-plume rongé comme si, avec l'encre qui les
souille, elles suçaient sans comprendre le lait, le principe, non pas
même d'une civilisation, de la poussiéreuse culture aux inutiles et
poussiéreux bouquins, mais de la vie même. (pp. 130-131)

In the novel then, consumption and consummation are intimately
linked in a metaphorical transfer which ultimately suggests a textual
parallel between knowledge gained from books and sexual knowledge.

Doubrovsky, in an analysis of Georges's quest for knowledge
through Corinne talks of 'une curieuse mise en équation de l'acte
érotique, de l'acte d'écrire et de l'acte de parler'.[10] However, the 'mise
en équation' of 'l'acte érotique' and the act of reading is no less
arresting, as the links we have already mentioned are further reinforced
by the striking textual correspondances established between various
parts of the novel. On page 54 we have a description of the documents
that Georges 'avait passé une nuit à parcourir'. This can be linked
directly to the night he spends with Corinne; we read: 'je n'en finissais
pas de la parcourir rampant sous elle explorant dans la nuit découvrant
son corps immense et ténébreux' (p. 257). The textual jump is in fact
suggested in the 'texte italien' (pp. 55-56) where the words 'femme
centaure', 'lire', and 'con' seem to hint at the analogy to be drawn
between the two sequences, and implicitly then between the two
activities. The accounts of the night Georges and Corinne spend
together also contain many elements that can be traced back to
descriptions of Pierre reading. On one occasion we find him 'sous le
grand maronnier où ils ont pris le thé, le maronnier en fleurs à cette
époque, ses multiples grappes blanches comme des candélabres
doucement phosphorescentes' (p. 243). However because of the fading
light he can no longer read, 'se contentant . . . de savoir que ces
caractères, ces signes sont là, comme dans sa nuit un aveugle sait —
connaît — l'existence des murs protecteurs . . . encore qu'il puisse au
besoin les toucher' (p. 244). In the descriptions of Georges and Corinne
in the hotel room Corinne's breasts are 'rose-thé' (p. 261); Georges's
penis is 'cette tige . . . cet arbre' (p. 257); he can feel 'le souffle sorti de
l'obscure fleur noire des lèvres' (p. 95); having sex with Corinne he
penetrates 'cette mousse ces mauves pétales' (p. 292). Like the

documents Pierre is studying, Corinne's buttocks are described as 'luisant faiblement phosphorescentes bleuâtres dans la nuit' (p. 257).[11] In addition, Georges on numerous occasions is compared to a blind man groping around in the dark; again the comparison with the description of Pierre is striking: 'mais une seule tête maintenant, qu'il pouvait toucher en levant simplement la main comme un aveugle reconnaît, et même pas besoin d'approcher la main pour savoir dans le noir' (p. 95).

In spite of Georges's explicit rejection of his father's naïve belief in the power of literature, it is obvious that his own quest for knowledge through Corinne exactly mirrors that of his father through books:

> *elle avait peut-être raison et que ce ne serait pas de cette façon c'est-à-dire avec elle ou plutôt à travers elle que j'y arriverai . . . peut- être était-ce aussi vain, aussi dépourvu de sens de réalité que d'aligner des pattes de mouches sur des feuilles de papier et de le chercher dans des mots. (p. 295)*

Georges himself eventually comes to this realization, and his admission, 'qu'avais-je cherché en elle esperé poursuivi jusque sur son corps dans son corps des mots des sons ausi fou que lui avec ses illusoires feuilles de papier noircies de pattes de mouches' (p. 274), underlines the fact that even in the sexual activity between himself and Corinne the concern with reading is dominant.

This metaphor of the female as book allows a striking parallel to be drawn between de Reixach and his ancestor and invites us, by paradigmatic association, to see de Reixach too as a 'deceived' reader.[12] If the captain is 'cocufié' by Corinne, his ancestor 's'était pour ainsi dire fait cocu lui-même, c'est-à-dire trompé: cocufié . . . non par une perfide créature féminine comme son lointain descendant mais en quelque sorte par son propre cerveau, ses idées — ou à défaut celles des autres' (p. 84). Both men are deceived, hypothetically by women, and implicitly then by their reading. The idea that de Reixach too is a 'lecteur trompé', is further suggested by another important intertextual reference which crops up in several of Simon's texts. In the second part of *Le Sacre du printemps,* Bernard's stepfather, like so many of Simon's protagonists, undergoes an initiation which makes him acutely aware of the falsity of his 'connaissances livresques' (p. 161). In a passage which can be linked directly to *Le Tricheur* he says: 'peut-être avais-je trop lu Nietzsche, espéré, cru, rêvé corriger le sort, et ainsi, triché. Mettons si tu veux un peu de tout' (p. 265); another example of someone who is duped by the books he has read. Now on two occasions Bernard's stepfather is

compared to the most famous of all fictional readers — Don Quixote
(pp. 250, 267). Don Quixote, we recall, 'so buried himself in his books
. . . filled his mind with all that he read . . . and so deeply did he
steep his imagination in the belief that all the fanciful stuff he read was
true, that to his mind no history in the world was more authentic'.[13]
This reference to Don Quixote is crucial in that it highlights a crisis of
reading. Don Quixote is the personification of the naïve reader, the
reader who fails to differentiate between the book and the world.
Karlheinz Stierle in fact writes: 'the quasi-pragmatic reception of
fictional texts is most strikingly illustrated by the literary figure of Don
Quixote. Don Quixote represents a reader for whom fiction changes
into illusion to such a powerful degree that it finally replaces reality'.[14]
It is revealing then that on numerous occasions we are invited to see the
de Reixach family as direct descendants of the famous 'hidalgo'. De
Reixach and the other 'cavaliers' appear to Georges as 'formes
donquichottesques' (p. 25); he imagines the earth concealing 'les
ossements des défuntes Rossinantes et des défunts Bucéphales' (p. 242);
the group of racehorses is described as a 'cortège hiératique et médiéval'
(p. 154), a 'groupe médiéval' (p. 153). In addition, both de Reixach and
his ancestor are accompanied by a 'Sancho Panza' their 'doubles fidèles'
(p. 25). Blum surmises of the ancestor that 'sans doute n'était-il pas
seul, avait-il lui aussi auprès de lui, s'était-il fait suivre d'un fidèle valet'
(p. 197), while de Reixach himself is accompanied by Iglésia, 'son frère
d'armes ou plutôt son frère en chevalerie' (p. 296). And what could be
more 'donquichottesque' than de Reixach's absurd gesture of
brandishing his sabre in the face of a German machine-gun, a gesture
'que lui avaient probablement transmis des générations de sabreurs' (p.
12)?

On a variety of levels then *La Route des Flandres* brings the problem
of reading to the fore. Pierre, Georges, de Reixach and his ill-fated
ancestor can all be seen in some way as 'fictional readers'. We suggested
earlier that, in learning to read, children undergo an initiation, an
initiation which results in a faith in the power of the word, an
acceptance of the ultimate value of the Book. The fictional readers in
the work of Claude Simon experience a second initiation, a second
'alphabétisation', a loss of virginity which is intellectual rather than
sexual in nature, 'comme si la virginité était moins une affaire de sexes,
de la chair déchirée, violentée, qu'une disposition, ou plutôt une
préservation de l'esprit' (*L'H,* p. 69). If the reading manuals analysed
by Delannoy lead to a confidence in the world and the Book, the novels

of Claude Simon seem to lead in entirely the opposite direction since this loss of virginity can be equated with a loss of faith in the power of the Book, a re-education in reading.

If *La Route des Flandres* documents the education (or rather re-education) of various fictional readers, it also constitutes an education for us, the readers. The process of the fiction and the thematics of the text seem to mirror and reflect each other. This is particularly true in the case of the suggested analogy between reading and sex. As we have seen, Georges's pursuit of knowledge through sexual activity with Corinne is constantly likened, metaphorically, to a process of reading and, ultimately, this pursuit is seen to be as futile and meaningless as Pierre's search for truth through books. However, the re-education is by no means entirely negative in nature, for, in equating reading with sex, we, as readers, have taken part in a complex textual 'accouplage', we have adopted a way of reading entirely contrary to that embodied by Pierre, we have exploited (and explored) the 'incantatoire magie du langage' (*RF,* p. 184). As Michel Foucault points out, Don Quixote represents not only the 'lecteur trompé', he can also be taken as a model for this new way of reading: 'la vérité de Don Quichotte . . . n'est pas dans le rapport des mots au monde, mais dans cette mince et constante relation que les marques verbales tissent d'elles-mêmes à elles-mêmes'.[15] It is this relation that the reader of *La Route des Flandres* is invited to explore. Reading, then, is now seen as a positive investigation of the text's *being* and not simply a passive assimilation of its *meaning.* 'Pourquoi ne pas prendre le roman moderne comme la peinture moderne', writes Simon, 'c'est-à-dire n'y chercher que ce qu'il propose? Il y a là, bien sûr, un changement dans la façon de lire'.[16] By focusing attention on the tragedy of defective reading in *La Route des Flandres,* Simon forces us, as readers, to reconsider the particular qualities of the literary work and invites us ultimately to redefine our relationship to it. We too then are asked to undergo an initiation or re-education as readers.

Obviously this brief study in no way exhausts the theme of the fictional reader in the novels of Claude Simon since we have concentrated almost exclusively on *La Route des Flandres.* Other aspects of the question need to be investigated in relation to other texts. *La Bataille de Pharsale* in particular abounds in references to readers and reading. Also, in view of Delannoy's suggested link between the illustration and the text in reading manuals, it might be worthwhile investigating how and if the reproductions of various illustrations in

Orion aveugle influence the way in which we read that text. The commentary on the reading of a textbook which forms an integral part of *Leçon de choses* would also seem to demand some attention, not to mention the reading of Orwell's *Homage to Catalonia* documented in Simon's latest work, *Les Géorgiques*. What we hope to have shown is that far from being simply the result of a current criticial fad, the reader, reading and the way in which they are portrayed, constitute an important if as yet largely unexplored aspect of the Simon text.[17]

REFERENCES

1. For a discussion of the various approaches to reading and the reader see Ruth Amossy, '(Re)lecture(s)', *Romanic Review,* 72 (1981), 226-242.

2. For a valiant attempt to distinguish between these various readers see W. D. Wilson, 'Readers in texts', *PMLA*, 96 (1981), 848-863.

3. Gilles Deleuze, *Proust et les signes* (Paris, 1971).

4. Jacques Dubois, 'Surcodage et protocole de lecture dans le roman naturaliste', *Poétique*, no. 16 (1973), 491-498 (p. 495).

5. Pierre-Alban Delannoy, 'L'Image dans le livre de lecture', *Communications,* no. 33 (1981), 197-221 (p. 199).

6. This belief in the Book is obviously at the centre of the 'logo-centrisme' attacked by Derrida, see *De la grammatologie (Paris, 1967), pp. 27-31.*

7. Lacan, 'Fonction et champ de la parole en psychanalyse', *Écrits 1* (Paris, 1970), pp. 157-8.

8. Verrier here is quoting the words of one of his students in 'Questions sur un parapluie', *La Français aujourd'hui*, no. 54 (juin 1981), 91-92, (p. 91).

9. Roland Barthes, *Le Plaisir du texte* (Paris, 197), p. 30.

10. Serge Doubrovsky, 'Notes sur la genèse d'une ecriture', *Entretiens: Claude Simon,* no. 31 (1972), 51-64 (p. 61).

11. The analogy between Corinne's body and Pierre's papers is even stronger when we remember that in *L'Herbe* these papers are described as 'feuilles blanches . . . vaguement phosphorescentes dans l'ombre' (p. 256).

12. For a more detailed analysis of the metaphor of the book as female see Michael Danahy, 'Le Roman est-il chose femelle?', *Poétique*, no. 25 (1976), 85-106.

13. Cervantes, *The Adventure of Don Quixote* (London, Penguin Books, 1950), p. 32.

14. Karlheinz Stierle, 'The reading of fictional texts', in *The Reader in the Text,* edited by S. Suleiman and I. Crosman (Princeton, 1980), pp. 83-105 (p. 87).

15. Michel Foucault, *Les Mots et les Choses* (Paris, 1966), p. 62.

16. 'Claude Simon, à la question', in *Claude Simon: colloque de Cerisy*, edited by J. Ricardou (Paris, 1975), pp. 403-31 (p. 407).

17. For a recent analysis of reading and intertextuality see Maria Brewer, 'An energetics of reading: the intertextual in Claude Simon', *Romanic Review,* 73 (1982), 489-504.

Fiction as process: the later novels of Claude Simon

Maxim Silverman

Claude Simon has described his development as a writer as 'une lente évolution par tâtonnements'.[1] Despite the progressive transformation in technique referred to here, Simon's work from 1960 onwards clearly falls into two distinct periods. I propose to explore both the continuity and difference between these two periods in order to highlight Simon's techniques in foregrounding the fiction-making process.

Simon's novels of the 1960's unsettle and challenge the reader by posing two fundamental problems. The first of these concerns the point of view or perspective adopted in the narrative. The narration appears to be both positioned from the limited point of view of the hero present at a particular scene (in true Jamesian style) and able to adopt a wider and more distanced focus (more akin to the all-embracing vision of the classic omniscient narrator of the nineteenth century). This ambiguity between what can be called the focus *of* a character and the focus *on* him is apparent in both the first-person narrations of *La Route des Flandres* and *Histoire* and the third-person narration of *Le Palace*. Thus, in *La Route des Flandres* the narration is characterized by a fluid movement between the perceptions of the hero in Flanders and the wider focus of the narrator reflecting on his past experience; in *Le Palace* the same balance is established between the focus of the student and the focus on him by the narrator. Despite the oft-repeated announcements of the limited point of view ('je pouvais voir', 'j'ai pu le voir', 'pouvant voir') the narration habitually includes information which clearly exceeds that limited point of view. The effect is that of a subtle and fluid contraction and expansion of focus.

These 'glissements' and condensations of focus, these camera-like 'zooms' and 'wide-angles' disrupt visual unity and clarity in the narration and challenge the traditional polarity between the 'objective' and 'subjective' novel. Perspective functions rather like a moebius strip to produce an impossible relationship between the outer and inner points of view. Simon is indebted here (and elsewhere) to Proust since a large part of the fascination of the narrative structure of *A la recherche du temps perdu* is to be found in the ambiguous relationship between the wide focus of the narrator and the limited focus of the hero. Yet, in Simon's case, the expansions and contractions of point of view produce a dizzy movement which is far more disturbing for the reader.

The second problem confronting the reader in the novels of the 1960's concerns the narrating voice. *La Route des Flandres, Le Palace* and *Histoire* all relate the memory of past events: the hero who returns to his ancestral house in *Histoire* and attempts to piece together the fragments of his past indulges in the same activity as the man who returns to Barcelona in *Le Palace* and Georges in *La Route des Flandres*. However, unlike more conventional narratives, these texts often blur the distinction between the time of the events narrated (or 'énoncé') and the moment of narration itself ('énonciation'). In all three novels the main narrative tense is a past tense. Yet the impression of a present-tense narration within the past tense is created by an over-abundance of present participles, of past participles used adjectivally, of descriptive detail de-temporalizing the action and of temporal indicators denoting a present action. The hero's sexual encounter with Corinne in *La Route des Flandres* is typical of this type of narration:

> *lappant son chose rose mais non pas rose rien que le noir dans les ténèbres touffues me léchant le visage mais en tout cas mes mains ma langue pouvant la toucher la connaître m'assurer, mes mains aveugles rassurées la touchant partout courant sur elle son dos son ventre avec un bruit de soie recontrant cette touffe broussailleuse poussant comme étrangère parasite sur sa nudité lisse. (p. 257)*

At these times the moment of 'énonciation' is equivalent to the time of the 'énoncé': the hero merges with the narrator narrating his experience in the present and the narration of past events takes on the appearance of a present 'stream of consciousness'.

Like the ambiguities in perspective, this past/present-tense narration clearly produces a fluidity and confusion in temporal relations between both narration and event and narrator and hero. The long account of the ambush of the squadron and the death of de Reixach in *La Route des Flandres* (see pp. 156-159), the Italian's account of the assassination in

the second section of *Le Palace,* and the interview between the hero and
the bank manager in *Histoire* (see especially pp. 70-75) all demonstrate
this: the narration appears to spring both from the character present at
the scene and from a narrator who is distanced from the event. The
'histoire' mode of narration — which Roland Barthes has described as a
world of established, free-floating facts in the past divorced from any
'énonciation'[2] — is penetrated by the present 'discours' of a
hero/narrator relating his own experiences. Such an unsettling
combination of the two types of narration disrupts the conventional
relationship between the two moments of 'énoncé' and 'énonciation'
and thus renders problematic the reader's ability to situate the moment
and source of the narrating voice.

These problems are accentuated by a further ambiguity. Specific
moments of 'énonciation' are frequently introduced only to be
immediately abandoned, causing the narration to drift into an
indeterminate area between (or rather, comprising) several levels of
'énonciation'. Each specification of who is speaking, from where and at
what point in time seems to have no effect whatsoever either on what is
being narrated or the manner and style of 'énonciation'. Indeed, the text
appears to ignore the fact that a new level of 'énonciation' has been
introduced at all. This is the most striking feature of the switches
between the first and third person in *La Route des Flandres* (see
especially pp. 26-27). But we can locate the same phenomenon in *Le
Palace,* where it is impossible to distinguish between the narrative of the
man who returns to Barcelona and that of the impersonal third-person
narrator, and in *Histoire,* where the narration of the hero is invariably
condensed with the present of the narrator. The different levels of
'énonciation' are indistinguishable in these texts because each voice
relates, repeats or reworks elements mentioned elsewhere. Resemblance
and repetition of 'énoncés' cut across the different moments of
'énonciation' so that there is, in fact, no way of distinguishing from
which 'énonciation' the narration comes.

Here we can locate an important aspect of Simon's narrative
technique in the novels of the 1960's. Each text consists of a series of
memories which seem to merge into one another and a series of voices
which are swallowed up in the single, continuous current of narration.
This should not lead us to conclude that everything is subsumed within
the voice of a single narrator or, as has been suggested, 'l'éternel présent
du souvenir',[3] but within the eternal present of a discourse in the
process of elaboration. Or, if the concept of memory is indeed to be

maintained, it must be re-defined (as with Proust), for it is no longer the classic, psychological mechanism for the reconstitution of the past but a present discourse which constitutes a text. Here is a voice which tries to reason, branches off through digressions, recapitulates, is attentive to the sounds of words, a discourse which is thus elaborated slowly and uncertainly by means of linguistic prompts and circuitous routes. It is a voice which draws attention, as Dominique Lanceraux notes, 'non point sur la scène donc, mais le mouvement par lequel elle s'énonce'.[4] Hence a proliferation of those features of 'énonciation' which allow the discourse to progress 'á tâtons': *peut-être, donc, il me semble, sans doute, je suppose, pour ainsi dire, je pense, j'imagine.*

Simon's narration is, in effect, the scene of a discourse which progresses through an exploration of language. The ambiguities in perspective and voice are the products of a narration which pays little heed to the 'vraisemblable' and the literary conventions of realism but concerns itself more with its own mode of discourse. Under these conditions the distinction between memory and imagination (the 'real' and the 'fictional') becomes blurred since both are subject to the demands of the writing. So, for example, the life of the ancestor 'imagined' by Georges and Blum (*RF*, pp. 80-88 and pp. 188-200) is narrated in exactly the same manner as Georges's 'real' experiences in the war; similarly, there is no distinction in mode of narration in *Histoire* between the narrator's description of Uncle Charles as a young man ('imagined') and episodes from his own past life ('real') (see especially pp. 266-300). Whether real, imagined or reported via a witness at the scene — the horse race in *La Route des Flandres* told via de Reixach's jockey Iglésia (pp. 144-180) or the political assassination in *Le Palace* told via the Italian (pp. 47-99) — all scenes merge into a common narration which is, properly speaking, the very process by which those events are produced, that is, through the act of writing itself. In this sense, these texts reveal specific aspects of the modernist tendency: fictional episodes are shown to be produced and developed according to the peripeteias of the narration and the 'histoire' mode is transformed into a 'discours' whose present is the moment of writing.

What is the poetic technique which underlies this discourse? The frequent switches between fictional episodes — a familiar and disturbing feature of Simon's novels — transform the text into a mosaic of sequences. The resemblance of these diverse sequences through a host of common elements suggests the importance of metaphor in the structuring of the Simonian discourse. Each transition is clearly operated through the perception of similarity (or similarities), in the same way that the taste of the 'madeleine' allows the association of two distinct spatio-temporal episodes in Proust's novel. Jean Ricardou, especially, has indicated the way in which certain words operate these transitions or 'aiguillages' in the narration.[5] So, in *La Route des Flandres*, the narration switches from Georges's father to the night ride in Flanders through the similarity between the 'piétinement' of the father's voice in the autumn night and the 'ruissellement' of the rain in Flanders (pp. 37-38); the darkness and silence of the barn in which Georges is lying after the night ride and the erotic images conjured up by the young girl who has shown the riders to their place of rest subsequently produce a switch to Georges's night of passion with Corinne after the war (pp. 41-42), and so on.

Yet the emphasis upon the metaphorical nature of these novels tends to obscure an equally important process at work here, namely the combination of diverse textual elements and the associations produced through a crossing of paradigms. This interchange of elements to produce new associations (and hence a cross-connection of motifs) is essentially *metonymic* in character. For example, colours which appear in diverse contexts are displaced from one element to another and therefore unite (in a metonymic chain) the disparate objects with which they are contiguously related. In *La Route des Flandres* the red and yellow of the empty wardrobe in the hotel room (p. 42) have already been seen in connection with the horses during the war, the horses at the horse race, Iglésia's jockey outfit and Corinne's dress, and therefore recall these diverse objects/characters while, at the same time, establishing a connection between them.

It would therefore be truer to say that Simon's narration is constituted by the joint action of metaphor and metonymy; that is to say, it is subject to the ceaseless process of resemblance and contiguity of elements. The extraordinarily dense nature of the writing is the product of an exploration of language on these two planes: each passage repeats and rearranges elements mentioned elsewhere and therefore recalls the network of associations already established in the narration.[6]

This play of language has much in common with that of the dream-text: through a process of condensation and displacement of meaning each sequence becomes 'over-determined' and the reader is thus held within the multitude of metaphoric and metonymic chains which constitute the text.[7] The description of the naked woman at the window in *Le Palace* (pp. 173-5) serves as a demonstration of the work of the writing: the framing of the woman in the window recalls the poster of a revolutionary in the office of 'le palace' (see p. 121) and the erotic pictures which formerly hung there (see p. 11); the position of the framing recalls other framed images, in all of which only the top half of the body is visible (see pp. 106, 109, 123, 130), this 'coupure' suggesting the disappearance of the sexual organs and the introduction of the theme of castration; the shape of the spear-head between the woman's legs relates to other references to the weapon as phallus-substitute (see p. 17, 99, 126) and hence reinforces the theme of castration through the revolution; the 'fruit solitaire' of the woman's naval refers obliquely to the rotting foetus which stands as a metaphor for the aborted revolution, strangled by its own umbilical cord (see p. 16); the comparison of the body with a baroque construction recalls the description of the baroque hotel itself (see pp. 10-14) and, on another level, can be read as a metaphorical representation of the mode of production of the whole description, and so on. In short, the body of the woman dissolves into a tissue of diverse meanings and hence can be read as the material body of the text since its construction is, fundamentally, the material process of the inter-relation and superimposition of verbal signs which constitutes the text.

The effect of this mode of narration on the wider organization of the narrative is striking. The continual switching through resemblance from one episode to another disrupts the linear, temporal progression of the narrative and transforms it into a spatial composition: the fictional episodes are produced by a montage of diverse scenes. The inter-cutting of spatial fragments means that the text is the scene of the progressive and parallel development of a limited number of fictional episodes which 'expand' spatially through the addition of each new scene or spatial syntagm.

The constant reappearance of the same elements across episodes also results in the creation of a number of powerful motifs. Each scene itself is therefore like a collage composed of an 'assemblage' of this cluster of paradigms; consequently, episodes as a whole become mirror-images of each other. This method of narration favours not so much the 'mise en abyme' (which, strictly speaking, is an internal reflection of the main subject) but, as Lucien Dällenbach has suggested, a 'chevauchement' of 'récits métaphoriques'.[8] In other words, the narrative becomes the scene of an amalgamation in composite form of its mutually-resembling fictional episodes. For example, de Reixach's ancestor in La Route des Flandres becomes confused with de Reixach himself (see p. 58) so that the episodes relating to the two characters, separated in time by 150 years, are condensed to form a single, composite image. The same process occurs in *Histoire* with the merging of the hero and Uncle Charles (see especially pp. 151, 291, 369). As Dällenbach points out, this process again recalls Freud's description of condensation in dreams by which diverse layers of meaning are superimposed, like a set of transparencies, to constitute a single image.

The 'Simonian imagination' is clearly governed by a centripetal movement and a desire for unity. The disparate pieces in a fragmented text ultimately converge and combine to produce a dominant, single image which is not only composed of the diverse fictional episodes but also refers back to the chain of disparate scenes which are 'present' behind this image. In *La Route des Flandres* the articulation of themes and episodes is finally transposed onto Georges's desperate exploration of the body of Corinne; in *Histoire* the description of the photograph taken in the artist's studio (see pp. 266-301) provides the central image of the text, since the condensation of the hero and Uncle Charles allows an explanation of the former's fragmented present through the medium of the latter's past life.

The ultimate reconstitution of a thematic and spatial unity thus restores a hierarchy and coherence in the narrative which the play of language had done much to fragment. This 'closure' of the text terminates the modernist game of combining disparate parts and reduces the plurality of meaning to a 'sens univoque' (thus terminating the game with language). In other words, the final coherence of the fiction tends to obscure the work of the narration that has produced that fiction. Perhaps we can say that Simon's novels of the 1960's fall between two stools: they present an unmistakeable challenge to the realist text (by highlighting the process of production of fictions through the practice of writing) while, at the same time, failing to break with a narrative unity which lies at the heart of realism. They are at a stage of transition between Barthes's 'texte lisible' and 'texte scriptible', that is, between the text whose meaning is finally fixed and closed ('une structure de signifiés') and the modern text which manifests a plurality of meaning ('une galaxie de signifiants').[9]

The development from Part I to Part III of *La Bataille de Pharsale* demonstrates the transition from the novels of the 1960's to those of the 1970's: the stratification of temporality (past/present) and voice (a diversity of 'énonciations') cedes to a flat, uniform, non-stratified 'space' occupied by the play of language. If the mode of narration in the novels of the 1960's is a convoluted, baroque discourse, then the narration of the 1970's can be seen as a new classicism. The narrating voice has become strictly impersonal, no longer attributable to discrete characters but transformed into the voice of the narration itself. Similarly, the narrative perspective no longer shifts disconcertingly between hero and narrator but is now determined by the impersonal voice that speaks.

In the 1960's the voice ruminates, reflects and generalizes as well as reports what can be seen; in the 1970's the voice restricts itself almost entirely to what it can see. This produces a series of visual descriptions in which what can be seen is the product of a purely linguistic game. So, the description of the sick man's view along a New York street in *Les Corps conducteurs* is not an attempt to reproduce the scene realistically but is constituted by a play of elements already introduced in the text and which themselves will subsequently generate others:

> *Au bout de la rue il peut voir l'avenue qu'elle croise . . . et au-delà la marquise de l'hôtel. Il y a environ une centaine de mètres jusqu'au croisement avec l'avenue et, après celle-ci, encore une quarantaine de mètres jusqu'à la porte de l'hôtel. Les feuilles clairsemées des arbres, d'un vert tirant sur l'ocre ou même rouille, cartonneuses et maladives, s'agitent légèrement devant le fond grisâtre du building qui s'élève au coin de la rue et de l'avenue en lignes verticales et parallèles, comme des orgues. Dans l'ouverture de l'étroite tranchée que forment les hautes façades on peut voir le ciel blanc. A travers l'épaisse brume de chaleur l'extrémité de la tranchée se distingue à peine. (pp. 8-9)*

The antithesis of seeing ('on peut voir')/not seeing ('l'extrémité . . . se distingue à peine') and the colours of the trees are merely two of the motifs which play an important role in the formal construction of descriptions in the text. We might also draw attention to the use of point of view here. There is, in fact, no difference between the personal focus 'il peut voir' (which introduces the horizontal vision along the street) and the impersonal focus 'on peut voir' (which describes the vertical line of the sky-scrapers); they are equivalent in that both are the focal points used in the elaboration of a formal geometry which is in the process of construction.

This type of narration can be described as the voice of a mobile camera-eye: the eye is the focus of the voice while the voice itself is directed by a formalized play of language. Simon's achievement in the

1970's is to harness the narrating voice completely to the exigencies of the writing itself, so that the terms narrator/'énonciation'/writing become synonymous with one another. In this sense, the impersonal, present-tense narration is clearly the culmination of preceding techniques: the complete incorporation of the 'histoire' mode into the present discourse of a narration in the process of writing a text.

This new narration is thus a formalization and systematization of the practice of the 1960's and establishes a far more complex network of associations than in the earlier texts. The rigour of this new formal organization of sequences is evident in *Triptyque* where two sequences — a couple making love in a darkened barn and two boys fishing in a nearby river — interweave in the narration. The development of each sequence is structured according to a complex transference of 'signifiants' and 'signifiés', the river sequence apparently reflecting, in reverse order, developments in the barn sequence. We are told, for instance, that, on looking into the water, one's vision becomes progressively *more obscure* until total darkness is reached at the centre of the *circular* 'bassin', whereas, on looking through the slit in the barn wall, one's vision becomes progressively *less obscure* as the eye slowly begins to distinguish objects through the *circle* ('la fente') (pp. 10-11); *one can see* the bottom of the river because of the *darkness* (provided by 'les silhouettes' of the two boys leaning over the bridge) and the *circle* of a rusty barrel is visible within the *form of 'les silhouettes'*, whereas *one cannot see* clearly in the barn because of the *darkness,* and the *'silhouettes'* (of the couple making love) are visible within the *form of the circle* ('la fente') (pp. 13-14); the trout *goes into* the old jug lying on the river bed, next to which is the *blue* pan with the *black hole*, whereas the phallus *comes out* of a *black hole* between *blue* thighs (pp. 14-15); the base of the phallus *disappears* and subsequently *moves in and out*, whereas the second trout *appears* from beneath the bridge and finally becomes *immobile* (pp. 16-17). This series of cuts between sequences is terminated when the trout moves into a zone in which the opposites light/dark are synthesized within the oxymoron 'le reflet aveuglant' (p. 18).

Clearly the connection between the two sequences is not simply metaphorical, based on the resemblance between the movement of the phallus and the appearance and disappearance of the trout. The narration is regulated according to a formal play of balance and antithesis of 'signifiants' and 'signifiés'. Hence, the diverse objects in the river are closely associated with the sexual act: through similarity and contiguity. In addition to the chains of metaphorically-related elements (for example, *oeil, fente, trou, centre du bassin, cercle de tonneau*) are interwoven metonymic chains constituted by the 'enchaînement' of contiguous elements. Furthermore, this network of associations is not forgotten but is instrumental in determining the development of subsequent sequences. The reappearance of several of the objects on the river-bed in the context of the original meeting of the two lovers (which occurs later, on pages 54 to 56 of the text) is not at all fortuitous but is a direct result of the associations established between the objects and the couple at the beginning of the text. Those discarded objects are 'retrieved', so to speak, through 'le système de renvois'[10] in which they figure.

The procedure by which objects which appear in the opening descriptions are subsequently scattered over the text is a paradigm for the formal construction of the fictional episodes in Simon's more recent work. Description is not used as the context for an embellishment of the action but is, instead, the generating and propelling force underlying the progression of the narration and the development of the fiction. Indeed, 'Générique' — the opening section of *Leçon de choses* — is both a description which will generate the text as a whole (through the transformation of initial elements) and a self-reflecting dramatization of that process. By informing us that the description of the room could continue indefinitely (see pp. 10-11), the narration not only undermines the mimetic illusion but also suggests that the objects which subsequently appear in the room derive their visible presence in the text from their *linguistic* relations with objects already described (that is, words already mentioned). This specific relationship established between words and objects makes it clear that objects in the text are not concrete objects (that is, equivalent to their referents in the world) but themselves no more than words generated by other words. In which case, we might re-name the 'leçon de choses' as a 'leçon de mots'.

Objects described (models in a shop window, broken pots and pans on a river-bed, designs on a book-cover) are not so much tied to a specific 'signifié' but are points at which a number of meanings converge and from which a network of associations diverge. Each object (that is, each word) is a 'signifiant' whose meaning is always sliding along the metaphoric and metonymic chains established in the practice of writing. If the book in *Leçon de choses*, for example, is merely an object amongst many that are scattered in the room, it is (like them) caught up in a network of associations in language by which meaning is continually being condensed and displaced. The process of connection and transformation of an initial grouping of objects/words thus denies their instrumentality/expressivity and makes them the points of 'intersection' and 'réunion' of a plurality of meanings.

Is this signifying practice stabilized (as in the novels of the 1960's) according to the convergence of themes and spaces to produce, ultimately, a narrative coherence? In *Les Corps conducteurs* the presence of the sick man in the most significant episodes clearly prompts a reading which unites these episodes into a single, centred fiction. Other episodes — the soldiers' journey through the jungle, Orion's journey towards the rising sun — subsequently become mirror-images of the journey of the sick man towards his hotel. Once again, Freud's description of the dreamer's construction of a single image through the superposition (condensation) of a number of mutually-resembling images provides an excellent analogy with the process of unification of episodes in Simon's text. Thus in *Les Corps conducteurs* a plurality of meaning is again forestalled by the ultimate condensation of meaning within a single 'space': narrative coherence is achieved at the expense of an open-ended play of language. Hence, the flat and impersonal narration (the total abolition of a hierarchy of voices and focuses) does not necessarily produce a non-hierarchized text.

Recognition of this fact prompted Simon to undertake *Triptyque* with the express desire to break with the 'composition unitaire'.[11] Consequently, the inter-relationships of the narrative episodes in *Triptyque* and *Leçon de choses* do not function according to simple mirror-images but according to a continual series of contradictions which block a final resolution of the text. Herein lies the fascination and modernity of these novels. The three fictions proposed in each text are involved in a constant circulation of inner and outer, of main 'récit' and 'mise en abyme', whereby each episode is both contained in the other two, in the form of representations, and is the container of the other two. The opening passage from *Triptyque* is an image of the coastal resort (represented in the form of a postcard) lying on a table in the country kitchen (p. 7); this hierarchy is inverted at the end of the text when the image of the country scene is represented on the jigsaw-puzzle being composed by the man in the marine hotel (p. 220). The urban scene is initially represented in the form of a poster stuck on the side of the country barn (p. 21); later, the sexual encounter between the maid and the hunter in the barn is the subject of a film being shown in the town (p. 195). Furthermore, each episode is forever the subject of a different mode of representation: the coastal resort, first seen represented as a postcard, is subsequently to be the subject of a piece of film negative (p. 29), a film shown on a screen (pp. 33-34), a poster advertizing a film (p. 64), a film being made in a studio (pp. 80-81) and so on. No longer, therefore, are the 'spaces' progressively unified; no single episode dominates. Instead, stratification is denied since each 'space' is constantly in process of transformation.[12]

In *Triptyque* and *Leçon de choses* it is impossible to find an overall schema into which each of the three fictional episodes will comfortably fit. Each fiction is intricately connected with the other two (through the complex patterning of the process of metaphor/metonymy) yet never mirrors them. The achievement of these texts is to establish a continual process of production of fictions by the work of the narration without ever allowing the text to 'congeal' into a stratification of 'récits métaphoriques'. The fragmented narration incites in the reader the desire to construct a unity — by fitting together the disparate pieces in the puzzle — but deliberately blocks the reader's attainment of that unity. Instead we are left with a complex network of associations and no totalizing structure into which they fit.

The refusal to reinforce the reader's desire for unity through the refusal of a 'sens ultime' thus keeps open the processes of 'suture' and the production of meaning in the text. Now we can talk of a genuine break with realism. The realist text tends to efface itself as 'une écriture' and hence effaces itself as a material practice. It offers itself as a product to be consumed, as a body of (apparently) given, free-floating 'signifiés' which pass between writer and reader and constitute a shared and understood knowledge of the world. In opposition to this, *Triptyque* and *Leçon de choses* are composed of a sliding and transformation of 'signifiants', of a displacement and condensation of meaning through the complex play of metaphor and metonymy which is not foreclosed by a convergence of meaning but maintained as a plurality of signification 'without centre or point of arrest'.[13] The text is therefore transformed into a process of production of meaning in which both writer and reader are always *in formation,* never formed, always dispersed within the perpetual sliding of signification.

Les Géorgiques surprisingly marks a reversal in the rigorous development of Simon's practice of writing. The diversity of voices, the re-introduction of the long, digressive sentence and the frequent modulations in tempo of narration are immediately reminiscent of *Histoire* and the practice of the 1960's. Perhaps the most striking comparison with these earlier novels is the re-discovery of a centripetal movement which governs the wider narrative structuring of the text. *Les Géorgiques* is a text where the play of resemblance and repetition favours the convergence and condensation of three major episodes separated in time by over 150 years. The familiar thematic concerns of the 1960's play their part in this process: the cyclical and repetitive nature of 'Histoire' (History/story) is mirrored by — and mirrors — the eternal process of disintegration and renewal in Nature. Thus, once again, the play of analogy and circularity and the superimposition of mutually-resembling fictional episodes to produce a 'composition unitaire' counters the plurivalence of the text (the multiplicity of voices and inter-texts and the formidable play of language).

In *Les Géorgiques* Simon appears to reject the formalistic experiments of the 1970's and re-discovers a practice which combines his thoroughly modern approach to language and writing with a more humanistic sensibility. This return to a circular and unified narrative is a movement away from the 'open' text in which writer and reader are held within 'le jeu de la signification'.[14] However, if *Les Géorgiques* eschews the narrative contradictions of *Triptyque* and *Leçon de choses,* it nonetheless shares with them a primary concern with the process of production of the text. Indeed, the same fundamental activity can be detected in all Simon's later novels: the dramatization of the fiction-making process.

REFERENCES

1.   'Réponses de Claude Simon à quelques questions écrites de Ludovic Janvier', in *Entretiens: Claude Simon,* no. 31 (1972), 15-19 (p. 17).

2.   *Le Degré zéro de l'écriture,* Seuil (Paris, 1972), pp. 25-28.

3.   Jean-Luc Seylaz, 'Du *Vent* à *La Route des Flandres:* la conquête d'une forme romanesque', *Revue des Lettres Modernes,* nos. 94-99 (1964), 225-240 (p. 236).

4.   'Modalités de la narration dans *La Route des Flandres',* *Poétique,* no. 14 (1973), 235-249 (p. 235).

5.   See 'Un Ordre dans la débâcle' in *Problèmes du nouveau roman* (Paris, 1967), pp. 44-55 (p. 48).

6.   Simon suggests this when he comments: 'Tous les éléments du texte . . . sont toujours *présents*. Même s'ils ne sont pas au premier plan, ils continuent d'être là, courant en filigrane sous, ou derrière, celui qui est immédiatement lisible, ce dernier, par ses composantes, contribuant lui-même à rappeler sans cesse les autres à la mémoire'. 'La Fiction mot à mot', in *Nouveau Roman: hier,*

aujourd'hui, vol. 2, 'Pratiques', edited by Jean Ricardou (Paris, 1972), pp. 73-97 (p. 89).

7.   Jacques Lacan's assertion that language is fundamental to the constitution of the dream-text has opened the way to an analogy of this sort between dreams and certain types of writing. (See 'L'Instance de la lettre dans l'inconscient ou la raison depuis Freud', in *Ecrits 1* (Paris, 1966), pp. 249-289). However, Lacan's equation of the Freudian concepts of condensation and displacement with metaphor and metonymy respectively seems too reductive (condensation surely relies on metaphor *and* metonymy) and is at odds with Roman Jakobson's description of condensation and displacement as both metonymic in character. (See his seminal article 'Two aspects of language and two types of aphasic disturbances', in *Fundamentals of Language* (The Hague, 1971), pp. 67-96). The use of the metaphor/metonymy model for the classification of genres has often been too dualistic (metaphor *or* metonymy) and far too general. (See especially David Lodge, *The Modes of Modern Writing: Metaphor, Metonymy and the Typology of Modern Literature* (London, 1977), where the view expressed that literature is metaphoric and non-literature metonymic (p. 109) does little to help us understand the particular aspects of a specific piece of writing.)

8.   'Mise en abyme et redoublement spéculaire chez Claude Simon' in *Claude Simon: colloque de Cerisy* (Paris, 1975), pp. 151-171 (see pp. 158-161).

9.   *S/Z* (Paris, 1970), p. 12.

10.   Martin Heidegger, cited in the 'exergue' to Part III of *La Bataille de Pharsale* (p. 187).

11.   He explaines the motives for his fresh project as follows: 'J'avais le projet de faire un roman où les rapports entre les différentes "séries" (ou "ensembles") ne relèveraient pas d'un quelconque enchaînement ou déterminisme d'ordre psychologique, ou encore de similitudes de situations ou de thèmes (comme celui de l'errance sans aboutissement qui dominait *Les Corps conducteurs)* et où encore il n'y aurait pas de personnages, de temps ou de lieux apparemment privilégiés, ce qui avait permis à certains critiques de résumer *Les Corps conducteurs* en disant: un homme malade marche dans une rue et se souvient . . .'. 'Claude Simon, à la question', in *Claude Simon: colloque de Cerisy,* pp. 403-431 (p. 424).

12.   For a more detailed discussion of the inter-relationship of fictional episodes in *Triptyque* see especially Jean Ricardou, 'Le Dispositif osiriaque' in *Etudes littéraires: Claude Simon,* 9, no. 1 (avril 1976), pp. 9-80 and Lucien Dällenbach, *Le Récit spéculaire* (Paris, 1977), p. 195.

13.   Stephen Heath, *The Nouveau Roman: a Study in the Practice of Writing* (London, 1972), p. 227.

14.   Jacques Derrida, *L'Ecriture et la différence* (Paris, 1967), p. 411.

Hierarchy and coherence: Simon's novels from *La Bataille de Pharsale* to *Leçon de choses*

Alastair B. Duncan

Critics of Simon's works from *La Bataille de Pharsale* to *Leçon de choses* can be divided roughly into two camps. There are those who find hierarchy, coherence and unity in these novels, for whom they are 'des ensembles centrés'.[1] For others, Simon's novels of this period are increasingly discontinuous, non-hierarchized, shifting, uncentred, open, 'writeable'.[2] There is nothing surprising about this division. Much British and some American criticism of Simon has sprung from strong traditional humanistic roots nourished by the New Criticism. While drawing sustenance both from the insights of Russian Formalism and from structuralist analyses of narrative, it has resolutely declined to swallow them whole. As a result, it presupposes, seeks and finds meaning in Simon's novels and various kinds of complex coherence. Progressively, however, and with increasing speed, the literary scene has been changed by the very different presuppositions of deconstructive criticism. Under the influence of the later Barthes, the fragmentary has become a value in itself. Following Barthes and Bakhtin, Kristeva has taught that no text is an autonomous whole but rather a place where other texts and various codes criss-cross. With Derrida, insofar as his thought can be accommodated within traditional boundaries, the aim of criticism becomes to set the text against itself by teasing out inconsistencies and self-contradictions.[3] Given this variety of critical practice, it is not even surprising that some critics should appear to have a foot in both camps.[4] But while it is possible that their assumptions are

inconsistent or self-contradictory, this essay starts from an alternative
hypothesis, namely that Simon's texts justify the variety of these
attempts to label them. I shall explore some of these terms and by
setting them in relation to one another try to establish ways in which
they can suitably be applied to Simon's novels from the late sixties to
the mid-seventies.

The novels of this period have been seen as discontinuous,
fragmentary and non-hierarchized not least because they advertize
themselves as such. *La Bataille de Pharsale* comments on its own
procedures and aesthetic preferences in passages which offer opposing
views of the German artists of the Renaissance.

> *on dirait que la nature est restituée pêle-mêle dans l'ordre ou
> plutôt l'absence d'ordre où elle se présente (. . .) tout pour l'artiste
> allemand est au même plan dans la nature le détail masque
> toujours l'ensemble leur univers n'est pas continu mais fait de
> fragments juxtaposés on les voit dans leurs tableaux donner autant
> d'importance à une hallebarde qu'à un visage humain à une pierre
> inerte qu'à un corps en mouvement dessiner un paysage comme
> une carte de géographie apporter dans la décoration d'un édifice
> autant de soin à une horloge à marionnette qu'à la statue de
> l'Espérance ou de la Foi traiter cette statue avec les mêmes
> procédés que cette horloge. (p. 174)*

The tone of this passage, quoted from Elie Faure's *History of Art,*
clearly expresses Faure's disapproval. To his mind, these German
artists lack any sense of order, of appropriate hierarchy among the
elements of creation. But Faure's disapproval is violently countered by
the character reading his book: 'O sort de sa poche un stylo-mine et écrit
dans la marge: Incurable bêtise française' (p. 238). It would be an
unsympathetic reader of *La Bataille de Pharsale* who did not take the
side of Faure's critic in this dispute since the characteristics of German
Renaissance painting, as Faure describes them, appear to conform so
closely to those of the novel he is reading.

'Un univers fait de fragments juxtaposés; Simon has long been
fascinated by the heterogeneous. It appears as a motif in the clutter of
Herzog's bedroom in *Gulliver,* the disparate contents of Marie's toffee
tin in *L'Herbe* and in the undifferentiated list of events in her account
book. In *Le Palace* the listing of random, unrelated events and objects is
given pride of place in the titles of the symmetrical first and last
chapters, 'Inventaire' and 'Le bureau des objets perdus'. Not until *La*

Bataille de Pharsale, however, does any novel as a whole give the impression of being formed from juxtaposed fragments floating free of any containing consciousness. Most obvious are the fragments of narrative: a sequence concerning characters and events in a particular setting may at any moment be displaced by another sequence concerning quite different characters and events in a different setting. But there are also fragmentary quotations from a heterogeneous range of authors: Elie Faure rubs shoulders with Proust, Plutarch, a popular history of the First World War, a sequence from a comic strip. In *Les Corps conducteurs* there are fewer quotations but the same heterogeneity in the range of pictorial images from which the text originated: a photograph of a telephone kiosk, an anatomical plate, an erotic drawing, classical and modern paintings. Partly in consequence, this novel is marked by a variety, almost a jumble of registers and tones: the factual encyclopedic, the grandiose mythic, the erotic, the analytically critical, the naïve historical, the oratorical. Yet in *Triptyque* the range of registers is much narrower; and in *Leçon de choses* only the colloquial stands out as contrast and relief against a contrary, or rather complementary trend in Simon's writing. The heterogeneous has given way to the homogeneous, as demonstrated in the following passage from *Triptyque.*

> *La femme est coiffée d'un chapeau de paille jaune foncé dont les larges bords sont rabattus de chaque côté de la tête par un foulard sombre passé sur la calotte et noué sous le menton. Des mèches grises en désordre s'échappent de la coiffe et retombent sur le front. Tout le bas de la figure et le menton saillent comme chez certains singes ou certains chiens. Sous la jupe flasque qui bat les mollets on aperçoit les chevilles maigres sur lesquelles tirebouchonnent des bas noirs. Les pieds sont chaussés de gros brodequins d'homme sans lacets. Les manches du caraco noir pointillé de pastilles grises sont retroussées et laissent voir les avant-bras osseux recouverts d'une peau jaunâtre. Au bout de l'un d'eux, horizontal et à angle droit par rapport à l'aplomb du corps, pend un lapin au pelage gris perle tenu par les oreilles, tantôt parfaitement immobile, tantôt agité de soubresauts et de coups de reins impuissants. Sortant de l'autre main aux doigts noueux et jaunes on peut voir par instants briller la lame d'un couteau. La fille couchée dans le foin accompagne de coups de reins le va-et-vient rythmé des fesses de l'homme dont on voit chaque fois briller le membre luisant qui*

disparaît ensuite jusqu'aux couilles entre les poils touffus, noirs et brillants, bouclés comme de l'astrakan. Le couple se tient dans une zone de pénombre à l'écart du cône lumineux que projette à l'entrée de l'étroit passage entre les murs de briques un réflecteur fixé au sommet d'un poteau métallique aux poutrelles entrecroisées. (pp. 24-5)

In one sense this is a passage of juxtaposed fragments. Context instructs the reader that within this passage there are two changes of scene, from an old woman holding a rabbit to a couple lying in the hay in a barn to another couple leaning against a brick wall at night in the rain of a grim Northern town. But the effect of difference is overlaid by the similarity of treatment ('traiter cette statue avec les mêmes procédés que cette horloge'), a treatment which contrasts with *La Bataille de Pharsale*, with *Les Corps conducteurs,* and even more strikingly with Simon's earlier novels. The prose of Simon's middle period, from *Le Vent* to *Histoire*, conveyed a sense of struggle, an attempt to capture, arrest and order a flood of memories and sense impressions, of words which sprang to the pen as he wrote. Here the detail of description is as precise, but it is a description without strain. The tone is uniformly unemotive. The sense of depth created by varied tenses has given way to the flatness of an unchanging present. The syntax, once precariously ordered, constantly under threat from additions and corrections, barely preserving subordination by the expedient of multiple parentheses, is now regulated and controlled in short sentences, simply constructed. In this passage there are no apparent hierarchies, of time, of intensity, of relative importance. Everything is on the same plane. There is neither foreground nor background; or rather, since the uninvolved, unplaced observer treats every detail with the same care, everything is successively foregrounded.

And yet, as Max Silverman points out in the fore-going essay in this collection, this treatment of detail is not in itself sufficient to create a non-hierarchized text. One must also take into account the form of the work as a whole and in particular how the narratives relate to one another. In *La Bataille de Pharsale* frameworks crack and split. The conventional hierarchy between what is real and what is represented vanishes when the characters in a 'real' scene are suddenly described as figures in a painting (pp. 224-5), or when the horseman on a frieze threaten to ride away (p. 259). *Triptyque* and *Leçon de choses* go further in that in these novels the narratives spill over into one another. Each is an image within the other, a poster, film, painting or calendar, which comes to life and in turn contains an image which in its turn contains an image, and so on. The effect is first to abolish the hierarchy of past, present and future: a comic *mise en abyme* of Simon's puzzled readers shows two small boys poring over the fragment of a reel of film, trying in vain to determine an appropriate chronological order (*T*, pp. 174-5). When in addition, as in *Triptyque*, three narratives have equal prominence, the effect is to deprive the reader of a conventional fixed centre of interest. The text seems to have become what Simon predicted in *La Bataille de Pharsale:* 'un mobile se déformant sans cesse autour de quelques rares points fixes' (p. 186).

Given the absence of a fixed centre, the constantly shifting perspectives, the progressive abandonment of hierarchies, it becomes tempting to apply to these novels as a whole a remark from *Le Vent:* 'nous-mêmes ballottés de droite et de gauche, comme un bouchon à la dérive, sans direction, sans vue' (p. 10). That experience, one might say, has been progressively textualized. In *Le Vent* it was true of the characters; from *L'Herbe* to *Histoire*, perhaps even as far as *Les Corps conducteurs*, it could be applied to the narrators; by *Triptyque* it is the reader who is tossed on a stormy sea, with no sense of direction, no overall perspective. But can one go further than this? Do these characteristics of the text imply a more fundamental absence of order? Has the writer lost or renounced control of his language, or perhaps merely recognised that he never had it? Is he the plaything of his words?

These questions arise in the case of Simon because by the mid-sixties they were already edging towards the centre of critical debate in France. In 1968 Roland Barthes declared that the author was dead.[5] By this he meant that the author should no longer be conceived of as the source of his works. Like Proust and Valéry before him he was attacking the continuing assumptions of a crude positivistic criticism: that the writer when writing is identical with the man, that the work expresses his subjectivity and that it can therefore be explained by reference to the man. Against this, Barthes insisted that the relationship between writer and text is complex and indecipherable, partly because the act of writing influences what is being said, but more profoundly because the writer's subjectivity is itself a product of language. Here Barthes goes beyond Proust or Valéry. His argument reflects the new prestige of Saussurian linguistics which was also pervading other spheres of thought. Lacan was showing how language shapes the child's accession to the Symbolic Order, Althusser how it moulds those concepts of the relationship between subject and society which constitute ideologies. Although each of these writers left an escape route, a glimpse of possible freedom for the subject, the dominant tendency of their thought was to replace the old psychological, biological or sociological determinisms with a new linguistic determinism. The risk, perhaps even the reality, was that we do not speak language, it speaks us.[6]

Of most direct relevance to Simon is the particular slant given to these arguments by Jean Ricardou, both in theoretical essays and in articles on Simon's novels. Ricardou repeatedly denounced what he saw as the chief presuppositions of the realist aesthetic: 'the two complementary doctrines of expression and representation'.[7] The novel, he claimed, was neither a representation of reality nor the expression of an inner self, a message or a preconceived intention. Although Ricardou never explicitly denies that the writer controls his material, his articles elevate language to a quasi-autonomous status. With breath-taking ingenuity he demonstrates how certain novels, among them notably *La Bataille de Pharsale,* grow from the expanding associations of a few initial generating words and phrases. One association is held to command another; whole sequences, once established, demand to be repeated in modified form.[8]

To much of this theory Simon was deeply sympathetic. His exploration of the theme of memory in novels from *Le Vent* to *La Route des Flandres* had led him to conclude that language could not capture the past: by endlessly suggesting new associations and combinations it prevented the writer representing reality or expressing what he had wanted to say. In *La Route des Flandres* that experience was perceived as a disappointment and a betrayal. But increasingly Simon came to see the fertility of language as a merit: it offered opportunities to be exploited. Thus his method of work corresponded more and more to the models proposed by Barthes and Ricardou. His novels began as unrelated fragmentary descriptions: 'Je crois qu'on peut aller à tout en commençant par la description d'un crayon'.[9] These descriptions were progressively expanded and related to one another thanks to a dynamic power which Simon attributed to language itself:

> *Chaque mot en suscite (ou en commande) plusieurs autres, non seulement par la force des images qu'il attire à lui comme un aimant, mais parfois aussi par sa seule morphologie, de simples assonances qui, de même que les nécessités formelles de la syntaxe, du rythme et de la composition, se révèlent aussi fécondes que ses multiples significations.*

A statement such as this from the preface to *Orion aveugle* emphasises signifier as much as signified. It marks the high point of the convergence of Simon's views with those of Ricardou.

Yet on the other hand Simon never wavered from the conviction that, though language proposes, the writer disposes. He repeatedly affirmed that his novels were not Surrealist experiments in endless free association.[10] To give free rein to language was at most a stage in their construction. The writer's task was then to select and edit in accordance with a project, not preconceived, but growing and changing as his work on the text advanced:

> *chaque fois qu'à chacun des mots carrefours plusieurs perspectives,*
> *plusieurs figures se présentent, avoir toujours à l'esprit, pour le*
> *choix qu'on va faire, la figure initiale avec ses quatre ou cinq*
> *propriétés dérivées et ne jamais perdre celles-ci de vue, faute de*
> *quoi (. . .) il n'y aurait pas* livre, *c'est-à-dire unité, et tout*
> *s'éparpillerait en une simple suite.*[11]

Simon aimed to control his writing, to make his novels unified wholes. What was the nature of the coherence he sought?

First, as the above quotation makes clear, Simon acknowledges that his kind of coherence necessarily implies hierarchy: the initial figure and its derivatives must dominate the work. In this context one may compare Simon's novels of this period with what he calls the 'academic' novel.[12] The 'academic' novel uses and encourages the reader to use familiar codes specific to the novel, for example, character, story or description. These codes have a conventional, albeit variable hierarchy. For instance, either character or story may predominate, but description will always be secondary: it will serve character or story. Simon disrupts these codes and their hierarchical relationships. Hence his novels appear non-hierarchized. There are however other, more general codes which we use in reading a novel as in interpreting other linguistic messages, for example that a title concentrates and summarises, or that what is repeated is significant. These codes Simon uses. Seen in this perspective his novels are hierarchized.

Formally, for example, the title *Triptyque* had led every commentator to discuss that novel as a combination of three stories, and to treat the circus episodes as secondary; just as *La Bataille de Pharsale*, as signifier and signified, is one of the 'points fixes' around which the text revolves and its critics have skirmished. Or again, although all words are called to be 'mots carrefours', few or relatively few are chosen. Thus *Triptyque* is written under the signs of the cross and the serpent, while in the second last section of *Leçon de choses*, 'La charge de Reichshoffen', Simon plays predominantly with the military and sexual connotations of 'tireur', 'tirer' and 'retirer', 'charge', 'chargeur' and, by implication, 'se décharger'. But there can be as much value in scarcity: some passages are specially prominent because they are unique, untypical, particularly dense or heightened in tone. An immaterial mass threatens to engulf the sick man in *Les Corps conducteurs* and breaks the surface realism of the text. Night falls in *Triptyque*, heavy with a lyrical, philosophical dew which distinguishes this passage from the rest of the novel. The mason's boiled egg in *Leçon de choses* concentrates and reflects the room, the world and the text.

Similarly, some themes are more equal than others. Chief among these is precisely an attack on conventional hierarchies. Simon's novels of this period are perhaps above all a series of critical commentaries on the conception of a natural hierarchy which puts man and his concerns above all else. In *La Bataille de Pharsale* fragments which begin to coalesce into a story of jealousy disperse again in a minuet of shifting points of view. In *Les Corps conducteurs* the human body itself is sectioned, divided, distributed, its parts reformed in new shapes. Thus attention is not focussed on an individual's sickness and suffering but conducted ceaselessly from one body to another. The three incidents of *Triptyque* are potentially full of human interest. They appear in all their garish drama on the cinema posters. One might sum them up as: bride-groom deserts bride on wedding-night; sex-mad nanny leaves girl to drown; baroness's son in drugs scandal. Yet in the novel itself these human dramas are no more than echoes, empty gestures. Like Orion in *Les Corps conducteurs*, 'partie intégrante du magma de terre, de feuillage, d'eau et de ciel qui l'entoure' (p. 77), Simon's characters are increasingly incorporated in the urban or more often natural environment from which they grow and into which they fade. *Leçon de choses* explores this same theme in a different way. The text-book 'leçon de choses' shows a world arranged to serve man; but as that text-book appears in Simon's *Leçon de choses*, fragmented and rewritten, its certainties are exploded: man and the world are seen as together subject to a constant process of deformation and reformation.

A particular aspect of this theme concerns human sexuality. In earlier novels, notably *La Route des Flandres*, the sexual act is rich in significance. It is associated both with a search for epistomological certainty and, simultaneously, with a desire for oblivion. It is conventionally treated in that sexual climax is represented by verbal climax: the pace quickens, the tone rises, images whirl and explode. Particularly in *Triptyque* and *Leçon de choses*, however, the homogeneity of Simon's style strips the sexual act almost entirely of cultural or personal, emotional significance. It becomes something purely material; and yet, though described with vivid precision, it is also lacking in sensual significance. Pornographic writing has its own conventional rhythm: a slow, teasing build-up to an inevitable climax. The sexual act in Simon's novels is subservient to a different rhythm; closely observed bodies come and go; there is no correspondence between sexual and textual climax. Human physical relationships are made to seem merely one activity among a thousand others; sex, in these novels, is nothing to get excited about.

Simon, then, questions hierarchies but, so long as he clings to coherence, cannot escape them: the figures must be limited; themes have their own hierarchy. This is the paradox and — if one is prepared to recognize the writer as conscious producer of his own text — the drama of these novels. In each of them, questioning hierarchy, Simon creates a new hierarchy, against his will. Time and again he renews the struggle to prevent hierarchies from hardening, to keep his mobile turning, to do away with the 'points fixes'. The impossible ideal would be a novel without hierarchy yet absolutely coherent.

Simon's determination to keep the mobile turning is particularly evident, for example, in the autobiographical element in his novels from *L'Herbe* onwards. In a first phase, even up to *La Bataille de Pharsale*, there are some relatively fixed foundations on which the reader may construct a scaffold of knowledge somewhere alongside a mythical 'real' Claude Simon. In a very conventional way *La Route des Flandres* is the continuation of *L'Herbe*. Not merely is the same family put on stage but in particular *La Route des Flandres* explains how Georges lost his illusions: there was something more to it than failing the entry exam to the Ecole Normale Supérieure. *Le Palace* and *Histoire* probe successively further back in time. The origins of a reasonably consistent central character are traced back to the foetus described on the last page of *Histoire*. But already the ground is shifting. In *Histoire* and again in *La Bataille de Pharsale* the contours of this central character become blurred as his experience blends with that of his uncle. And when the references to familiar family names — Corinne and de Reixach —, absent entirely from *Les Corps conducteurs*, reappear in *Triptyque* and *Leçon de choses*, they have an air of self-quotation, almost self-parody, a nod and a wink to the reader that these characters are drawn from other texts, not from life. The old mason of *Leçon de choses* is a specially humorous reshuffling of the cards. He recounts experiences of war blended from the Simon of *La Corde raide* and Georges of *La Route des Flandres* but in the style of Iglésia, the jockey, if one can imagine Iglésia having become garrulous in old age.

Can the same effect of motion be achieved within a single novel? Simon increasingly tackles this problem head-on. Not all words can be cross-roads. But what if one multiplies the cross-roads so that, as far as possible, all words, figures, themes are continuously present, explicitly or 'en surimpression', 'en filigrane'? A last return to the lengthy passage quoted earlier from *Triptyque* can demonstrate the heroic failure and paradoxical triumph of this endeavour. Some elements recur so often as to be almost continuously present, for example the yellows, greys and blacks which colour each scene, or the frequent references to male and female: 'la femme . . . Les pieds chaussés de gros brodequins d'homme . . . la fille . . . l'homme . . . le couple'. Others echo passages elsewhere in the novel. The old woman's stockings cling round her ankles, just like the man's trousers a few pages before. The cone of light and the right angle between the rabbit and the old woman refer backward and forward in the text, to the circles, triangles and tangents of the schoolboy's geometry problem which frames this extract. The passage comes nearest to perpetual motion however in a cluster of motifs which combine the play of light, shapes with sexual connotations, and a suggestion of movement:

> *Sortant de l'autre main . . . on peut voir par instants briller la lame d'un couteau . . . l'homme dont on voit chaque fois briller le membre luisant qui disparaît ensuite jusqu'aux couilles . . . à l'écart du cône lumineux que projette à l'entrée de l'étroit passage . . . un réflecteur fixé au sommet d'un poteau métallique. (p. 25)*

Yet as an attempt to abolish hierarchy this passage is a failure since the rule of frequency continues to apply. Despite Simon's best efforts, not everything is present all the time; that which is most consistently present gains ever greater prominence. This then is the triumph: the passage coheres tightly along the axes formed by the various repetitions, similarities, reminiscences, comparisons and contrasts. Thus the repetition of male and female draws attention to a contrast between decaying age and vigorous youth, a contrast further refined and heightened by the similar gesture of rabbit and young couple: the death throes of the rabbit resemble the movements by which the young couple create life, the 'coups de rein' of the young woman and the 'va-et-vient rythmé des fesses de l'homme'. One can go further. The rabbit's movements are 'impuissants'; this evaluative word, the only one in the passage, comments ironically on the young couple's activity. It focuses attention on the old woman's knife which the recurring motifs place in such menacing proximity to 'le membre luisant qui disparaît jusqu'aux couilles': to truncate that phrase is to leave the last four words of it open to an alarming double meaning, an answer to the implied question: how much of the male member disappears? Turn where you will in this passage, light falls on sex and in particular on classic male fears and apprehensions. The extract coheres by virtue of its themes no less than by the recurrence of figures which summon them.

A superficial reading of some 'mises en abymes' in Simon's novels from *La Bataille de Pharsale* to *Leçon de choses* might lead one to suppose that Simon's response to the crisis of language was one of renunciation: having discovered that language could not be tamed to say what he wanted, he decided to give it free rein. In fact the reverse is true. Simon resolves to meet language on its own ground. Since language produces meaning he will set out to exploit that capacity, making words resonate with words, combining their manifold connotations and associations of sound but mainly of sense. In *Triptyque* Simon describes a child colouring in a picture-book by drawing a continuous line back and forth across itself and across the outline of the images beneath. Similarly the continuous line of Simon's writing blurs familiar patterns, conventional contours, but in traversing and retraversing them creates new patterns which bind the old more closely together. Or, to change the image, his aim is to weave a densely-textured cloth. He forces each thread again and again through the figures of the warp so as to leave no visible loose ends. The scale of his ambition is extraordinary. It is an attempt both to control language, by exhausting its possibilities of combination, at least within a circum-scribed field, and an attempt to control the reader. Simon's novels are 'open' works in Eco's sense of the term.[13] They break with established codes and set up their own. By various stratagems of internal reduplication they guide the reader as to how they should be read. Their ideal reader is one who is prepared to follow the adventures of their figures.

To what extent however does Simon achieve the control he seeks?

Any victory over language is partial and temporary. The material is too rich; there are always loose ends, new possible combinations. To take one example: 'la description (. . .) peut se continuer (ou être complétée) à peu près indéfiniment' (*LC*, 10). The battle continues until the writer is exhausted.[14] It can have no other outcome. The end is always arbitrary. Over the reader, Simon's control is no more complete. Undoubtedly Simon forces readers to abandon old reading habits and adopt new ones. But if a reader accepts Simon's invitation to play, to follow the varying figures, nothing ensures that he or she will respect the limits of Simon's game: 'la figure initiale et ses quatre ou cinq propriétés dérivées'. Only connect: the habit is catching. Is that passage from *Triptyque* primarily, predominantly about the fear of castration? At some point the reading proposed above has set in concrete what in the text itself was fluid and fleeting. Does it perhaps tell more about the reader than about the text? Simon's novels of this period are eminently 'writeable' in that they encourage readings which go beyond the hierarchies established in the text.

In another sense, to raise the question of control is to move fully into one area of deconstructive criticism. What gulfs exist in these novels between rhetoric and practice? It is characteristic of all these texts to denounce the view that words represent reality. Whatever seems real quickly becomes representation, as film, painting, postcard or snapshot. Step by step the reader is forced back until compelled to acknowledge that words refer only to other words. Yet, despite this, Simon's novels remain profoundly mimetic, and not just in the sense that he uses language to describe the physical world in vivid detail. Beyond that, Simon shapes his novels to reflect what he sees to be realities. Philosophical realities: that man is 'one thing among other things rather than . . . a being placed above other things';[15] that we live in an exclusively material world subject to constant transformation; and also artistic realities. For Ricardou, *La Bataille de Pharsale* was the story of its production. But in an earlier article in this collection Jean Duffy has shown how much work, how much rewriting, it takes for Simon to create that kind of effect. *La Bataille de Pharsale,* like other novels of this period, tells not *the* but *a* story of its production. That is to say it imitates the processes by which it came into being because Simon wants to tell us how his works are written. In general, Simon's novels of this time illustrate to the full one of the paradoxes which Frank Lentriccia claims to be at the heart of Modernism: they seek to instruct us about reality, while denying that words can do so.[16]

Beneath this paradox lies another. As we have seen, Simon's chief theme is that there is no preordained hierarchy in the natural world, man is not the king of creation. There is a way to demonstrate in writing that one thing is no more important than any other. It is to let words tumble out in random sequence. Yet in this instance Simon rejects mimesis. He opts instead for coherence and with it, inevitably, hierarchy. The reason for this choice is clear. Though conscious of the weight and shaping force of language Simon wishes to demonstrate his control of words. In 'The death of the author' Barthes conceded that the writer has 'the power . . . to mix writings, to counter the ones with the others, in such a way as never to rest on any one of them'.[17] Simon is, like Barthes, an arch-challenger of conventional codes. By mixing writings he attempts to demonstrate his freedom. Of course, *La Bataille de Pharsale*, *Les Corps conducteurs*, *Triptyque* and *Leçon de choses* may not ultimately be Simon's novels: there is no way of telling if we have free will. But Simon believes that they are, and they can be read as such. Like the writings of Barthes, Simon's novels represent a form of Humanism: they affirm that man creates meaning.

REFERENCES

1.   In this category, despite varying methods and perspectives, one might include, for example, both J. A. E. Loubère in *The Novels of Claude Simon* (London, 1975), and S. Sykes in *Les Romans de Claude Simon* (Paris, 1979). The phrase 'des ensembles centrés' was used by Simon himself and is to be found in *Nouveau Roman: hier, aujourd'hui*, 2, *Pratiques* (Paris, 1972), p. 92.

2.   The critic who has gone furthest along this line is probably C. H. Gosselin in 'Voices of the past in Claude Simon's *La Bataille de Pharsale*', *New York Literary Forum*, 2 (1978: 'Intertextuality: New Perspectives in Criticism'), 23-33. Others moving in the same direction have been R. Mortier, 'Discontinu et rupture dans *La Bataille de Pharsale*', *Degrès*, 1, no. 2 (avril 1973), c1-c6; F. Jost, 'Les Aventures du lecteur', *Poétique*, no. 29 (1977), 77-89; C. Gaudin, 'Niveaux de lisibilité dans *Leçon de choses* de Claude Simon', *Romanic Review*, 68 (1977), 175-96; and Max Silverman, in the essay which precedes this one. The trend has also affected reading of earlier novels, as in L. Hesbois, 'Qui dit ça? Identification des voix narratives dans *L'Herbe* de Claude Simon', *Revue du Pacifique*, 2 (1967), 144 59. Umberto Eco launched the word 'open' on a new career in *L'Œuvre ouverte* (Paris, 1965); 'writeable' is an English version of Roland Barthes's coining, 'scriptible', in *S/Z* (Paris, 1970).

3.   In *S/Z* Barthes analyses Balzac's *Sarrasine* by fragments, in order to 'apprécier de quel pluriel il est fait'; the ideal 'writeable' text, however, is more

D

irreducibly polysemic, therefore more fragmentary. J. Kristeva introduced the notion of intertextuality in 'Bakhtine, le mot, le dialogue et le roman', *Critique*, no. 239 (1967), 438-65. The reference to Derrida is a reformulation of Barbara Johnson's definition of deconstruction: 'the careful teasing out of warring forces of signification within the text', in *The Critical Difference: Essays in the Contemporary Rhetoric of Reading* (Baltimore, 1980), p. 5.

4. To be fair, most of the critics mentioned in 3. above could be placed in this category. A somewhat unexpected member of this company seems to me to be J. Ricardou. In 'Le Dispositif osiriaque', *Etudes littéraries*, 9, no. 1 (1976), 10-79, he dismisses the ideas of coherence and unity by associating them with consistency of character or story; but he illustrates his replacement term, 'discoherence', with an extremely rigid unifying schema (fig. 14, p. 67).

5. 'La Mort de l'auteur', *Mantéia*, 5 (1968). Reprinted as 'The death of the author' in *Image, Music, Text* (Glasgow, 1977), pp. 142-48.

6. A helpful summary of these developments is to be found in C. Belsey, *Critical Practice* (London, 1980), Chap. 3, pp. 56-84.

7. 'Nouveau Roman, Tel Quel' in *Pour une théorie du nouveau roman* (Paris, 1971), p. 261.

8. 'La Bataille de la phrase', *Pour une théorie du nouveau roman*, pp. 118-58.

9. J. Duranteau, 'Claude Simon. "Le Roman se fait, je le fais, et il me fait"', *Les Lettres françaises*, 13-19 avril, 1967, 4.

10. For example in 'Réponses de Claude Simon a quelques questions écrites de Ludovic Janvier', *Entretiens: Claude Simon*, no. 31 (1972), 26; 'La Fiction mot à mot', *Nouveau Roman: hier, aujourd'hui*, 2, pp. 84 and 88.

11. 'La Fiction mot à mot', p. 88.

12. In the 'Interview with Claude Simon' at the beginning of this book, p. 13.

13. See *The Role of the Reader* (London, 1981), pp. 9-10.

14. 'Ainsi ne peut-il [mon trajet] avoir d'autre terme que l'épuisement du voyageur explorant ce paysage inépuisable': Claude Simon, in the preface to *Orion aveugle*.

15. 'Interview with Claude Simon', p. 13.

16. *After the New Criticism* (London, 1980), pp. 36 and 58.

17. *Image, Music, Text*, p. 146.

The Orpheus myth in
Les Georgiques

Michael Evans

> La décroissance du jour me plongeant par le
> souvenir dans une atmosphère ancienne et
> fraîche, je la respirais avec les mêmes délices
> qu'Orphée l'air subtil, inconnu sur cette
> terre, des Champs Elysées.
>
> Marcel Proust, *La Prisonnière*

The Orpheus myth has held the attention of writers at almost every period in the history of western literature. In many ways, it is the supreme myth of literary creativity. But like all recurrent legends, and indeed more so than most, the story has undergone many transformations and aroused a clamour of differing interpretations, beginning with the oracular status anonymously bestowed upon Orpheus as patron of a religious cult and author of sacred writings. Yet the myth's ability to accommodate a rich diversity of interpretation argues against any attempt to ascribe a univocal, archetypal significance to its appearance in contemporary fiction; above all in a work which, through self-conscious intertextual and metaphorical awareness, is as open to plurality and creative complexity as that of Claude Simon.

It is true that, on one level, the Orpheus myth is concerned with the primordial accession or initiation to a hidden world of truth and idealism. Thus, for Mircea Eliade, Orpheus's *'descensus ad infernos* constitutes the initiatory ordeal par excellence'.[1] But rather than disclosing any particular symbolic truths regarding the precise nature of this initiation, or perhaps because its symbolism has proved to be so polysemic, the myth is best read as an allegory of the process of mythical inquiry. Thus the relevance of this myth to modernity lies less in its allusion to particular archetypes expressing the 'primordial experience' than in its depiction of the search for archetypes. With Claude Simon, this search, prominent and obsessive as it is in novels like *La Route des Flandres, Histoire* and *Les Géorgiques,* pivots around a hollow epicentre, a focal absence. The transparency of cosmogonic revelation, as propounded by the Orphic doctrine, is eclipsed by the opacity of textual and sensual experience.

Direct allusions to the myth in *Les Géorgiques* are indeed scant but, as is often the case with the use of intertextuality in Simon's novels, this apparent reticence thinly veils an implicit background of associations which informs and guides the narrative. Textually, the few direct references to the Orpheus myth which appear in the novel act as points of intersection between the separate yet intertwining strands of narrative. References to the Gluck opera are a case in point. The opera is watched by the narrator as a boy and by his grandmother, and it is also heard by a group of soldiers many years later when the radio 'operator', a self-conscious pun, inadvertently tunes in to a broadcast of the same piece of music: 'Comme parvenant à travers des épaisseurs du temps et d'espace la voix fragile d'un ténor chante *Che faro senza Euridice? Dove andrò senza il mio ben?*' (p. 39). A further link is created, on the same page, between Orpheus's lament, *'Dove andrò'*, and L.S.M.'s persistent question, *'Et où irez-vous?'* However, apart from this local, structural use of the myth, one can discern a more widespread implicit involvement with its allegorical connotations. And it is on this latter level of association that I shall focus in this essay. But before proceeding to show the ways in which Simon's novel weaves its own allegories out of the Orpheus myth it is necessary to prepare the premises of my argument by recalling some of the salient aspects of the 'original' version.

Bearing in mind the novel's title and the references to Virgil in *Les Géorgiques,* one is justified in turning to the version of the myth which appears at the end of the *Georgics* as the source or matrix from which Claude Simon has shaped his own treatment of the myth. Virgil relates the Orpheus story after prescribing a floral remedy as a cure for sickly bees. When the latter are too close to death to respond to this treatment, the sole recourse left is the divine prescription recounted in the legend. Thus, the catabatic myth of Orpheus, dwelling on the theme of death and its transgression, is introduced into Virgil's poem on the pretext of a last-ditch defiance of death. Aristaeus, the mortal son of the immortal nymph Cyrene, feels that the gods are deliberately frustrating his efforts to keep bees and descends to his mother's underwater palace in search of an explanation. She refers him to Proteus, advising him to shackle the sea-god in his sleep so as to prevent him from deploying his infinite powers of metamorphosis to escape. Aristaeus follows his mother's instructions and learns from Proteus that he had incurred Orpheus's wrath for having caused the death of his wife, Eurydice, who was bitten by a venomous hydra while fleeing from Aristaeus's lustful advances. Proteus recounts that Orpheus lamented Eurydice's death by singing to the accompaniment of his lyre. He descended to the Underworld whose inhabitants were awakened and charmed by Orpheus's music. Finally, Eurydice appeared and followed behind her husband as he led the way back to the Upper world. But as they approached the threshold Orpheus committed the irrevocable error of looking back at Eurydice and thus broke the conditions set by Proserpine for Eurydice's release. She was once more overcome with the sleep of the dead and abducted to the Underworld. Orpheus poured out his grief for seven months on the banks of the river Strymon. There he played his lyre and sang so beautifully that he enchanted the tigers and made the trees follow him. However, his unswerving devotion to Eurydice eventually earned him the anger of the Thracian Bacchantes who tore him to pieces during an orgy in honour of Bacchus and dispersed the severed parts of his body over the land. His head fell into the river Hebrus but continued to sing for Eurydice as it drifted past the banks which echoed her name. Having completed his narration, Proteus escapes without revealing the means by which Aristaeus can win back the gods' favour. However, Cyrene, who has been eavesdropping and has learnt the cause of her son's misfortune, provides him with the requisite prescription.

Virgil's adaptation of the myth contains several narrative dramatisations of the accession to the land of the dead; and these are embedded within the wider thematic scenario of mythic triumph over death. Apart from the initial framing of the legend within the *Georgics* on the basis of the miraculous remedy for plague-ridden bees, both Aristaeus's descent to the underwater home of his mother, and Orpheus's abortive attempt to retrieve Eurydice from the Underworld are set in the context of a sharply-defined line of demarcation separating the nether world from the land of the living. This dividing-line is also represented by the numerous allusions to rivers: such as Peneus, the abode of Cyrene; the Styx, encircling Hell; and Hebrus, whence the severed head of Orpheus continues to sing Eurydice's name. Orpheus's ultimate triumph over death has been interpreted by some commentators as the perennial endurance of myths throughout time. Such a reading certainly conforms to the view of the legend as a myth of myths, self-consciously mirroring the process of archetypal creation. But Orpheus is also the father of poetry and through his eternal abode in the river Hebrus he inhabits the very threshold between the two universes: 'ici' and 'ailleurs'. The poet, inspired by an irrecuperable absence is constrained to dwell on the limits of re-presentation and invocation. This dual role played by the Orpheus myth (as an archetype of myths in general; and as a symbol of the poetic impulse) is subtly developed in Simon's novel and takes the form of an allegorical expansion. Three allegories emerge from the myth, each of which sheds light on the compositional and ideological principles against which *Les Géorgiques* is set: the allegories of transgression, initiation, and reflexivity.

Whilst the Orpheus myth in *Les Géorgiques* may be said to introduce and highlight the motif of transgression as a dramatic allegory of the poetic desire for the breaking of limits, the most immediately discernible appearances of the myth in Simon's novel elicit a negative or parodic allegorical reading. It is L.S.M., the illustrious regicide and Napoleonic general at the centre of the novel whose life can in part be seen as a re-enactment of the archetypal Orphic yearning for transgression. Like Orpheus obsessed with the memory of Eurydice, L.S.M. is haunted by the memory of his first wife, Marianne. The letter in which he speaks of her is written in a style which is almost self-consciously classical: 'au milieu des plus grands dangers j'ai bien souvent cru voir l'ombre de cette femme adorée me couvrir d'une égide et me frayer un chemin à travers les périls' (p. 49). Apart from the reference to the aegis and the ponderous, mannered tone, the lines echo the words uttered in Gluck's opera, *Orfeo ed Euridice*, quoted in the novel: 'ombra cara ove sei?' In many ways, L.S.M. is a 'resurrected Roman',[2] one of the heroic figures of the French Revolution, draped in the costumes of classical tragedy, acting out their parts on the stage of history. Although undeniably a man of action whose courage and boundless energy were put to the service of social and historical change, he is none the less also shown to be a man for whom heroism was largely a matter of posture based on a mimicry of archetypal behaviour. The Roman affectation is nowhere more tangible than in the marble bust of L.S.M. which, centuries later, the modern descendant, a fictional incarnation of Simon himself, attempts to recover. Thus the awe and respect which is conveyed in the depiction of this ancestral colossus is mitigated by an ironical deflation of the mythical pretensions in his personality. After all, as the narrator points out, 'cette femme adorée', once lured away from her native Holland, was thoroughly neglected in a remote corner of France while the heroic spouse valiantly strode the war-torn continent. But the element of travesty is most sharply focused in the novel on the depiction of Adelaide, L.S.M.'s second wife. Described by the narrator as Briseis, Agamemnon's captive mistress, she embodies much of the neo-classical pretensions of the bourgeoisie of post-Revolutionary France. In a sense, Adelaide is presented as the antithesis of L.S.M.'s idealised, Orphic view of his first wife. She is the Eurydice whom Orpheus-L.S.M. successfully retrieves from the Underworld. The hero meets her by chance, during the period of the reign of terror, in prison awaiting execution, and he succeeds in snatching her away from the jaws of death. But the reality of Adelaide, who was later to betray all that L.S.M. stood for, is no more than a parodic inversion of the absent ideal.

It is not only the glimpses, real or imagined, of L.S.M.'s life which cast an ironic shadow over the allegorical purport of the Orpheus myth. The same parodic disenchantment is conveyed, more directly, in the description of the Gluck opera performance attended by the boy protagonist and his grandmother.[3] Seen through the eyes of the boy, the statuesque figures on the stage strike postures 'd'éternelle passion, d'éternelle agonie'. They resemble bishops and prostitutes officiating at some mysterious initiation ceremony:

> comme des sortes de divinités mineures dont la fonction ne pouvait être que celle d'intermédiaires, comme si au prix de quelque dégoutante et redoutable épreuve elles avaient la charge de faire accéder derrière les façades closes à quelque connaissance dont elles détenaient les clefs et qui se situait en dehors de toute logique, de tout désir et de toute raison, échappant à toute explication. (p. 224)

Although the allegorical motif of accession to a hidden world beyond is present in the description of the visit to the opera, the ultimate effect is negative. In the boy's eyes the theatre building is like a vestige 'd'un passé révolu' and the atmosphere inside is one of a fusty and antiquated world of 'haute bourgeoisie' temporarily resuscitated for the duration of the performance. It is the leaden form of the spectacle and the apparent sterility of the audience and auditorium which renders the opera ineffective as a medium for metaphorical transgression. The Orpheus myth, in Gluck's operatic version, is no more than a fossil. The whole episode is placed in counterpoint to the boy's impressions of the film shows he regularly attended at the local cinema. The wild, flea-ridden tribes of gypsies who take up the seats in the stalls, 'les populaires', are also archetypal in that they seem to the boy to emerge from 'ces profondeurs, cet au-delà (ou cet en-deçà?) où ils semblaient être tenus en réserve' (p. 214). They seem to him like 'la délégation vivante de l'humanité originelle' (p. 208). Above all, it is the 'ombres lumineuses' of the fluid images on the screen and the brusque succession of unconnected time spans which provide a specular complement to the protagonist's adult experience of apocalyptic initiation. It is, in fact, in mid-sentence that the narrative leaps from the cinema to the midst of explosions and gun-fire:

> *le garçon — c'est-à-dire plus un garçon alors, devenu un homme*
> *par une brusque mutation en l'espace d'une fraction de seconde,*
> *projeté aussi démuni qu'un nouveau-né dans ce qui est pour ainsi*
> *dire comme la face cachée des choses. (p.215)*

As this passage illustrates, the motif of transgression to an 'au-delà', a mythical space lying beyond reach, is closely bound up with the allegory of initiation which is also incorporated in the Orpheus myth. Here, Claude Simon is following in the footsteps of a time-honoured literary tradition. Mircea Eliade has analysed this myth in terms of shamanistic initiation ceremonies, and has linked it with the 'initiatory' works of writers like Nerval and Goethe:

> *But in* Dichtung und Wahreit *the old Goethe described the*
> *turbulent experience of his* Sturm und Drang *in terms which*
> *remind one of a 'shamanistic' type of initiation. Goethe speaks of*
> *the instability, eccentricity, and irresponsibility of those years. He*
> *admits that he wasted both his time and his gifts, that his life was*
> *purposeless and meaningless. He lived in a 'state of chaos', he was*
> *'dismembered and cut into pieces' . . . As is well known, the*
> *dismemberment and cutting into pieces, and also the 'state of*
> *chaos' (i.e. psychic and mental instability) are characteristic traits*
> *of the shamanistic initiation. And just as the would-be shaman*
> *reintegrates, through his initiation, a stronger and more creative*
> *personality, one can say that after the* Sturm und Drang *period*
> *Goethe conquered his immaturity and became master both of his*
> *life and of his creativity.*[4]

In Eliade's view, Orphic dismemberment and the state of chaos described by Goethe are assimilable in so far as they both mirror the transient phase of shamanistic initiation, the 'rite of passage' through which the individual gains access to a more unified and enhanced conception of himself. Despite the religious optimism and the neo-Aristotelian faith in the notion of one-ness, both of which are alien to the Simonian text, Eliade's comments can shed useful light on some of the mythical presuppositions underlying *Les Géorgiques*. Echoes of Goethe's metaphor of dismemberment reverberate throughout Simon's oeuvre, perhaps most strikingly in the lines from Rilke which serve as epigraph to *Histoire:*

> *Cela nous submerge. Nous l'organisons. Cela tombe en morceaux.*
> *Nous l'organisons de nouveau et tombons nous-mêmes en*
> *morceaux.*

In the context of Simon's work 'cela' is both history and story; fragmentation is the effect of both time and language. In *Les Géorgiques* it is L.S.M. (whose revolutionary zeal did not preclude an indomitable desire for order as manifested in the compulsive and meticulous instructions to his house-keeper, Batti, concerning the upkeep of his estate) who finally succumbs to the archetypal fatality of disintegration. L.S.M.'s grave is desecrated when a new road is built, 'amputating' a section of the cemetery. His bones are scattered by a bulldozer and the cross from his tomb is hoisted onto the steeple of a nearby church. It is only on the basis of a narrative repetition that one can compare the dispersal of L.S.M.'s remains with the dismemberment of Orpheus. The symbolic significance of the act is diametrically opposed in each case. No spiritual accession is gained by the scattering of L.S.M.'s bones, which the narrator interprets as being caused by the relentless internal logic of matter. Fragmentation here is not a religious or psychic process of initiation leading to a transcendental state of being, but a dynamic force in its own right. In a previous chapter, the narrator describes, along similar lines, the experience of the soldiers marching aimlessly over the snow-covered valleys of Alsace during the 'phoney war' period which preceded the German invasion of France in 1940. The squadron's disintegration is described in three phases, the last of which 'ne peut être décrite que de façon fragmentaire à l'image du phénomène de fragmentation lui-même' (p. 97). Again the description is coloured by a strongly demystifying vision which empties the apocalyptic experience of any further significance beyond its immediate

physical reality:

> *Sans doute fallait-il que d'abord ils (les hommes, les cavaliers)*
> *passent (comme au cours de ces initiations rituelles que pratiquent*
> *des ordres ou des confrèries secrètes) par la série des épreuves*
> *qu'avait consacrées une longue coutume . . . avant d'en arriver au*
> *printemps, à cette suprême et dernière consécration: celle du feu,*
> *soudaine, violente, brève, juste le temps d'apprendre ce qu'on (les*
> *commandements réglementaires et les métaphores de poètes) leur*
> *avait caché, c'est-à-dire que ce que l'on appelait le feu était*
> *véritablement du feu, brûlait. (p. 130)*

The reference to 'ces initiations rituelles', as well as the description of
the troop captain as 'un messager du royaume des morts, élyséen' (p.
123) clearly acknowledges the mythic background to the narrative, but
the allusion is pointedly critical. Moreover, it is not only myths and
myth-inspired leaders who have been responsible for creating deception
and false expectations but 'les métaphores de poètes' as well. Whether
or not this refers to the visionary poetry of Romantic literature (one
thinks, for example, of Nerval's 'Les Filles du *feu*') it is clear the
narrator is here suggesting, as he does earlier in the passage about
fragmentation, that the formal qualities of literary language cannot be
divorced from the ideological or allegorical inferences they elicit. By its
very nature, metaphor is transcendental: it creates the illusion of a two-
part reality, consisting of the immediate and the beyond, and it affects
to bridge the intervening gap.

But the denial of this dualistic perspective does not entail an outright rejection of Eliade's description of the primal 'state of chaos'; it
merely demystifies it. The poet's metaphor is halved and the tenor
jettisoned; only the vehicle, the turbulence, remains. Thus, the narrator
is fascinated by Orwell's description of the 'magic quality' of the time
he spent in the trenches during the Spanish civil war. The same
paradoxical atmosphere of enchantment in extreme physical adversity
recurs in the lives of all the main characters in *Les Géorgiques*. For
instance, L.S.M.'s renegade brother fleeing from the Revolutionary
police walks unwittingly into a bed of quicksand. Despite being panic-
stricken at the imminence of his own death, his perception of the colours
and sounds surrounding him becomes acute. He has passed, the
narrator says, 'de l'autre côté', into a world which has been turned inside
out: 'révélé dans son envers ou plutôt perverti en ce sens que plus rien
n'y avait la même signification, sinon de signification tout court' (p.

426). The initiatory experience is, therefore, a de-signifying experience. However, the phrase, also singled out by the narrator, which Orwell uses to describe his sensation when a bullet pierced through his neck — 'Roughly speaking it was the sensation of being *at the centre* of an explosion' — also calls to mind the spiritual diffraction of the shamanistic 'state of chaos'. But, as Simon makes explicit in an interview, the experience of war is a process of initiation which does not lead to transcendental enhancement but to an awakened sensitivity to nature:

> *Enfin, dans la guerre, l'homme se trouve au contact direct de la nature. Il apprend à connaître intimement les saisons, le sol, les intempéries, les nuits, les aubes. Initiation acquise au prix d'une épreuve terrible à laquelle il faut être contraint pour y accéder, mais qui compte.*[5]

The allegory of initiation has been transferred from the mythical and psychological realms to the phenomenological plane. Jean-Marie's engulfment in the marshy quicksand is thus the narrative reflection of a sensual absorption in nature. Equally, the frequent use of animal imagery and the figurative metamorphoses (0. is a hunted rat; Jean-Marie a hunted fox) can be interpreted in the same way.

This inititiatory vision of Orphic experience is interwoven with a third strand of thematic development in *Les Géorgiques:* namely, that of temporal retrospection. Orpheus, the poet figure, awakens the dead with his songs; so too, autobiographical writing brings about a fictional resuscitation of the past. And yet, as the chapter concerned with Orwell's *Homage to Catalonia* indicates, the method of writing about one's past determines the degree of success. Thus whilst one can detect a deep feeling of sympathy on the part of the author for Orwell the man, there is a strong condemnation of Orwell the chronicler of personal experiences during the tumultuous events of the Spanish civil war:

> *Peut-être espère-t-il qu'en écrivant son aventure il s'en dégagera un sens cohérent. Tout d'abord le fait qu'il va énumérer dans leur ordre chronologique des évènements qui se bousculent pêle-mêle dans sa mémoire ou se présentent selon des priorités d'ordre affectif devrait, dans une certaine mesure, les expliquer. (pp. 310-11)*

In his re-writing of certain passages from *Homage to Catalonia* Simon substitutes for Orwell's neutral, detached style a form of writing which more accurately reflects the disordered superimposition of memory. The contrast between Orwell's deadpan narrative (he is described as a corpse looking back on a past life) which fumbles with statistics and acronyms in an attempt to render a logical, ordered reconstruction of the tempestuous events and Simon's 'phenomenological' or 'vivid' re-writing of some passages re-iterates the contrast I have already discussed between the operatic performance and the life-teeming atmosphere exhaled in the cinema. If one compares the 're-written' passages in this chapter with the 'original' accounts by Orwell, such as the description of the long-awaited nocturnal assault on the Fascist redoubt, one notices that Simon reduces the 'discursive' element of the narrative (the explanatory insertions and expressions of opinion) and concentrates on the emotional and physical sensations aroused under the particular circumstances. The traditional corner-stones of 'realistic' or journalistic prose, strategic points of reference informing the reader as to the chronological and causal order of the events, are faded out and what generally serves as background depiction, subservient to the main thrust of the narrative, is brought to the forefront. Merleau-Ponty's acute observation, made with regard to Simon's earlier work, still holds true: 'Le travail ne consiste pas seulement, d'ailleurs, à "convertir en mots" le vécu; il s'agit de faire parler ce qui est senti'.[6]

Temporal retrospection is a form of reflexivity: it entails a backward gaze, albeit an Orphic gaze which is doomed to dissipate the very past it seeks to revive. For Roland Barthes, the Orpheus myth is an allegory of theory that is reflexive, of a 'discours qui se retourne sur lui-même':

> *Au fond, le héros éponyme, le héros mythique de la théorie,*
> *pourrait être Orphée, parce que précisément c'est celui qui se*
> *retourne sur ce qu'il aime, quitte à détruire; en se retournant sur*
> *Eurydice il la fait évanouir, il la tue une deuxième fois.* Il faut
> faire *ce retournement, quitte à detruire.*[7]

Like the other novels before it, *Les Géorgiques's* fascination with the past is not based on a desire for accurate reconstruction. Despite the extensive use of textual material relating to 'real' people and events, *Les Géorgiques* is neither an historical novel nor a chronicle. By inter-mingling fact and fiction, and by interweaving the lives of three protagonists, Simon adds a further twist to the reflexive allegory suggested by the Orpheus myth. The historical authenticity of the three main protagonists is not at stake: they 'co-exist', as Alastair Duncan has rightly said, 'as fictions in the domain of words'.[8] With this novel

Simon has created a kind of biographical bricolage whereby what comes alive is not the past, seen 'in a glass, darkly', but writing itself.

REFERENCES

1. Mircea Eliade, *The Quest. History and Meaning in Religion* (Chicago and London, 1969), p. 123.
2. Harold Rosenberg, *The Tradition of the New* (London, 1970), pp. 140-58.
3. The connection between the boy's grandmother and the Orpheus myth may be fruitfully compared with the first of two allusions to Orpheus in Proust's *A la recherche du temps perdu* (the second occurrence I have already quoted as epigraph to this essay). The allusion is made after a telephone conversation between Marcel and his grandmother leaves the former with a premonition of his grandmother's imminent death: 'Il me semblait que c'était déjà une ombre chérie que je venais de laisser se perdre parmi les ombres, et seul devant l'appareil, je continuais à répéter en vain: "Grand'mère, grand'mère", comme Orphée, resté seul, répète le nom de la morte.' (Paris, 1954), vol. 2, p. 136.
4. Eliade, pp. 124-5.
5. Claude Simon, quoted in J. Piatier, 'Claude Simon ouvre *Les Géorgiques*', *Le Monde,* 4 septembre 1981, p. 13.
6. Maurice Merleau-Ponty, 'Cinq notes sur Claude Simon', *Entretiens: Claude Simon,* no. 31 (1972), p. 45.
7. Roland Barthes, *Le Grain de la voix* (Paris, 1981), p. 136.
8. Alastair Duncan, 'Claude Simon's *Les Géorgiques:* an intertextual adventure', *Romance Studies,* no. 2 (Summer 1983), 90-107 (p. 97).

Intertextuality and fictionality: *Les Géorgiques* and *Homage to Catalonia*

John Fletcher

Les Géorgiques, it has been said, processes a large amount of material from a variety of sources and offers 'historical biography on a grand scale'.[1] Most of it, of course, is derived from the papers of Claude Simon's ancestor General Lacombe Saint Michel, but another important element is *Homage to Catalonia*, George Orwell's classic *reportage* on the Spanish Civil War, first published in 1938. The French translation of this work appeared in 1955 under the title *La Catalogne libre*;[2] this is the text which Simon uses in *Les Géorgiques*, most extensively in chapter IV, but in a few places in chapter I as well. His quotations and adaptations from *La Catalogne libre* raise interesting questions of intertextuality and fictionality which it is my purpose to discuss in this essay.

Simon read *La Catalogne libre* with close interest — that much is evident from the amount and distribution of his quotations from, and allusions to, the book — but his reading was clearly 'filtered' by his own experience of the Spanish war, fictionalized in two earlier novels, *Le Sacre du printemps* (1954) and *Le Palace* (1962). Because he took part in the struggle in his youth, and because like Orwell he wrote about it (both before and after *La Catalogne libre* was published in France), the tone which his narrator adopts towards the English socialist writer is never a neutral one. At times the narrator suggests a critique; at others, something approaching respectful homage. In other words, the novel's attitude to Orwell is ambivalent. There are good reasons why Simon should have left matters in this ambiguous form, as I hope to show.

As one might expect, *La Catalogne libre* is not the only 'Spanish' element intertextually present in *Les Géorgiques*. Another civil war passage is placed in chapter III. This italicised section (*LesG*, pp. 226-7) is set in the 'palace de Barcelone' from which Simon's novel of 1962 takes its title. The 'palace' is not named, but it was in real life the Hotel Colón, the headquarters of the Communist organisation on the Plaza de Cataluña, and as such is mentioned by Orwell in passing.[3] Indeed, Simon's reference in chapter III to 'l'odeur écœurante d'huile chaude et rance qui imprégnait la nourriture servie aux volontaires étrangers' could just as well be Orwellian, as could the restrained description of the prisoner 'resté là vingt-quatre heures assis sur une chaise, les bras et les jambes croisés, comme dans un salon, refusant de manger et de s'étendre, jusqu'à ce qu'on l'emmène pour le fusiller'. But however close to the tone and spirit of *Homage to Catalonia* these observations are, they happen not to be quoted from it.

Even so, Simon devotes, in all, over a hundred pages to reflections upon Orwell's *témoignage*, a remarkable enough fact in itself. *Homage to Catalonia*, written in England after Orwell had managed to escape from the police in Barcelona and slip out of Spain, covers the six months or so he spent in the Republic. His narrative falls naturally into four parts. The first — corresponding to chapters 1-7 in the French edition — describes his enlistment in the militia of the POUM (Partido Obrero de Unificación Marxista) in December 1936, and his three and a half months of active (or, more accurately, largely inactive) service on the Aragon front during the winter and early spring of 1937. The second section (chapters 8 and 9) deals with the fighting in Barcelona early in May between the Republican authorities and the POUM, in which he participated while on furlough after his long period in the line. In the third part (chapter 10) Orwell tells how, on his return to the front later in May, he was badly wounded in the throat. He was evacuated in stages from the battle zone until he finally reached Barcelona. The last section (chapters 11 and 12) relates how, the POUM having been declared illegal, Orwell — still recovering from his injuries — had to go into hiding until he was able to escape to France in late June 1937.

As a result of these experiences in Spain, Orwell's anti-communist position hardened, and he wrote *Homage to Catalonia* in large measure to vindicate the POUM and to expose what he saw as the Communists' betrayal of the Republican cause. It is a truly powerful and effective book, indeed in the view of Raymond Williams — recorded in a monograph which Simon also read when preparing *Les Géorgiques* — it is Orwell's 'most important and most moving' work.[4] Simon's interest in it is all the more understandable in that he had experienced the same events, also at first hand, but had early on felt less idealistic about them. Indeed, he told me in 1982 that what he himself had understood 'au bout de quinze jours' Orwell had taken months to come to terms with. Although the two men seem never to have met, Orwell's later admission is true of his younger French colleague earlier in the conflict: 'I suppose there is no one who spent more than a few weeks in Spain without being in some degree disillusioned' (*HC*, p. 172). Simon's own recollection of disillusionment with what Malraux in *L'Espoir* called 'l'illusion lyrique' is already fairly directly expressed in *Le Sacre du printemps* and in *Le Palace*. In *Les Géorgiques* he conveys it just as effectively but by more oblique means: by the intertextual exploitation and critique of Orwell's autobiographical account.

In the French edition, which Simon used, the chapters of detailed political commentary (5 and 11 in the original) are relegated to appendices at the end of the volume. This has the advantage of making Orwell's narrative clearer and less cluttered. Since he is primarily interested in the story, Simon does not quote from this political material, although he does refer to it obliquely at one point (*LesG*, p. 342). Even within the main body of the French text he is selective: he quotes a great deal from some sections and not at all from others. His borrowings take the form sometimes of direct quotation with, or more often without inverted commas; sometimes of paraphrase; and sometimes of précis or other less direct kinds of intertextual exploitation.

In chapter I of *Les Géorgiques* especially, he switches to and from *Homage to Catalonia* without warning, so that one needs to be conversant with Orwell's text in order to be sure when it is being cited or referred to, and when the narrative has moved on to another topic. In the following passage, for example, the reader is only aware that the narrative has shifted from the struggles of 1937 to the 'phoney war' of 1939-40 by internal evidence, in this case the fact that Orwell, sleeping rough in Barcelona during June, needed no overcoat to protect him from the snow. The break occurs after the words 'bains publics':

> *Il couche dans une église incendiée. Il couche dans un terrain vague, dissimulé par les hautes herbes, dans un chantier abandonné, recroquevillé dans l'escalier d'un abri anti-aérien au fond rempli d'eau croupie. Pendant la journée il échappe à ses poursuivants en fréquentant les restaurants de luxe et les bains publics. Il couche à même le sol enveloppé dans son manteau.*

*Quand il ouvre les yeux au réveil ils sont obstrués par une matière grenue, scintillante, d'un blanc grisâtre et opaque. Son visage et son manteau de cavalerie sont couverts de neige. (*LesG, p. 31; original in italics)*

In this chapter of *Les Géorgiques*, most of the references are to the second 'part' of *Homage to Catalonia*, the May street battles in Barcelona, but there are some allusions to the first 'part' (the winter campaign) and — as in the extract above — to the last (the period when Orwell went to ground before his final departure). In most cases the text of *La Catalogne libre* is adapted, developed and augmented with comments of the narrator's own; it is not simply quoted. This passage, for instance, embroiders considerably on what Orwell writes; there is no mention in *Homage to Catalonia* of the foliage on the plane trees, or of the branches being sliced through by gunfire:

*Les pousses duveteuses aux extrémités des branches sont d'un roux pâle aussi. Il est armé de deux bombes accrochées à sa ceinture et d'un pistolet. La ville secouée d'explosions est immobile sous le soleil. Le sol de l'avenue est jonché par places de rameaux sectionnés par les balles. (*LesG, p. 33; in italics)*

In fact, this is more of a pre-echo of Simon's own text (p. 301) than it is an echo of Orwell. The effect in this first chapter of *Les Géorgiques* is in any case modified by the fact that references to Orwell's text are scattered randomly; they stand next to quite different material and blend curiously into it, as for instance with the two sentences which follow immediately upon those which I have just quoted:

*Les feuilles sont encore vertes mais commencent à se friper. Le ténor chante Euridice Euridice ombra cara ove sei? (*LesG, p. 33; in italics)*

It is in chapter IV, however, that Orwell is most extensively used. *La Catalogne libre* is handled in any of three ways: some passages are not discussed or referred to at all; others are quoted or alluded to in fairly straightforward ways; others again are rewritten, lyrically or vulgarly as the case may be, in other words substantially altered.

In chapter I of Orwell's book, for instance, the enlistment, the sight of the Italian militiaman, and the triumphal departure of the recruits for the front are reflected in *Les Géorgiques*, but not so much the humdrum aspects of the militiamen's training. In chapters 2 to 5, the winter period at the front is drawn upon only lightly; matters picked up include the characteristic stench in the trenches (*CL*, p. 28; *LesG*, p. 344), the dilapidated rifle with which Orwell was issued (*CL*, p. 30; *LesG*, p. 343), the overriding need to forage for firewood even in places exposed to enemy machine guns (*CL*, pp. 48-9; *LesG*, pp. 345-6), the dropping of leaflets from a solitary enemy aeroplane flying too high to be shot at (*CL*, p. 65; *LesG*, pp. 280-1), the lamentable state of munitions available to both sides (*CL*, p. 71; *LesG*, p. 283), the potato patch in no man's land which troops from each camp raided in turn (*CL*, p. 72; *LesG*, p. 282), the Army and Navy Stores provisions which somehow got through to Orwell (*CL*, p. 76; *LesG*, p. 284), the detective novel called *The Missing Money-Lender* (translated as *La Disparition de l'usurier*, *CL*, p. 84; *LesG*, p. 284), and the pun on the letters DSO ('Dickie shot off', *CL*, p. 85; *LesG*, p. 282). Orwell's chapter 6 — the 'coup de main' or attack on the Fascist redoubt — is fairly thoroughly rewritten and abridged by Simon (*CL*, pp. 90-111; *LesG*, pp. 285-93), whereas chapter 7, which concludes Orwell's first 'part', is hardly touched upon at all.

In the second part (chapters 8 and 9), the May troubles are closely annotated, particularly chapter 9 which deals with the actual street fighting (*CL*, pp. 139-78). This is covered in two main passages in *Les Géorgiques*, pages 293-308 and 355-60, although once more selectively, and at shorter length. In chapter 10 — which deals with Orwell's brief return to the front — only the actual wounding is reworked, and the subsequent tedious trail through military hospitals is only briefly mentioned (*CL*, p. 186; *LesG*, pp. 309-10). Finally, the last two chapters, covering Orwell's experiences as a wanted man, his escape to France and return to peaceful England, are retold in some detail in *Les Géorgiques* (particularly on pp. 263-80 and 310); the longest episode from this time concerns Orwell's vain attempts to secure the release from prison of his superior officer (Major Kopp, not actually named in Simon's version, *LesG*, pp. 274-9; *CL*, pp. 231-8).

It is thus clear which incidents in *Homage to Catalonia* particularly interested Simon: those which are visual or 'graphic' in Orwell's account, such as the inflated heroics of the departure for the front and the struggle over the potato field; those which struck him as funny, such as the bawdy pun on 'DSO' and the absurd meticulousness of the police search of the Orwells' hotel room, in which each individual cigarette paper was scrutinised for secret messages; and finally those which are exciting — a feature known in the trade as 'action-packed' — such as the skirmish over the redoubt, or the frenzied *démarches* on Kopp's behalf. These fragments are not of course inserted *seriatim* in *Les Géorgiques* but in achronological order, as the following table — this time taking the Simon text first — makes clear:

LesG pp.	*CL* pp.
263-80	213-48
280-1	65
281-2	55-6
282-93	70-111
293-308	144-76*
309-10	186
310	251
311	134*
332	11
333-4	13
335	16
336	25
343	30
344	28
345-6	48-9
348	118
349	124
353	134*
355	139-40
357-60	140-9*

Such a table is of course of only limited usefulness since it over-simplifies what is a complex interaction between two texts. It does however have the advantage of showing, firstly, how Simon's borrowings are scattered through this chapter of *Les Géorgiques,* and secondly how certain passages (asterisked above) come to be used more than once by him, and finally how, roughly half-way through chapter IV, he quotes or paraphrases less and offers instead a commentary or meditation on Orwell's document. The table also reveals that quite a number of pages in chapter IV (notably 259-62, 308-9, 311-32, 336-43, 346-7, 350-3, 354, 356 and 360-2) bear little or no relationship to *Homage to Catalonia*. It is into these passages that Simon injects material of his own, for instance the detailed description of a photograph taken (by Simon himself?) during the civil war (*LesG*, pp.

259-62), or the references to Lytton Strachey's *Eminent Victorians* (pp. 308-9, 351, 354), or the long meditation on Orwell writing up his memoirs back home and attempting, through the literary act, to understand what he has experienced (*LesG*, pp. 311-32). This last is an aspect which Simon is well-placed to understand since this is, as I have said, the third occasion on which he has tried to do the same about Spain; the reader is therefore not surprised to find him mentioning the name of 'Patrocle' and the term 'homme-fusil', both of which are lifted from *Le Palace* (*LesG*, p. 341; *P*, pp. 47 and 101).

Equally interesting is what Simon passes over in silence. I have already mentioned the political commentary offered by Orwell and largely ignored by Simon. In addition there are many other pages in *Homage to Catalonia* which did not hold Simon's attention, chiefly where the narrative is straightforward or even pedestrian. In not specifically recalling these passages Simon is behaving as most readers would. (Does not Beckett say, after all, that 'à l'homo mensura il faut du staffage'?[5]) Other omissions can be explained by the temperament and outlook of this particular reader. It is not surprising, for instance, that the heroics of this passage did not appeal to Simon:

> *The men who were well enough to stand had moved across the carriage to cheer the Italians as they went past. A crutch waved out of the window; bandaged forearms made the Red Salute. It was like an allegorical picture of war; the trainload of fresh men gliding proudly up the line, the maimed men sliding slowly down, and all the while the guns on the open trucks making one's heart leap as guns always do, and reviving that pernicious feeling, so difficult to get rid of, that war* is *glorious after all. (HC, p. 184)*

It is not particularly surprising, either, that Simon fails to pick up Orwell's very British jokes, such as this witty aside:

> *One morning it was announced that the men in my ward were to be sent down to Barcelona today. I managed to send a wire to my wife, telling her that I was coming, and presently they packed us into buses and took us down to the station. It was only when the train was actually starting that the hospital orderly who travelled with us casually let fall that we were not going to Barcelona after all, but to Tarragona. I suppose the engine-driver had changed his mind. 'Just like Spain!' I thought. But it was very Spanish, too, that they agreed to hold up the train while I sent another wire, and more Spanish still that the wire never got there. (HC, p. 183)*

But Simon does echo the more sardonic comments, such as 'It was no use hanging on to the English notion that you are safe so long as you keep the law. Practically the law was what the police chose to make it' (*HC*, p. 201; *LesG*, p. 268). Finally, and rather curiously, Orwell's occasional 'knowing' manner, in asides like 'artillery is the determining factor in street warfare' (*HC*, p. 129), his untroubled assumption of military expertise although he was in fact the merest of amateurs, does not appear to have annoyed Simon as it must some readers.

Instead, Simon dwells at considerable length on Orwell's public school background and speculates on how his years at Eton may have affected him, particularly in inculcating the death-wish which the text attributes to him (see *LesG*, p. 352). This is a very Simonian slant, not at all what the average reader would find in Orwell's writing (indeed which is frankly contradicted by it; see *Homage to Catalonia*, p. 70, a passage which occurs in the first appendix to the French translation, p. 279, so probably was not read by Simon). To take the view that Orwell wished to be killed in Spain makes him into a Simonian character, like de Reixach in *La Route des Flandres* or the student in *Le Palace*. Simon's view of Eric Blair is in fact influenced more by Lytton Strachey's essay on Cardinal Manning in *Eminent Victorians* than by Raymond Williams's monograph on Orwell: Simon sees Blair as coming from the same stable as Manning, 'endowed', like the latter and his Oxford friends, 'with an infinite capacity for making speeches',[6] a phrase which Simon renders, a shade contemptuously, as 'doués d'une capacité infinie à faire des discours' (*LesG*, pp. 308, 351 and 354). Simon's narrator sees Orwell's political stance as tinged with hypocrisy, a 'subtil mélange de tricherie et de naturel', and ascribes this to the traditional educational background of the British élite, which reduces everything to that 'qui est de règle dans les pugilats disputés autour d'un ballon' (p. 353).

In advancing this opinion he gives no weight to Orwell's own clear statement that, much as he wished to be transferred to the Madrid front where the 'real' fight against Franco was taking place, he could not take the necessary first step towards the achievement of his aim, since this would have meant joining a Communist-controlled unit. He was against doing this not just because the Communists were bent on suppressing their left-wing rivals, the POUM — which in any case he never actually joined, although he fought in their militia — but also because he knew that 'sooner or later it might mean [his] being used against the Spanish working class' (*HC*, p. 140). In other words Orwell's objections to the

Spanish Communists were more pragmatic than ideological: he had
seen them, with his own eyes, denounce a socialist workers' party, the
POUM, as a Fascist front organization which had in the name of
revolutionary efficacy to be wiped out. They manoeuvered, in fact, to
have government troops and police drive the rival movement
underground. That, Orwell maintains, is what the May troubles were
all about, and why in June he and his comrades had to choose between
going to prison and running to earth. In the end, as we have seen,
Orwell was obliged to flee from Spain before he was murdered, as Bob
Smillie allegedly had been (Smillie, a member of the British
Independent Labour Party and a POUM activist, died in a Valencia jail
in mysterious circumstances). Orwell joined in the May street-fighting
almost by instinct: 'when I see an actual flesh-and-blood worker in
conflict with his natural enemy, the policeman', he wrote afterwards, 'I
do not have to ask myself which side I am on' (*HC*, p. 119). As
Raymond Williams argues, Orwell emerged from this experience a
revolutionary socialist, with his position as an anti-communist
confirmed. So although he joined the POUM militia almost by
accident, he came to share its political stance, and rather to regret that
he had not actually joined the party while he had the opportunity (*HC*,
p. 70). As Williams says, he made up for that to some extent by joining
the Independent Labour party (which had close links with the POUM)
on his return from Spain (*W*, p. 13), thus consummating his break with
the orthodox British left. It is certainly neither accurate nor fair to
suggest that 'O.' (as Simon's narrator refers to him) at any time
's'apprêtait à renier' his POUM friends (*LesG*, p. 358).

Reading *Homage to Catalonia* with Raymond Williams's study of
Orwell thus gives one a rather different picture than *Les Géorgiques*
presents, and yet as I have shown Simon drew on both works for
material in writing his novel. Since Simon's narrator shows himself as
anti-communist as Orwell was (see for example the heavy irony of the
remark about 'le seul drapeau authentiquement rouge', *LesG*, p. 355), it
is all the more surprising that Simon ignores significant passages in
Homage to Catalonia such as those which I have quoted and with which
he could be expected to sympathize. It is almost as if he wished to
simplify, even to distort Orwell's political position for his own purpose.
That purpose is betrayed by the fact that *Les Géorgiques* is as much a
meditation upon *Le Palace* as it is upon *La Catalogne libre*. Indeed it can
even be argued that Orwell's book was a pretext — as well as a pre-text
— a convenient hook on which to hang the Simonian narrator's fears

and obsessions about a past event in which Orwell happens also to have been an actor. Hence the fact that Orwell's positive tone — heard in several passages which claim that, however the war turns out, it will have been worth fighting Franco, that the outcome need not necessarily be 'disillusionment and cynicism' (*HC*, p. 220) — is not carried over into *Les Géorgiques*, which stresses instead the pathos and futility of Orwell's position, and by extension that of all idealists who threw in their lot with the Republican troops. That explains why the coda of chapter IV — the meditation on the 'eternal' poor and on 'cette indécourageable ferveur et cette infinie patience des pauvres' (p. 362), which they display in all circumstances and under all régimes — is such a telling comment by the narrator on the fate of all political idealisms, not least, no doubt, the young Claude Simon's own. But it is a view which, on the evidence of his writings, Orwell would not share. In another, later essay, 'Looking back on the Spanish War', he wrote that it was better to have fought and been defeated than to have surrendered to Fascism without a struggle (*IIC*, p. 242). At bottom, therefore, Simon is not really interested in what Orwell says. In *Le Sacre du printemps* he probes his own dilemmas by the simple, even crude device of setting up a debate between an idealistic youth and a disillusioned older man. In *Les Géorgiques* he adopts the subtler method of intertextualizing an idealistic text with which his own *text* sets up a debate. The argument, in other words, is not in the last analysis with Orwell at all: it is, as always in Simon, an introspective act, a tussle with himself.

When he is not 'interpreting' Orwell's position in this way to probe his own political attitudes and past experience of a similar situation, Simon uses his narrator to comment on, to lyricize and also to vulgarize different moments in *Homage to Catalonia*. Orwell, for instance, tells us that the hunt for Trotskyists even took the police to the public baths where they arrested a number of people 'in a state of nature' (*HC*, p. 205). This story is considerably expanded in *Les Géorgiques* and made to seem even more crude:

> *il y avait bien aussi les établissements de bains publics, avec leurs*
> *suintantes parois de briques émaillées, leurs fades relents de stupres*
> *et cette vague, émolliente et libidineuse atmosphère qui imprègne*
> *ces sortes de lieux, les corps exténués, flottant laiteux et sans poids*
> *dans les transparences couleurs d'huître d'où s'élevaient en grises*
> *fumerolles rampant et se tordant à la surface de l'eau brûlante*

d'impalpables et convulsives vapeurs, comme les ectoplasmiques
exhalaisons d'innombrables étreintes masculines, d'innombrables
orgasmes tarifés d'innombrables gitons (pp. 271-2)

Orwell, who was prudish in sexual matters, would never have written
that. The same applies to remarks about the Barcelona brothels which
O. and his friends might have frequented in their attempts to elude the
police (*LesG*, p. 263); needless to say, this is not a suggestion one finds
in *Homage to Catalonia*, which is content to state, in a brief aside, that
the brothels, closed by workers' patrols in the early days of the
revolution, had reopened by April 1937 (p. 111).

Apart from introducing greater sexual explicitness, Simon's text
amplifies Orwell's account by laying stress on the nightmarish aspects
of the police hunt in June, and thus makes the story 'cloudier' and more
sinister than the original. The whole atmosphere of political intrigue is
harsher and more cynically described in Simon's account, as if he were
implying that Orwell was a naive English radical who had little idea
how vicious things really were, a man for whom the Penguin Book had
not been written which could enlighten him about the true nature of the
crisis (*LesG*, p. 302). So although he retells Orwell's story of how his
hotel room was searched by the secret police, he omits the wry
conclusion that the detectives 'had some of the spirit of the Gestapo,
but not much of its competence' (*HC*, p. 202). Indeed, Simon's narrator
suggests that hard men with Russian-sounding names manipulated the
Republican leaders to carry out the will of governments thousands of
miles away (pp. 356-7); likewise he speaks sarcastically of the POUM
(not actually named but clearly implied) as a mere 'secte philosophique'
(p. 298).

On the other hand, Orwell's narrative is frequently expanded and
improved by a writer of much greater literary gifts, for instance in the
retelling of the account of the attack on the redoubt (pp. 287ff). In any
case, Simon introduces relevant memories of his own, such as the
graffiti in the ruined cathedral at Lerida (pp. 334-5), the 'on' here being
Simon's narrator, not Orwell. The same narrator offers commentary of
a 'lit. crit.' kind on Orwell's document, making judgements, or drawing
attention to what that book leaves out (such as the funeral processions
which figure so prominently in *Le Palace: LesG*, p. 331), or scrutinizing
dispassionately what it does feature prominently (such as the Italian
militiaman, p. 332), or, again, speculating on what Orwell was doing
and thinking before he enrolled at the Lenin barracks (pp. 328-9).

There is even a short biography of Orwell (based on material in Williams) offered by the narrator in his 'objective' tone of voice (*LesG*, p. 318), and a disquisition on Spain and on Barcelona which helps the reader understand the context in which Orwell's *témoignage* needs to be read (pp. 319-20).

In all this, of course, Simon's narrator imputes to Orwell the wish, 'en écrivant son aventure', to 'en dégager un sens cohérent' (p. 310), which is the same as Simon's own in *Le Palace* and indeed in most of his novels. He sees Orwell as a writer first and foremost, 'assis devant une table' and looking out of the window as he tries to make sense of his experience and render it comprehensible to his readers (*LesG*, pp. 312, 314). In doing so he raises the question of how 'fictional' *Homage to Catalonia* is. One of Simon's great merits in this meditation on Orwell, it seems to me, is that he has drawn our attention to this fundamental question. Since Orwell's book was published we have become more conscious of the blurred line which separates documentary on the one hand from fiction on the other. We now recognise that seemingly factual texts are rhetorical, even manipulative, and thus function in ways not dissimilar from those of works of the imagination. By the same token *Les Géorgiques* is characteristic of much contemporary writing in incorporating factual material and putting it to uses which are, overall, 'fictive'. Today's reader of *Homage to Catalonia* is more likely to notice the dramatic devices and other rhetorical effects which Orwell uses to make his account more graphic and persuasive, and Simon's commentary in *Les Géorgiques* serves paradoxically but importantly to demonstrate that *Homage to Catalonia* has much in common with a work of fiction, just as *Le Palace* has much in common with a work of *témoignage*.

If it is agreed that, through references to other texts, *Les Géorgiques* has the effect, as Alastair Duncan says, of acknowledging the fictional status of its own text, I want in conclusion to ask why Simon undertook this elaborate and detailed homage to *Homage to Catalonia*. Why, indeed, should Simon so painstakingly annotate Orwell's narrative, so self-absorbedly — and at such length — intertextualize it? There can be only one explanation: that, in spite of everything, he basically admires and respects Orwell's political attitude, which is radical, a shade anarchistic, and deeply committed to ideals that are democratic and socialist with a small 'd' and a small 's'. One sees what Orwell meant when he said, 'I am glad to have been . . . among Anarchists and POUM people instead of in the [Communist-dominated] International

Brigade'[7], at one with the working class and not with trend-following intelligentsia whom he despised so much; and one suspects that Simon agrees with a view thus shorn of illusions, but not devoid of ideals.

But the homage is also a critique. Duncan is correct in saying that Simon's tone is critical and that there is an ironic distance between the narrating voice and O. Nevertheless, I would not accept that chapter IV 'attacks the whole temper' of *Homage to Catalonia* (Duncan, p. 105), nor would I agree that Simon sees Orwell's self-image as 'bland'. O. is not Orwell, after all, as Duncan himself points out, but an intertextualized and therefore fictionalized version of the self-image projected in *Homage to Catalonia*, with inevitable and fruitful interferences from the images of the protagonists of *Le Sacre du printemps* and *Le Palace*. As Duncan aptly puts it, 'the artist is not a creator, but an adaptor; all his texts are second-hand' (p. 101). It so happens, in this case, that both the text and its metatext are remarkable, if very different, works of art.

REFERENCES

1. See, in particular, Alastair B. Duncan, 'Claude Simon's *Les Géorgiques*: an intertextual adventure', *Romance Studies*, no. 2 (Summer 1983), 90-107 (p. 91). In what follows, this essay is referred to as 'Duncan'.
2. *La Catalogne libre*, tr. Yvonne Davet (Paris, Gallimard, 1955); abbreviated as *CL*. It is worth remarking that Simon does not slavishly follow this text, but takes liberties with it of a factual kind, and sometimes makes mistakes through inadvertence. At the same time he greatly improves on it stylistically, as one would expect; compare, for example, *LesG* p. 307 with *CL* p. 158.
3. *Homage to Catalonia* (London, Penguin, 1975), p. 126; abbreviated as *HC*.
4. Raymond Williams, *Orwell* (London, Fontana/Collins, 1971), p. 59; abbreviated as *W*.
5. Samuel Becket, *Molloy* (Paris, Minuit, 1951), p. 95.
6. Lytton Strachey, *Eminent Victorians* (Penguin, 1948), p. 15.
7. *Collected Essays* (Penguin, 1970), vol. 1, p. 301.

Facing the matter of history:
Les Géorgiques

Anthony Cheal Pugh

> The belief in a hard core of facts existing
> objectively and independently of the
> historian is a preposterous fallacy.
>
> E. H. Carr, *What is History?*

PREAMBLE

If indeed there are no such things as objective 'facts', history can hardly
be said to exist outside the texts which narrate it. 'History', therefore, is
both what is presupposed by a certain kind of narrative, and what is
produced by it. It is not surprising, therefore, if positivist theorists of
history, such as Maurice Mandelbaum, have played down the narrative
element in historical writing in favour of *explanatory* and *interpretive*
forms:[1] once 'events' are sequentially ordered, the question of *what
happened* is taken as read.

I shall not be claiming in this essay that *Les Géorgiques* is what we
term an 'historical novel'. I shall seek to demonstrate, however, that it is
a text which gives novel forms to history, and that in so doing it gives
poetic answers to some of the philosophical questions currently debated
in the field of historiography.

In order to discuss 'the matter of history', as treated in the novel, I
am therefore obliged to make use of a commonsense definition of the
concept, for which 'History', having existed, can in some way be
recovered, reconstructed, or otherwise represented. It should be noted,
nevertheless, that even mainstream theorists admit that this involves
what is called the 'temporal paradox', even if they claim to circumvent
it by means of appeals to causal laws, and objectivity, however
'limited'.[2]

If we accept, with Derrida, that 'la première écriture est . . . une image peinte',[3] and that the 'languages' of art (painting or literature) do not deal with 'perception', but with systems of reference,[4] then it is clear that the modern preoccupation with the 'existential' status of representation, whether in art or in historical writing, must be taken as an index of a certain *anxiety* regarding not just the reality of past events, but also the means adopted to represent them.

This is evident from the example of annals listing important 'events': if nothing notable happened, a number (a date) stands for the time that has past. In an even more archaic form, the genealogical list, regeneration is simply recorded: it does not seem to involve the 'perpetual fear' of which Hobbes speaks in *Leviathan* (it is he who uses the word 'anxiety' regarding 'causes' of good and evil fortune[5]). It is thus when events are linked by the devices of narrative that 'anxiety' finds a concrete literary form, and the 'temporal paradox' begins to become apparent, as writers take up a 'perspective' upon the past. Much has been written about the role of scientific rationalism, and the 'metaphysical' concepts of 'presence' and 'subjectivity' which appear to be its historical concomitants. For present purposes, it will suffice to note, in passing, that the epistemological basis of what we commonly call 'history' has been challenged from a number of angles. Thus, as one of the more extreme examples of such a challenge, we have Lévi-Strauss, for whom history is 'a method with no distinct object corresponding to it.'[6]

To cut a long story short, therefore (and leaving aside for the present the whole question, however vital it may be, of the relationship between history and the novel), we can observe that the present state of the art is one in which a certain degree of dissension appears to obtain. Thus we have Roland Barthes, paraphrasing Nietzsche, and asserting that 'the fact can only be defined in a tautological fashion.'[7] Barthes defines the historian, moreover, as 'not so much a collector of facts as a collector and relater of signifiers; that is to say, he organizes them with the purpose of establishing positive meaning and filling the vacuum of pure meaningless series.'[8] Mandelbaum, on the other hand, will require that 'a historian's account of a series of events be true not only of that series when viewed as a whole, but that its account of all the components included in the series also be true.'[9] Going in a totally opposed direction are 'narrativists', such as Louis O. Mink, who roundly declares that 'History is not writing, it is the rewriting of stories.'[10]

This brings us back to representation, which happens also to be the first topic dealt with in *Les Géorgiques*: the novel, before it starts to tell its stories, confronts what we have seen to be the fundamental issue in history, one that is logically prior to the question of *why* things happened. It is summed up in a phrase that echoes from novel to novel in Simon's mature work, 'mais comment savoir?': *what happened, exactly?* Clearly, the novelist is fascinated by the 'temporal paradox', even if he tends to explain it away on aesthetic grounds, in order to defend himself from over-inquisitive interviewers.

What I have described elsewhere as the 'prologue' to *Les Géorgiques*[11] consists of an elaborate allegory of representation and reading. In my analysis of this 'prologue' I have claimed that what it demonstrates above all is that artistic representations in general depend upon the maintenance of a contradiction rooted in a denial. Briefly stated, this denial consists in believing that an 'image' (whether pictorial, or produced in the mind by a description in a text) has the power to effect a 'transport' from the sign 'back to' the real, when what is 'visible' in a figurative depiction is in fact signifying the invisibility of the thing, object or scene signified; what is 'seen in the mind', when reading, designates an even more radical form of absence.

Literary theory, in the past two decades, has been saying little more — even if in a sometimes rather more long-winded fashion. In the most concise formula I have come across, J.-F. Lyotard sums it all up: 'la "réalité" est ce qui échappe.'[12] Both history, and fiction, consequently, are caught up in a 'paradox' that is both temporal and epistemological.

THE GROUND OF HISTORY

The meaning of a novel's title is not always evident until at least a first reading of the text has been accomplished. '*Les Géorgiques*' is no exception here, for beyond (or before) the intertextual references (Virgil, Orwell, *La route des Flandres*), there is the etymological meaning: 'Earth + Work' (gē + ergon). The question 'what is history?' is thus answered in the most literal way: the 'ground' upon which historical figuration is based is the earth itself. But the soil worked by peasants, in harmony with nature's cycles, is regularly trampled upon and churned up by soldiers who march along Europe's invasion routes as one political visionary after another attempts to 'change the face of Europe'. Thus whereas the novel's title indicates an ideal of stasis within a pattern of change regulated by geophysical time, rather than human intervention, 'l'histoire événementielle' superimposes upon the natural rhythms of life and death a more brutal and unpredictable kind

of change in the form of war: *Les Géorgiques* systematically investigates
the powers of narrative applied to such circumstances in its evocations
of the French Revolution, the Spanish Civil War and the defeat of the
French armies on the Meuse in 1940.

In examining the 'ground' of history, before looking, in the latter
part of this essay, at history as a 'figure', I shall concentrate upon the
retold autobiographical fragments relating (to) the author's experiences
as a cavalry trooper sent forward into Belgium to head off the German
attack which commenced on 10th May, 1940. We return, therefore, to
the question of 'facts', in an apparent reversal of the quotation from
What is History? which serves as the epigraph to my commentary on
Simon's novel. Perhaps, therefore, it is worth stressing the way in
which in order to 'refer' to these events, above, I have been obliged to
play the part of the historian. The point about tautology, therefore,
remains to be disproven.

THE ORDER OF EVENTS

The first descriptions of the writer's first-hand experience follow a
rapid survey of the military career of his ancestor, the Revolutionary
General Jean-Pierre Lacombe St. Michel (referred to in the text as
'L.S.M.'). It is noteworthy that this survey is not so much narrated as
set down in the purely sequential (but, here, not necessarily
chronological) form of historical annals: 'Il signe au nom du Comité de
salut public la promotion de Pichegru au commandement des armées
réunies de Moselle et du Rhin. Il joint ses félicitations personnelles au
décret. Il exhorte les représentants à défendre la Meuse sans esprit de
recul.' (p. 24). And in fact, brief mentions of parallels in the writer's
life, with particular reference to the crossing and recrossing of the
Meuse, have already occurred, in italicized fragments inserted in the list
of the General's campaigns: *'Le soir du dimanche de la Pentecôte il
repasse précipitamment la Meuse avant que les ponts sautent.'* (p. 23).
Whether we are concerned with the general's or his descendant's life,
the events described constitute historical 'facts'. What is also evident,
however, is that these 'facts' cannot be verified other than by cross-
checking with other *texts:* 'intertextuality' defines, amongst other
things, the essence of historians' practice as readers and writers.

Claude Simon, as an artist 'for whom the real exists' (but is only
knowable in its present manifestations), is thus concerned more with
the truth of his activity as a writer than with the philosophical and

theoretical problem of the truth value of historical 'facts'. It is therefore not so much a question, for Simon, of disbelieving in history (which would be doubly absurd given his direct involvement in the kinds of event traditionally defined as 'historic') as of accepting that men do not 'make history', but are constantly made, and unmade, by it. Writing about it, clearly, can only ever be a 'supplementary' activity.

The next sequence relating to the events of May 1940 is clearly situated from a chronological point of view:

> *L'épisode suivant se situe le surlendemain de la nuit passée auprès des artilleurs. En dehors de son caractère sanglant, son importance tient à ce qu'il marquera pour les survivants la fin de la phase pour ainsi dire cohérente de la bataille, ou plutôt qu'il n'y aura des lors aucune sorte d'ordre, même désastreux. Ils se trouvent alors entre la Meuse et la Sambre hors de tout système structuré chacun ou par infimes petits groupes dans une complète errance, privés d'informations, se guidant au juger d'après la position du soleil, handicapés par leur état d'épuisement et le manque de sommeil. (p. 44)*

The retreat continues the following night, and the next day the horsemen find themselves apparently alone in the midst of a vast plain, with no cover, seemingly far from the battle (p. 46). But it is then that they run into an ambush, and it is at this point in the narration of events that the crucial issue is raised:

> *Ils comprennent alors qu'ils sont tombés dans une embuscade et qu'ils vont presque tous mourir. Aussitôt après avoir écrit cette phrase il se rend compte qu'elle est à peu près incompréhensible pour qui ne s'est pas trouvé dans une situation semblable et il relève sa main. (p. 47)*

The 'event' and its narration have collided, not just because of the doubt concerning the reader's capacity to 'comprehend' such a situation, but because of a more radical doubt over the power of narrative to 'communicate' anything beyond the common-places of experience. Thus behind the implied opposition experience/inexperience, that is, the 'humanist' reading of the passage, there is another set of questions. Individuals may have 'experiences', and, indeed, gain *experience* from them, but when narrated or described — and *read* — the signs employed become part of a far more complex system of references: they will always 'differ' from their 'originals', and the effects they produce, being deferred, can never be made to match their source. To the extent that discourse can only function through the discourse of the other (and other sets of references), it cannot produce effects of presence unless we choose to believe in them. In conventional narratives (fictional or historical) no choice is offered; in the passage quoted above, the writer's hesitation, the flicker of doubt (or the 'framing' effect — it can be defined in many ways), creates the necessary distance for the setting out of the preconditions of such 'belief'. The extreme case of an experience of almost certain death (we have no reasons for treating the 'original' as inauthentic — it is simply unverifiable and unavailable) thus shakes the whole narrative enterprise to its foundations, and with it a number of commonsense assumptions about communication via texts. At a more theoretical level, the novel bears out deconstructionist critiques of the communication model as used in early structuralist analyses of the relationship between the sender and the receiver: the message is not a medium, unless, that is, we mean a vehicle for spiritualist transference.

By highlighting this central misapprehension regarding the relationship between writing and reading, and by distancing the writer's *persona* from his person by the use of the narrative 'He', Simon (his *text*, properly speaking) shows why historical and fictional writings which reject out of hand or purport to be unaware of the problems outlined above cannot achieve *poetic* status, that is, a degree of self-recognition in the form of indices of the processes involved in their fabrication, an awareness of their formal heterogeneity, or admissions that whatever unity they have is the result of the papering over of numerous gaps. In the same way that we say that a net consists of a lot of holes tied together with string, a text consists of a series of discontinuous fragments strung together in phrastic units. In *Les Géorgiques*, as in a number of Claude Simon's previous novels, this is the starting-point for a search for another kind of compositional logic: 'il existe aussi, quoique non codifiée, une logique interne de la langue qui exige une syntaxe du texte dans son ensemble, de la première à la dernière ligne, et que si on parvient à suivre ces lois cachées, alors "quelque chose" se dira, tandis que dans le cas contraire, tout discours n'est que bavardage conventionnel. (. . .) Et naturellement, de ces fragments discontinus d'histoire ainsi ordonnés et mis en rapports d'une façon qui m'a semblé propre à former une continuité, de cette *composition,* ne ressort pour moi aucun "message", aucune "morale", aucune "fatalité", qui, comme on l'a dit pompeusement, "introduirait

la tragédie grecque dans le roman", aucune dérision non plus: en
somme, aucune espèce d'enseignement allant au-delà du seul constat de
ces "correspondences" thématiques ou (j'en demande pardon aux
pourfendeurs de "l'humanisme") simplement émotives.'[13]

It is not my purpose, here, to try to discover what might be the
overall logic at work in the composition of *Les Géorgiques*, but where the
fragments relating to the cavalryman are concerned, it seems that their
retelling — with the addition of a certain amount of contextual detail
missing from *La Route des Flandres* — is intended to retrospectively
reinforce that novel's 'historical' status.[14] The criterion of 'truth', so
readily used by historians, is, however, replaced by that of 'fidelity',
which implies recognition of the 'differences' stressed above. The
allusion to the other work is itself neither a direct reference, nor a
cryptic 'clin d'oeil': it is 'a novel', no more, no less:

> *Il rapporte dans un roman les circonstances et la façon dont les*
> *choses se sont déroulées entretemps: en tenant compte de*
> *l'affaiblissement de ses facultés de perception dû à la fatigue, au*
> *manque de sommeil, au bruit et au danger, des inévitables lacunes*
> *et déformations de la mémoire, on peut considérer ce récit comme*
> *une relation des faits aussi fidèle que possible: le carrefour et les*
> *champs parsemés de corps, le blessé ensanglanté, le mort étalé au*
> *revers du fossé, sa progressive reprise de conscience. (p. 52)*

This passage brings the demonstration to a head, for having made the
event and its narration 'collide' previously, it is now the turn for history
and fiction: no categorial distinction between the two concepts now
seems to be possible. But this depends, of course, upon what we mean
by 'history', and the novel has a great deal more to say about it, as we
shall see in due course.

There is one more passage in the novel dealing with the events of
May 1940 that I want to examine in connection with the notion of
'order', not just because it encapsulates the issues of sequentiality and
arbitrariness in narrative, but because it bring us to a further problem
that I have so far elided: that of point of view, or narrative perspective.
This problem raises the possibility of a totally different reading of the
novel, unlike the one proposed hitherto in which appeals to lived
history and felt experience have been prominent — although a doubt
has been expressed, in the text, as to the possibility of communicating
such experience, as opposed to producing in the reader a *different* set of
emotions, elicited not by the events narrated, but by what could be

E

called 'the event of narrative', an experience belonging to that category of effects derived solely from *the act of reading.*

The passage I want to look at, although it follows the previous one quoted (in the text that is) refers to an incident chronologically prior to it, the first attack by aircraft (which occurred, in 'historical' terms, during the afternoon of the 11th May, when Simon's regiment had crossed the Meuse and advanced further into Belgium near the town of Natoye):

> *Tout se passe en effet en quelques instants, presque simultanément, et il lui sera impossible de dire avec certitude dans quel ordre se succèdent les diverses phases de l'action (soit, par exemple: le bruit des moteurs des avions, puis la dispersion et les cris de terreur des réfugiés, le bruit de l'explosion, le moment où il a tourné la tête et vu le buisson de fumée grise (gris brun) troué d'étincelles, de lueurs — ou si, au contraire, les réfugiés se sont d'abord mis à courir avant de les entendre sans qu'il en comprenne la raison, si ce sont les cris affolés des réfugiés qui, avant même qu'ils se mettent à courir et s'égaillent, ont donné l'alerte, ou si le paquet de bombes est tombé avant qu'on entende les moteurs et si c'est l'explosion qui a déclenché la fuite et la dispersion de réfugiés, ou encore tout autre ordre). (pp. 176-7; original in italics)*

'*ou . . . tout autre ordre*': how can there be a natural or necessary order in narrative when the events it aspires to represent are multiple, simultaneous, discontinuous and disordered? If we accept the cavalryman/narrator's view, we must conclude that narrative has no natural basis in history as it is lived by human subjects, and that any order, or orders, that it produces are therefore falsifications of lived time. From this vitalist-phenomenological angle, then, there is no 'ground' for history either prior to or subsequent to the intervention of writing; history is simply a matter of memory, a subjective illusion.

This position is further reinforced by the narrator's critique of O.'s account of his involvement in the Spanish Civil War:

> *Peut-être espère-t-il qu'en écrivant son aventure il s'en dégagera un sens cohérent. Tout d'abord le fait qu'il va énumérer dans leur ordre chronologique des événements qui se bousculent pêle-mêle dans sa mémoire ou se présentent selon des priorités d'ordre affectif devrait, dans une certaine mesure, les expliquer. Il pense aussi peut-être qu'à l'intérieur de cet ordre premier les obligations de la*

> *construction syntaxique feront ressortir des rapports de cause à*
> *effet. (pp. 310-1)*

In narrative, whether historical or fictional, causality thus appears to be merely an effect of narrative sequence. But as the cavalryman's previous story has shown, narrative need not be sequential in order to produce persuasive effects. 'O.', however, jumps immediately to the conclusion that if history cannot be narrated on the ground, as it were, it must have another rationale, albeit an unseen one. Since he cannot, however, explain what this might be, another voice intervenes to 'correct' his account:

> *Maintenant il avait simplement par-dessus la tête de cette histoire*
> *dont il doutait (en quoi il se trompait encore) qu'elle méritât qu'il*
> *l'écrivît avec un H majuscule et qui ne l'intéressait décidément pas*
> *. . . il lui semblait de moins en moins probable qu'il participât à*
> *une action historique: en tout cas, si action il y avait, elle*
> *apparaissait sous une forme, bruyante certes et tapageuse, de non-*
> *action, à moins d'admettre . . . que l'Histoire se manifeste*
> *(s'accomplit) par l'accumulation de faits insignifiants, sinon*
> *dérisoires, tels que ceux qu'il récapitula plus tard. (p. 304)*

The parenthetical but authoritative intervention has the immediate effect of bringing into question the convention of third person narration which enables events, in stories and in histories, to 'just happen'. In the passage following the intervention, by contrast, there is a more overt ambiguity: the reader is faced with the problem of 'identifying' an origin for the narrative voice, hitherto safely anonymous. But the 'correction' of 'O.'s misapprehension simply makes the question rebound, by revealing the constant temptation to hypostatize 'history' by naming it, and to promote it to the level of the master-concept by capitalizing it. Such an 'authorization' thus runs the risk of suggesting that if history can be identified, and named, it must consist of a transcendent process, or alternatively that, by naming it, it can be understood, whereas such 'understanding' consists of no more than an 'after-effect'. The problem is, therefore, one of authority, and thus one of authorship also.

AUTHORITY

The passages quoted thus criticize, from the point of view of something called 'History', both accounts of events derived from subjective sources, such as the memory, and accounts that attempt to make events conform to what are merely linguistic and narrational conventions. For events to merit the capital 'H' of History, they must constitute, it seems, a totalizable series. Since the events in which 'O.' participates do not appear to him to correspond to any such order, they do not deserve raising, at this stage, to the level of the historical. On what basis, therefore, does the authorial voice — or the dissonant voice that we may wish to refer back to an author — contradict 'O.'? Is 'O.' merely an incompetent writer, unable to exploit fully the privileges of authorship, or is his grasp of the theory of history (Marxist theory, as implied by the expression 's'accomplit') simply inadequate? Does the author of *Les Géorgiques*, or his *persona*, enjoy a superior perspective upon history? Is this based upon better information, greater political acumen, or merely the universal and proverbially useless advantage of hindsight?[15] To follow this line of questioning is to exit from the text of *Les Géorgiques* to find oneself in territory that historical writing is familiar with (or claims to be able to deal with), but which the fictional text, by definition, has to avoid. But this is precisely the point, for by apparently breaking what we could call the fictional 'contract' that guarantees the autonomy of the fictional world (however closely it imitates the reality that the theory of mimesis presents as extratextual and extralinguistic) *Les Géorgiques* brings to our attention the fallacies upon which both exclusively mimetic and exclusively anti-mimetic theories of fiction are built. Thus whereas the alternatives seem to be fiction *or* history, or the 'referential illusion' versus some self-guaranteeing 'real' referentiality, a text that upsets the formal distinctions upon which such oppositions depend opens up a problem that has bedevilled literary theory for some time. As recent work has shown, it is quite possible to argue for a theory of meaning, based upon Frege's distinction between sense and reference, which is neither intralinguistic (like structuralism) nor based upon 'realist', or extralinguistic, premises, yet which accepts an anti-realist view of language.[16] In other words, to accept that the way in which a text 'refers' to reality can *always* be problematic is very different from deciding that certain texts call up 'real' referents and others 'illusory' ones. It would appear, to judge from the conclusion of a recent article by Hayden White, that historiography is in the process of grasping this point: 'Is it not possible that the question of narrative in any discussion of historical theory is always finally about the function of imagination in the production of a specifically human truth?'[17]

This is equivalent to saying that 'imagination' is part and parcel of 'cognition', and as such it is a sign of a return to health in the field of theory, to the extent that it is not so much the so-called 'referential illusion' that is abnormal, as its condemnation by certain theorists. For the illusory images provoked by texts can be qualitatively distinguished, according to the ways in which they are 'framed' by critical, theoretical or ironic commentary: 'referentiality' is not absolute, but relative, and conditional not so much on 'experience' as such, as on the experience of using language and reading texts.

As Umberto Eco has shown, the relationship between a text and its extralinguistic referents, fictional and real, can only be established by careful plotting of the routes followed by readers when trying to 'make sense' of what they read. These involve what Eco calls 'inferential walks' through other texts, and a complex relaying of meaing via a whole series of cognitive frames from the local and the personal to the encyclopaedic.[18] Every meaning, therefore, whether 'fictional', 'mythical', 'historical', or whatever, has a number of possible histories, and a fictional work that would aspire to total 'self-referentiality' denies the reality of the processes by which meaning is created in a constant coming and going between the subject and, again, not the world 'as such', but what can be known of it beyond our spatio-temporal limits by means of representations. Both novels and histories, however, are texts that are signed by 'authors', even if, well aware of the problems outlined above, they sometimes deny their responsibility for their progeny.[19] But like everything else that such texts refer to, directly or indirectly, the biographical author remains absent from his text: his 'identity' is no longer in his possession; it has become one among many other potential meaning-effects. *Les Géorgiques* emphasises this aspect of the writing and reading processes by avoiding using proper names where its principal narrators are concerned. 'Claude Simon' is not present in his text, any more than 'George Orwell', and if 'O.' stands for Orwell it is doubly distant from its referent, since it refers in the first instance to a 'nom de plume'

FROM HISTORICISM TO FICTIONALISM

In the same way that a reaction against 'historicism' has provoked a renewal of interest in history as narrative,[20] so literary theorists have re-examined the concept of fiction in the context of critiques of structuralism and a spate of so-called 'metafictional' writing.

Les Géorgiques, by adopting the device of initials standing for names of real persons, makes an implicit appeal to the conventions of the eighteenth-century memoir novel. Fiction and history, brought face to face at one level, are therefore also confronted 'in disguise'. Such a strategy brings out, by requiring that we 'discover' hidden identities, the need for a critical reappraisal of the ways in which modern fiction, by sometimes overstressing its own 'fictionality', runs the risk of substituting mystification for the genuinely problematic issues of representation in narrative.

Frank Lentricchia's term 'fictionalism' usefully defines the positions adopted by both the cavalryman/narrator and 'O.' in the passages quoted earlier, positions which, as we have seen, are thrown into critical relief by authorial interventions which themselves invite an inquiry into the concept of authorship.

Such positions involve an 'internal contradiction' that Lentricchia sees as one of the central presuppositions of literary modernism: 'Self-consciousness is thought to perform the magical act of mediating between fiction and reality. It not only declares reality off-limits to fictive (playful, nonreferential, operationally invalid) discourse, but while doing this it enables us to "find out", it teaches us something about reality by telling us that fictions are *not* mimetic. Like all strictly formulated dualisms, however, the fiction-reality antithesis cannot be mediated without at the same time destroying the antithesis itself, and thus destroying what confers the opposed values of fiction and reality, and the traditional ontological opposition conveyed by those terms. . . . Once the Kantian turn from realism is made there is no way to disguise our "inventions" with the mask of discovery, no way back to an uncritical position.'[21]

Les Géorgiques, standing as it does within the Proustian and Faulknerian tradition, in which fiction and fictionalism (as misreading) are represented as the texture of experience itself, is thus typical of the kind of modernist text described by Lentricchia. The superimposition of narratorial and authorial self-consciousness upon the fictionalism within the fiction that also characterises Simon's novel, in common with those of his acknowledged masters, is also a recurrent feature of many modern texts. It could thus be said that the reality-fiction antithesis functions at all levels in such writing, since as soon as author, narrator, character or reader emerge from one fiction (or misreading) they are engulfed by another. Fiction cannot therefore escape from itself unless it opposes the fabricated heterogeneity of its own elements (narrative, dialogue, description, and metaphor) to the heterogeneity that also inhabits performative and pragmatic, or 'non-fictional' discourses, or otherwise exposes itself to the 'outside' that it attempts to enclose.

A major problem here is of course the very fruitfulness of the reality-fiction antithesis: art can set itself up, endlessly, as the only possible mediator between what it portrays as the fictions of life and the real that it claims only to be able to represent as fiction. *Les Géorgiques*, however, is fully aware that the machine of fiction,[22] if it continues to rely for too long upon such premises, is bound to break down as irony contaminates all levels of meaning, both formal and representational. Even so, the novel continues to produce meanings that are not generated solely by the antithesis and its 'internal contradictions', meanings that will take us, in the latter part of this essay, into a series of further problems arising out of both the 'unavoidable critical position' described by Lentricchia, and the 'fundamental metaphysical proclivities'[23] that he sees in modernist writing, problems that can be seen reflected in *Les Géorgiques* not only in its treatment of narrative perspective, but also in its handling of figural language.

But Fictionalism requires an absolute, Fate, Destiny, or Chance: in *Les Géorgiques* history is all these things, and thus none of them, merely the reflection of a desire for an order which would deny the reality of change and death. 'History' thus becomes the figure signalling the repression of that knowledge:

> *the fundamental repression that shapes discourse is the repression of death, of final absence, the intellectual certainty that I will die, very soon . . . . That fundamental, inescapable, mis-recognition that is not a mis-perception of the real world isn't (only) rooted in the Oedipal trauma; it persists as long as bodies persist. Which is for ever, within history; but they'll be somebody else soon.*[24]

For the self-conscious subject, death is final; for Nature, however, it is merely an aspect of what in *Les Géorgiques* is described as 'l'interne logique de la matière' (p. 352). History, in this sense, is already written in the 'implacables mécanismes' (p. 352) governing the constant redistribution or energy and matter. However, as scientific knowledge, or as philosophical wisdom, such awareness provides little solace for mortals. Thus, although it may be claimed, as in the *prière d'insérer* of *Les Géorgiques*, that Nature, is 'le principal personnage du livre',[25] its cycles can only be seen as eternal from a transcendent perspective. The novel does not romanticize nature by placing it *above* history, rather, it identifies Nature and history as absolutes beyond the scope of finite human knowledge which are nevertheless forces that pre-script individual and collective human histories. Both are supremely indifferent to the fate of Simon's fictional/historical characters, as is made abundantly clear when the ground gives way under the fugitive brother's feet as he wanders into a marsh, while the butterflies continue their ritual mating dance over his head (pp 422-4).

BURNT OUT TROPES

It has been claimed that literarity consists in the foregrounding of the 'poetic function' (Jakobson). Deconstructive criticism goes further, by demonstrating how literary texts reveal not so much their radical difference from other types of text, as a linguistic self-awareness that can teach us to un-read (or de-scribe) rhetorical and poetic effects in all discourse. *Les Géorgiques* draws attention to its scriptural texture in Section II, where the experience of coming under fire for the first time is described: 'cette suprême et dernière consécration: celle du feu, soudaine, violente, brève, juste le temps d'apprendre ce qu'on (les commandements réglementaires et les métaphores des poètes) leur avait caché, c'est-à-dire que ce qu'on appelait le feu était veritablement du feu, brûlait . . .' (p. 130). The initiatory ritual consists as much in the unmasking of linguistic fictions, military *and* poetic, as in the physical experience itself. 'Fire', that most poetic of metaphors, can only burn outside language, and no words can adequately convey the nakedness of flesh exposed to bombs and bullets. The figural and the referential meanings are effaced by reality, and all that remains is the burnt out carcase of a metaphor, not so much a poetic figure (a substitution), as a residue of meaning, or black sooty traces of what has been consumed: 'de longues traînées noirâtres, aussi prosaïquement sales qu'une cheminée mal ramonée ou le fond d'une poêle à frire' (p. 131). In the very act of deconstructing the poetic metaphor, and of replacing it with prosaic comparisons, the text metaphorizes its own material ground: the black traces of writing, signs standing in the place of what has gone (history), or what never was (fiction), are all that we have.

In *Les Géorgiques*, history is regularly personified. The personification moreover, metaphorically designates itself as a *figure*: it has a face even if it hides it much of the time. In the remarkable passage describing gypsies in a cinema, time is 'la face cachée des choses' (p. 215), the fundamental unknown precisely because time and the past itself can only be represented as illusions. But this image puts the rhetorical figure back into contact with the human figuration upon which fiction depends, and 'History' becomes another character in the novel when it is glimpsed 'à visage découvert' (p. 385). Is history given a face because the human figures in the text (and in any text) are in some sense faceless, their identities, in *Les Géorgiques*, merged into the ubiquitous third person? Or are these figures, as linguistic entities in a text, turned into 'characters', because they are authorized by language and by narrative, and by that author of authors, 'History itself'?

Thus although History sometimes shows its face in *Les Géorgiques* it is the face of many characters, who, like the narrators, all resemble one another: 'la même face, un peu épaisse un peu large, et derrière, en plusieurs exemplaires, le même imperturbable personnage connu tantôt sous le nom de Grigoriev, tantôt sous celui de Grigoriévitch. (p. 340): Stalinist robots unconsciously parody their own roles in the name of History as the Absolute Value. But History, Nature, and the text, all deface and de-compose their figures: 'comme si . . . le temps, l'Histoire pourrissaient eux-mêmes, se décomposaient' (p. 210).

The attack upon absolutes, in *Les Géorgiques*, is thus pursued at a level that is not only structural and philosophical, but tropological. It is suggested, for example, in the same description of night manoeuvres referred to earlier, that History may operate according to its own laws, and that these may simply be invisible to both protagonists, narrators, and metanarrators. Where these perspectives might end is of course something of a problem. The text, however, cannot avoid the temptation to describe these 'laws' in figural terms: 'Des lois peut-être (un ordre ou plutôt une ordonnance impossible à détecter mais d'une nature aussi imprescriptible, aussi mathématique, que celles qui président aux spirales des coquillages' (p. 131). A 'law' should entail an element of predictability, whereas the order imagined here is 'imprescriptible': if a 'law' is in any way mathematical moreover, it should also be computable. In fact, the text has already denied any such inferences, preferring the word 'ordonnance', and thus suggesting something more akin to an aesthetically pleasing patterning comparable to what can be observed in nature (but not necessarily understood). The very statement that produces the hypothesis of an order thus modifies, and then undoes its own hypothesis: the order posited is a purely metaphorical one. Ironically, the comparison that invests itself with the prestige of mathematical logic — and which thus blinds us with figures, in more than one sense — goes on to reveal its fragile figurality in another trope, well-suited for the expression of a circular and repetitious, but non-final logic: the spirals of a sea-shell. But once again, not only the form, but also the substance of the metaphor (more properly, the absent substance it evokes) is empty: the conceit is as hollow as what it represents, and both what it represents and the signifier performing the representation have, in any case, taken the place of something indescribable. The text therefore demonstrates, in the very spirals of its metaphors, the process by which each and every figure deconstructs the one for which it has been substituted just as protagonists, narrators and metanarrators comment upon, and criticise, each other's view of history. There is always another metaphor, just as there is always another possible narrative instance.

Formal and figural models do not, however, provide an aesthetic refuge for meaning — at least in those texts which admit the contradictory presence/absence of something called 'history' both outside them, and inside them (that is, in the form of references to historical and autobiographical events, and in the form of traces recording the generation, the growth, and the transformation of the texts themselves). Neither metaphysics nor aesthetics can 'save' the text: it is necessarily inhabited by its own madness, like any absolute, such as 'history itself': 's'affolant alors, se précipitant, se mettant à fonctionner à vide, emballée, tournant à la parodie, au bouffon' (p. 385). There is no proper meaning, or ground, upon which the text can construct its figures: *Les Géorgiques* clearly shows that its meanings, and its final absence of meaning (for the subject-for-death), can only be played out by promoting figures (tropes) to the level of *characters*.

SUPPLEMENT

The true modernity of Claude Simon's writing lies in how it faces up to its own awareness of its 'supplementarity'. Derrida's concept is used by Edward Said to explain how modern fiction reflects the writer's recognition of his marginality, and the eccentricity of his medium with regard to the real world: 'History and society seem to have forced upon the novel its supplementarity, to which the novelist's answer is a very difficult art whose connections with reality are seldom obvious'.[26] What is no longer obvious, however, is how written memories (memoirs) can resist the orders imposed by the textually and materially more immediate realities (for writer and reader) of language, fabulation, and composition. Even the place names on the 'Route des Flandres', the names which have inscribed themselves so indelibly in history and in the writer's memory, produce more fictional matter: 'le dernier (Anor) avec ses consonances sombres (comme une contraction d'Anubis, Nord, Noir, Mort)' (p. 227). A page later, a reference to opera (Gluck's *Orfeo*) presents a seemingly gratuitous variant, 'ou Norma' (p. 228); the text *works*: it points out its own productivity.

Les Géorgiques, a text which faces and de-faces its figures ('persons', 'characters' and tropes), and in so doing 'loses its head' [27], questions the pertinence of the very concept of thought as 'knowledge' in literature. [28] Novels can *speculate* about an 'unknown knowledge' that might be the property of the ideal author we call 'History', and they can ironically subvert the pretensions of their own and other discourses by means of forever incomplete and self-deconstructive effects of meaning, but the diversions they offer lead inevitably back to problems of interpretation inherent in all and any attempts to represent the real within the medium that represents not the real but the reality of thought processes articulated in language. *Les Géorgiques* transforms *ground* (Earth, History, Reference, 'original' and 'intentional' meaning), by the productive *work* of writing, into *figures* that trace and efface the trajectories of meanings which, like history, will not stand still. [29]

REFERENCES

1. Maurice Mandelbaum, *The Anatomy of Historical Knowledge* (Baltimore and London, 1977), p. 26.
2. Ibid., pp. 145-168, ('Objectivity and its limits').
3. Jacques Derrida, *De la grammatologie* (Paris, 1967), p. 401.
4. 'Structure, sign, and play', in *The Structuralist Controversy* (Baltimore and London, 1970). The point is made in the discussion following Derrida's paper.
5. *Leviathan* (Glasgow, 1962), p. 129, ('On religion').
6. *The Savage Mind*, (London, 1966), p. 262.
7. 'The discourse of history', *Comparative Criticism. A Yearbook* (Cambridge, 1981), p. 16.
8. Ibid.
9. Mandelbaum, p. 9.
10. Quoted by Paul Ricoeur, *Temps et récit*, vol. 1 (Paris, 1983), p. 222.
11. In 'From drawing, to painting, to text. Claude Simon's allegory of representation and reading in the prologue to *Les Géorgiques*', forthcoming in *The Review of Contemporary Fiction* (Spring 1985).
12. J.-F. Lyotard, *Discours, Figure* (Paris, 1978), p. 126.
13. 'Réflexions sur le roman', Claude Simon's address to the New York University colloquium on the *nouveau roman* (1982), forthcoming (in translation) in *The Review of Contemporary Fiction*.

14. See my articles: 'Defeat, May 1940: Claude Simon, Marc Bloch and the writing of disaster', *Forum for Modern Language Studies,* 21 (1985), 59-70, and 'Supplementary history: before and after *La Route des Flandres',* forthcoming in *The Second World War in Literature,* ed. I. Higgins (Edinburgh, Scottish Academic Press), for a discussion of some of the many problems arising from such a reinterpretation of the past. The second of these articles includes Claude Simon's own account of his experiences in 1940, in the form of a short chronicle entitled 'petit historique'.

15. 'What experience and history teach us is this — that people and governments have never learnt anything from history, or acted upon principles deduced from it.' (Hegel)

16. See Stephen Gaukroger, 'Logic, language and literature: the relevance of Frege', *The Oxford Literary Review,* 6, no. 1 (1983), 68-96.

17. 'The question of narrative in contemporary historical theory', *History and Theory,* vol. 23, no. 1 (1984), p. 33.

18. See Umberto Eco, *The Role of the Reader* (London, 1979), pp. 3-43.

19. See my article 'Authorial personae in Pinget's fiction: Mahu, Mortin and Monsieur Songe', *The Review of Contemporary Fiction,* 3, no. 2 (Summer 1983), 208-213.

20. See Ricoeur, *Temps et récit,* Part II, 'Histoire et récit', for a summary of 'narrativist' theories.

21. Frank Lentricchia, *After The New Criticism* (Chicago, 1980), pp. 58-9.

22. See Stuart Sykes's description of the text as an 'ensemble grinçant', in *'Les Georgiques:* "Une reconversion totale"?', *Romance Studies,* no. 2 (Summer 1983), p. 87.

23. Lentricchia, p. 60.

24. Bernard Sharratt, *Reading Relations* (Brighton, 1982), p. 157.

25. Signed by Jérôme Lindon.

26. Edward Said, *Beginnings* (New York, 1975), p. 151.

27. The theme of decapitation in the novel is itself worthy of examination: as Derrida remarks of Genet's *Notre-Dame des Fleurs,* '. . . cette écriture est de la décapitation, elle n'a pas de centre'. *Glas I* (Paris, 1981), p. 100. I shall follow this up in a sequel to this essay.

28. 'Puisque l'acte de langage remet en question la simple *connaissance* linguistique, il ne peut savoir ce qu'il fait ni non plus savoir *ce qu'il ne sait pas.'* Shoshana Felman, *La Folie et la chose littéraire* (Paris, 1978), p. 24.

29. 'Ni le repérage d'un topos, ni l'opacité d'un *pathos,* ni la transparence d'un *logos,* la figure produit tout à la fois un effet de topos, un effet de pathos, un effet de logos qui se déconstruisent réciproquement, et entre lesquels elle est, justement, le mouvement de l'*inadéquation, et le travail même de la différence,',* ibid., p. 25.

The generative image: an exploration of Claude Simon's *La Chevelure de Bérénice*

Mary Orr

La Chevelure de Bérénice is the latest text by Simon to be published by Minuit. As text, however, this is its third appearance, the only, and very vital change being the new title.[1] This distinguishing feature makes it a different work of art, and poses interesting questions as to literary development within an opus (authorial generation) and contextual changes from one reprint to another (contextual generation). It is these two areas which are the subject of this essay.

Most readers assume chronological development within an opus as the writer explores his subject with each succeeding text. In Simon's oeuvre as a whole, *La Chevelure* is a new development going beyond *Les Géorgiques* in its exploration of language and writing. However, it is also a direct reprint of *Femmes*, a text of Simon's so-called middle period, and therefore becomes both a precursor of itself and questions, retrospectively, its own development. Simon's authorial generation can thus be seen to be both linear and circular, diachronic and synchronic, depending on a reworking of components from itself and Art, both literature and painting. The central concern remains the act of composition, but visual images (the Miró reproductions in *Femmes*) are superseded by pure text, its language encompassing the linear progression of words and, by association, the spatial grouping of image clusters.

Simon's authorial generation as he works on his material requires the reader to respond to changes in the context, and to be aware of the importance of new detail. The titles *Orion aveugle* and *La Chevelure* refer to constellations and offer a metaphor for this process. Each star (word) is part of a whole pattern. As in a child's dot-to-dot book, a picture emerges when a line is drawn between the numbered dots in the prescribed order. With Simon, the dots are unnumbered, which allows different pictures to appear as the reader draws lines between images. There is no 'right' reading (one numerical sequence), but 'wrong' readings may be discerned if they do not conform to certain patterns that the text and its structure suggest. This textual drawing (association) also mirrors the paintings and collages reproduced in *Orion aveugle* and the Chinese-style hieroglyphs, the Miró's, in *Femmes*, but as the reader's mental images. Contextual generation, therefore, has to do with the relationship between pattern maker (the writer) and pattern remaker (the reader), both free to draw from and within the patterns of language.

I now want to consider this contextual generation from *Femmes* to *La Chevelure* by taking, as generator, each title in turn, to show how Simon's change of one element of the pattern is not a trivial concern in the new text,[2] but intrinsic to further enlightenment of the Text in progress.

Femmes is a fiction in parallel with some 'toiles' by Miró. It begins, not with the plural, but from a single woman, reduced to the pronoun, 'elle'.

> *lourde tout entière vêtue de noir la tête couverte d'un fichu noir*
> *elle traversa la plage déserte arrivée près du bord elle s'assit sur le*
> *sable fit asseoir l'enfant à côté d'elle après quoi elle resta là les*
> *deux mains posées un peu en arrière les bras en étais le buste*
> *légèrement renversé regardant la mer les jambes allongées croisées*

Description takes precedence. Bulk (physical presence) and blackness delay the subject, which unleashes action and the rest of the text. This first stanza contains key descriptive techniques which are enlarged as the writing progresses. The forms and shapes of the body, the grouping of the woman and her child echo the cumulative formation of the text. Their movement or fixity translate into textual dynamism (active verbs) or stasis (description). Colour, the play between background and foreground, narrative angle and perspective are also contained in this opening section, to be developed as contrasts and changing viewpoint shape and enrich the text.

'Elle' not only generates the subject matter; she also forms the structural framework. There is complete balance and harmony between 'elle retira ses bas . . .' (p. 8) and the penultimate stanza 'elle remit ses bas' (p. 24). Within the overall structure, 'elle' punctuates the text, marking off the three main segments by her physical presence. The first of these is mainly erotic in tone and gathers energy for a new departure by reworking old motifs:

bas noirs aussi quoique jeune

peut-être en deuil

amies (p. 18)

From the eroticism of removing stockings, the emphasis is now 'deuil'. This new textual segment moves to the second phase of the Eros-Thanatos interrelationship, using juxtaposition to direct new content. 'Amies' has a whole line to itself, implicitly suggesting the correspondence between womb and tomb, although on a superficial level, it relates to the bonds between the women. The embodiment of youth and young motherhood, the generator 'elle', disappears and the stage is set for her counterpart, 'vieille qui saignait des poulets'. In a grotesque way, she evokes the 'trame' of the young woman's stockings on page seven with her 'tablier *quadrillé* de fines raies ardoise'. The second segment is framed by the reappearance of 'elle', who activates the final thematic section, war, the third panel of the triptych.

'Elle' controls the text and also helps proliferate it, by taking her place among 'trois s'en allant là-bas au loin' (p. 9). This multiplying of description by three allows the interplay of harmonies and discords. Contrast becomes a 'corps producteur' within the entity of the group *Femmes*. The original 'elle', in her black dress, acts as a foil for 'le corsage géranium de la seconde' (p. 10). This burst of colour off-setting the 'black' woman is similar in technique to Miró's paintings, which rely heavily on the juxtaposition of blacks and violent colour. The women also introduce the first continuous present verb. The past-historic actions ('elle') can now be slowed into present, on-going text, because the initial motion has been set off, and the expanding text can generate itself through the comparison of entities when new elements are drawn in (in the artistic and magnetic senses).

Contrast is produced also by variations on a theme. The women introduce other subjects, inanimate and human, which then become thematic and chromatic groups in their own right. The dockers are a case in point. Similar to the 'elles' in dress, it is their differences which make them a separate entity, '. . . allongés comme endormis mais trop immobiles . . . les pieds sales chaussés *d'espadrilles* aussi' (p. 15). These men in turn watch another group of women '. . . les festons javellisés se retroussant leur chair tout entière . . . décolorée . . . grisâtre à l'exception des visages violemment coloriés *cyclamen noir* leurs yeux d'oiseaux fardés de bleu ou de vert' (p. 17). These prostitutes act as a parodic mirror of the initial 'elles', the colours repeated, but as violent make-up, colour painted on. Their individuality is totally suppressed.

For the reader, 'elle' also traces perspective, the narrative viewpoint. As the subject, she controls and is seen from the stance of textual anonymity. At closer range, a particular vision of her emerges by the use of 'on'. When 'elle' creates a reaction, a memory or sensation, 'je' becomes more prominent. Three readings or narratives are executed simultaneously, depending on whether text, writer or reader controls the emphasis of perspective. From the anonymous viewpoint, 'elle' is in charge; the reader follows the connections cerebrally. The 'on' of middle-distance and reported speech creates greater reader involvement on both the cerebral and sensual levels, but with the autonomy of the text preserved. The 'je' reading could be described as sensual, where the text becomes secondary, or subjected to reader experience, and a stimulant to personal imagination or interpretation.

'Elle' is also involved in *text*ure. The visible cloth of *La Chevelure/Femmes* parallels Miró's paintings, in which the hessian shows through the paint. Simon transposes this into text, 'une toile de sac servait de porte elle l'écarta apparut vêtue de noir criant . . . à travers la toile on pouvait voir la flamme de la lampe c'est-à-dire plutôt une tache diffuse safran bue par la trame de ficelle comme par un buvard' (pp. 12-13), and later,' la toile de sac retomba obstruant la porte elle resta là se profilant en ombre chinoise'. These extremely important and evocative quotations highlight Simon's reliance on, and departure from, Miró. Instead of painting his text onto the canvas — content (surface) taking precedence over structural framework (form) — Simon puts 'elle' behind the 'trame', in the movable doorway between the two. The 'trame' is visible but, because of its texture, 'elle' remains visible too. 'Silhouette', 'ombre chinoise' epitomize Miró's style, but also Simon's intent: to describe writing in action. 'Elle' is the thin silhouette line traced on text, which acts as a blotter, diffusing fixed images. The metaphor of writing materials thus becomes highly appropriate. No clear distinguishing story or characterization (the traditional novel) emerges because of this 'blended-blotch' text-making on the writer's palette.

Blackness produces colour. This seeming contradiction has been noted in the contrasting dress colours, but it is more than a simple foil or juxtaposition. It plumbs the layers of writing and, by assimilation, draws together separate fragments within the textual space, imbuing them with new significance. Throughout the text, the line of black ink produces images in the reader's mind, just as in the same way the word 'géranium' produces a mental picture. The first explicit erotic image is unleashed by the use of assimilation, colour and the act of drawing and writing, 'poils collés moites dans les plis obscurs de son corps noirs embrouillés semblables à ces griffonages d'enfants appuyant fort la mine de plomb crevant le papier se déchirant fente rose cyclamen' (p. 12). The 'elle' who produced the colour has receded to leave pure colour open to the play of the imagination. The text develops this colour, applying its erotic connotations to both sexes, through the use of synonym (pp 13, 16 and 17). 'Cyclamen' becomes 'lilas fané', 'vermillon pâle', 'cramoisi', 'mauve foncé', before culminating with 'ce dard *encre* et coquelicot' (p. 24).

In the only critical article on *Femmes,* Raillard notes, 'chez Miró le chromatisme tend à l'érotisme, chez Simon l'érotisme s'accomplit en chromatisme'.[3] A close inspection of Simon's text shows that his chromatism inclines to the erotic as well, and to its concomitant, death.

> *pâtés de langues de rossignols ou quels oiseaux rouge-gorges colibris que des esclaves leur apportaient sur des plats ciselés dans mon esprit d'enfant il me semblait par l'effet d'un habile mécanisme caché devait en sortir un gazouillis mélodieux cristillin l'exquis concert de ces oiseaux morts les imaginant (ces pâtés) sous forme de buissons ou de dômes (sans doute par <u>assimilation</u> avec ces globes recouvrant des arbres miniatures peuplés d'oiseaux empaillés et multicolores) hérissés de fines langues pointues triangulaires pourpre foncé comme ces bizarres préservatifs que je vis plus tard exposés dans une vitrine de pharmacien à Barcelone en même temps que des gaines en caoutchouc pour la langue pourvues de languettes roses ou couleur de viande crue. (pp. 20-21)*

The nightingales' tongues are associated with the erotic aspect of the women in the first half of the text. Here, transformed into pâté, and assimilated to stuffed birds and other lifeless objects, the death aspect is

F

heavily underlined. Both eroticism and death are on display throughout the text, joined by language.

Colour not only produces visual or erotic images. By synaesthesia, it generates the whole gamut of the senses. The nightingales, above, bridge colour and sound, divorcing colour from sight in a very explicit manner, 'on dit que pour qu'ils chantent mieux on leur crève les yeux lançant alors dans leur nuit les notes stridentes indigo pervenche turquoise canari rouge-gorge déchirant l'obscurité (p. 13). Further layers of meaning are exposed as bird names and colours are superimposed. Colour also releases olfactory images, for example: 'cet âcre et *noir* parfum d'humus' (p. 19). Smell becomes more prominent in the latter sections of the text and impregnates it with decaying, rotting images, underlining the death theme, without separating them from the female generators and the strands of eroticism.

Colour, form, shape, themes, frame, perspective; Simon merges all aspects of pictorial art and Miró with fiction to create *Femmes*, exploring the impressionistic effects and verbal depths of language. His 'toile' has the solidity of collage, and the concreteness of the title suggests that this is a major consideration. What more can *La Chevelure* uncover since *Femmes* has led the reader to 'see' form, content, description, imagery, and the text at work?

The change of emphasis wrought by *La Chevelure* as title generator highlights the descriptions in the space around 'elles', but related to them by parallel and analogy. Description is thus seen as an attempt to capture space. Converging ideas can intersect and radiate out in non-linear directions. Concrete fixity and the objects of the physical world are insufficient to capture vacillating existence. To do this, rhythmic movements between opposites are used, 'l'air de s'allonger et de se raccourcir tour à tour rétractiles' (p. 24). Description is elevated beyond the static and solid to the abstract and intangible. Image gives way to a swirling impression and the text moves forward in a centrifugal way. The text achieves new depth as objects, often trivial, are superimposed. The knot in the wood (p. 8) exemplifies this. Lines become a star which breaks into waves, an image condensing key topoi of the text. Similarly, the image on the stamp fuses together associations from the animal, mineral and vegetable worlds. Enumeration and juxtaposition of physical objects can even have the effect of producing a dense, non-material image, 'montagne constellée de scintillantes étoiles de rubans' (p. 24).

As constellation, *La Chevelure* is the child's dot-to-dot book on a

cosmic scale. In *Femmes,* the timespan was approximately one day.
Now the emphasis is on a-temporality; time is swamped in eternity. We
considered the text in connection with pictorial space (Miró). Spatiality
now takes on more limitless proportions. The new title changes the
scene from the expanse of the beach to the dimensions of space and the
universe. The text leads us to the universality of art, and the timelessness of themes such as eroticism, war and death. We progress beyond
the object per se, beyond personality ('elle', the women, 'on', 'je') to
myth and poesis.

The cosmic arena of space is also an expansion of the contrast
between blackness and colour studied above. Set in opposition to the
darkness of space, there is the whiteness of light, white light being the
synthesis of the seven colours of the spectrum from ultra-violet to infra-
red. The prominence of these colours takes on new significance,
especially as they appear at opposite ends of the spectrum, with 'vert
pomme' midway between the two extremes. The three women therefore
embody the components of light and space, and the text concludes with
this impression, 'celle en noir' disparue les deux corsages géranium et
vert même plus visible maintenant'. Juxtaposition of colour or
composite colours transcend fixed chromatic associations, to produce a
kind of supra-colour, for example, 'couleur de crépuscule d'aubes' (p.
24). Sunrise and sunset violets and reds unite in a cosmic time beyond
the diurnal, in the realms of poetry.

La Chevelure also investigates such avenues of descriptive language
as simile, metaphor and metonymy. The title points to the richness and
ambiguity in language, its crossroads of meaning. 'Chevelure' has two
meanings; a head of hair and the tail of a comet. The shift between the
two senses is traced in the text. The literal, physical action of the comb
pulled through the woman's hair becomes a simile, where the
woodgrain is compared to 'une chevelure après le passage d'un peigne'
(p. 8). The modification to the allegorical and cosmological meaning
occurs when the physical and abstract combine, 'un instant le peigne
aux dents noires se détachant sur le ciel disparaissant passant deux ou
trois fois dans sa chevelure' (pp. 22-23). The title epitomizes the fluidity
of language and the imprecision of meaning, where *Femmes* evokes a
fixed image.

Simon goes beyond 'toile' to the 'étoile' of this text. Microcosm and
macrocosm are interreflexive. Simon takes mundane topoi and explores
their potential as modes of mythopoeic imagery. Take the rusty tin,
'lune orange' (p. 17). This topos is developed into the 'lune de sang' in

the old woman's bowl. A grotesque figure, killing chickens and gutting fish, she becomes Death personified. The image combines all the classical evocations of the moon with death, the drops of blood dotting the white porcelain bowl; a kind of inverse parallel of the stars in the sky.

Actions, even the most simple, can generate into myth. The image of 'elle' paddling became sensorial when 'je' experienced the same action of water rushing round his legs. This act expands to a picture of communion with the elements: 'énorme barque se profilant monstrueuse noire sur le fond des constellations le Bouvier les Chiens de chasse l'Hydre femelle leurs jambes *pataugeant* dans les étoiles entrechoquées la masse obscure gémissant oscillant mais toujours désespérément inerte' (p. 11). This curious harmony between movement and stasis textualizes oxymoron and paradox. The same image also unifies opposite elements into a macrocosmic synthesis: 'à chaque vague les étoiles rapides se ruaient autour de leurs jambes les éclaboussant puis se retiraient la Chevelure de Bérénice Pégase' (p. 12). The sea reflects a sea of stars. Note, too, how the names of constellations mythologize small-letter words like 'bouvier' and imbue 'barque', already present as a physical object, with capital-letter significance. References to classical monsters like the Hydra serve to underline the mythic potential of the text. Simon takes them, reworks them and produces this constellation of language and writing within a rich cultural heritage.

The title thus leads the reader to draw mythic patterns. Lévi-Strauss, in his studies of South American tribal mythologies, confirms this important factor of archetype in language. Concerning the constellation 'la Chevelure de Bérénice' he writes, 'que c'est à son lever matinal qu'(elle) est associée à la saison sèche'.[4] It is also closely linked with the concomitant constellation, Orion, bearer of rain. Published after *Femmes, Orion aveugle* employs South America and this constellation among its thematic threads. Simon is a 'bricoleur' of language, not an anthropologist, but his texts show the universal depths of myth in the patterns of their poetic language.

The study of *La Chevelure* shows how the alteration of one detail can change the whole emphasis of the same verbal structure. In his article on *Femmes*, Raillard noted that: 'A l'inverse du peintre, l'écrivain trouve le mot "femme" pris dans une multiplicité d'engagements syntaxiques, lourd d'un passé de discours. Il s'agit de dépouiller le mot de sa monotonie et ses vagues incertitudes pour rendre son histoire formellement nécessaire et par là — intelligible au présent'. *La Chevelure* continues this process still further, demonstrating   the revolutionary nature of Simon's authorial generation, in the sense of the epigraph to *Le Palace*. With each completed cycle there is the potential for a new departure.

In this study, I have limited contextual generation to a microscopic treatment of detail and its intrinsic function in the density of highly poetic language. By following our generators, a little more of the mechanics of writing in progress has been explored. Contextual generation in its wider sense, how motifs develop and repeat themselves throughout the whole oeuvre, lies outside the scope of this essay, but it would be an equally valid and rewarding way of reading Simon, requiring a more telescopic approach to the whole. The tracing of motifs like the old woman from *Le Tricheur* to *La Chevelure* would raise different issues, and bring further insight to the question of increasing maturity in the writer and the on-going creativity of his writing.

REFERENCES

1.   The editions in chronological order are: *Femmes*, Editions Maeght, 1966, a limited edition with reproductions of some paintings by Miró. *Femmes*, in *Entretiens: Claude Simon*, no. 31 (1972), a reprint of the text alone.
        La Chevelure de Bérénice, Editions de Minuit, 1983. All page references are to this edition, henceforth shortened to *La Chevelure*.

2.   There was one purely practical reason for the change. In an interview with C. Paulhan, Simon explains that he had to choose another title as Gallimard had just published *Femmes* by Sollers, *Nouvelles*, no. 2922, 15-21 mars 1984, pp. 42-45.

3.   G. Raillard, '*Femmes* — Claude Simon dans les marges de Miró', *Cahiers du XX siècle*, no. 4 (1975), 123-137.

4.   C. Lévi-Strauss, *Mythologiques: le cru et le cuit* (Paris, 1964), p. 238.

Parmi les aveugles le borgne est roi. A personal survey of Simon criticism

Stuart Sykes

'There has never been anything premeditated about the way I work', declares Claude Simon on another page of this volume, and a comfortless thought it is for someone asked to condense a quarter of a century's critical writing on this prolific novelist into a few pages. There is at least the consolation that Simon's novels, and the responses to them, can be taken in a series of distinct phases. My approach will therefore be chronological, avoiding some of the repetition inherent in any attempt to group items by theme or methodology. Moreover, the chronological system lets history organize the material for us in its own meticulous fashion: work on Claude Simon can arguably be divided into two broad categories on either side of the years 1969-70, a watershed for the novelist in his practice of writing, and remarkable for having brought forth two of the most influential essays on his novels that we have yet been able to enjoy.

Before that date there was relatively little concerted work on Claude Simon, despite his own productivity. There were short notices on individual texts, increasing in number after publication of *Le Vent*, but until 1960 there was not a single major article. Professional reviewers were content to dwell on his Faulknerian concern with death, despair and difficult syntax, and even the special number of *Esprit*[1] devoted to the emergent *nouveau roman* gives little space to Simon, seen as a minor luminary of the latest literary fashion. The same applies to the special issue of *Yale French Studies*,[2] where Guicharnaud acknowledged the Proustian side of Simon's writing but said little of lasting importance.

The novel that brought Claude Simon to the attention of a wider audience was also the first to attract serious critical attention. Jean Ricardou's study of *La Route des Flandres*, 'Un Ordre dans la débâcle',[3] introduced the concept of the *métaphore structurelle*, stressed the loss of referential substance, and pointed the way to a closer analysis of the language-based complexities of the literary text. Its influence can be read in practically every essay since written on Simon's best-known book. Amongst other articles on *La Route des Flandres*, Yves Berger's 'L'Enfer, le temps'[4] and Merleau-Ponty's dense and thought-provoking 'Cinq notes sur Claude Simon'[5] were the most notable at that time.

Again it was the publication of a new Simon novel that produced the next essay of consequence.[6] Michel Deguy's 'Claude Simon et la représentation' was perhaps the most developed reading of any Simon text (in this case, of course, *Le Palace*) to that date. Simon himself expressed both admiration and some scepticism where Deguy's article was concerned, during the 1974 conference at Cerisy,[7] but he was unstinting in his praise for its first section. 'Dans le déploiement de l'imaginaire transissant tout réel', wrote Deguy, 'la différence entre le présent et le passé est secondaire; la remémoration et la perception sont homogènes sous le règne du caractère de *représentabilité* du réel' (p. 1019). Already we were moving away from the thematic approach to an examination of the conditions in which a novel such as *Le Palace* can even begin to take shape.

While our American friends ground away dutifully at their introductions and their 'samplers', the mid-sixties produced few examples of important work on Simon himself. It may be worth nodding in the direction of a special number of the diligent *Revue des Lettres Modernes*,[8] grouping three very different essays on Simon, ranging from his use of syntax to Biblical echoes in his novels and a worthy if unadventurous study of his concern with form.[9] But the year 1964 is significant for the appearance of the first full-length essay on the *nouveau roman*, Ludovic Janvier's *Une Parole exigeante*.[10] Janvier pays particular attention to the various 'temptations' put in the way of Simon's characters: time itself, games of chance, woman, and the escape from anguish offered by death. Summing up the substance of what had been said on Simon's themes, Janvier's book cleared the ground for much of what was to follow. Read in conjunction with Kurt Wilhelm's essay, 'Claude Simon als "Nouveau Romancier"',[11] it rounds off an initial phase in critical reception of Simon's work — but it also heralds a period of almost total silence about him. The one voice crying in the wilderness was that of John Simon,[12] who made a useful study of metaphor in *L'Herbe*, perhaps the most neglected of all Simon texts until recent times.

The relative silence of the mid-sixties can be explained in two ways. Simon was not to produce another novel for five years after *Le Palace*, and the intellectual climate in which he was working was being substantially altered by the appearance of several theoretical studies that transformed critical thinking in France in the following decade. Foremost amongst these was Todorov's anthology of essays by the Russian Formalists,[13] to which Simon has openly acknowledged his debt.[14] He was particularly impressed by Shklovsky's 'L'Art comme procéde', where the following definition appears:

> *Et voilà que pour rendre la sensation de la vie, pour sentir les objets, pour éprouver que la pierre est de pierre, il existe ce que l'on appelle art. Le but de l'art, c'est de donner une sensation de l'objet comme vision et non pas comme reconnaissance; le procédé de l'art est le procédé de singularisation des objets et le procédé qui consiste à obscurcir la forme, à augmenter la difficulté et la durée de la perception. L'acte de perception en art est une fin en soi et doit être prolongé; l'art est un moyen d'éprouver le devenir de l'objet, ce qui est déjà 'devenu' n'importe pas pour l'art. (p. 83)*[15]

When set alongside the *Théorie d'ensemble*[16] unleashed by the Tel Quel group in 1968, Todorov's text forms a crucial landmark in the development of critical practices: the response to Simon's novels, as to many others, would have to be radically rethought in the immediate future.

Ricardou confirmed his position in the forefront of critical writing when he published *Problèmes du nouveau roman* in 1967, giving us the classical antithesis of 'écriture d'une aventure' and 'aventure d'une écriture' (p. 111), but Simon's *Histoire* in the same year gave rise only to the usual crop of notices. Still, *La Bataille de Pharsale*, with its dramatic shifts in method, was to change all that. From now on, confirming the promise of *Histoire*, Simon's textual practice was determinedly materialist: for his critics, especially outside France, life would never be quite the same again. . . .

But before examining new directions opened up by that novel we must linger over the book which English-speaking readers still tend to consider the best yet written on Claude Simon.[17] John Sturrock's splendid study *The French New Novel* made the work of Robbe-Grillet,

Butor and Simon more readily accessible to an English audience, setting the *nouveau roman* in philosophical context and analysing its themes exhaustively. Where Simon is concerned, it has the added merit of demonstrating the continuity of his work from its beginnings through to *Histoire* and is especially convincing on that novel and *La Route des Flandres*. Strong in its examination of the baroque tendency in Simon's writing and thought, Sturrock's book is essential reading, the culmination of a decade of critical writing that was about to give way to a new, language-based approach.

Unsurprisingly, that new attack was led by Ricardou. His response to *La Bataille de Pharsale* was the artfully titled 'La Bataille de la phrase',[18] an ingenious yet almost wholly persuasive reading: again taking metaphor as its starting-point, Ricardou hunts down echoes of Valéry's Zeno stanza in the body of Simon's novel and breaks down the barriers between *écriture* and *lecture* as he works towards a restatement of what it is to make a literary text. It cannot be read without reference to his other essay on the same novel, 'L'Essence et les sens',[19] where Ricardou develops the electrifying concepts of *générateurs* and *transits* that will become the *lieux communs* of so many secondary texts in the seventies. If he fails at times to show just why the sum of parts is not quite equal to the whole, Ricardou's rigorous and dazzling use of language, and the clarity of his mental processes, form a vital complement to such work as Sturrock's. Taken *cum grano salis*, his writings are the starting-point for serious study of Simon's later work.

The other critic to have responded most readily to *La Bataille de Pharsale* was Françoise Van Rossum-Guyon. Her first essay, 'Ut pictura poesis',[20] stresses the novel's insistence on its own composing and takes it as the Simonian equivalent of *Le Temps retrouvé*: for Simon, the work of composition is akin to Proust's reliance on the notion that literature is 'la vraie vie'. Taking Horace's phrase in two ways — the novel is 'like' painting, but each has its specific rules — she concentrates on the *spectacular* in Simon, as all her work has done, in an engagingly committed reading of the novel. Again finding its foundations in Proust, her second essay, 'De Claude Simon à Proust: un exemple d'intertextualité',[21] is more developed if less conclusive. With specific reference to the final section of the novel, it treats words in Lacanian terms as *nœuds de signification* whose metaphoric riches have to be set in meaningful relationship: Proust is the antecedent for a work of radical transformation. Van Rossum-Guyon makes a valiant attempt to systematize Simon's borrowings from Proust, levelled out into the language that surrounds them and making a text that corresponds to Ricardou's memorable 'masse bruissante de rapports'.[22]

At the same time, on this side of the Channel, the editors of 'Directions in the nouveau roman'[23] said: 'A cycle is complete, and a new perspective must consequently be revealed' (p. 5). Anthony Cheal Pugh's essay on 'Claude Simon: the narrator and his double' (pp. 30-40) made no reference to *La Bataille de Pharsale*, but this thoughtful and productive writer examined the troublesome relationship between the figure of the narrator and the shadowy uncle in *Histoire* in the context of Simon's preoccupation with the visual. Pugh's conclusion to that essay also made a point to which I shall return at the end of my own.

Hard upon the heels of the 'theoretical' preface which Simon gave to *Orion aveugle* came the first *nouveau roman* workshop at Cerisy, where the leading writers were given the opportunity to account for their work in public. Simon's characteristically unassuming paper, 'La Fiction mot à mot',[24] dwelt on the 'logique interne du texte' (p. 78) and the 'crédibilité picturale' his art is seeking (p. 81). In general terms, the most useful essays here for the Simon specialist are Mansuy's 'L'Imagination dans le nouveau roman' (I, pp. 75-92) and Lotringer's 'Une Révolution romanesque' (I, pp. 327-48). In the same year as that Cerisy gathering, the relentless Ricardou came out with a second volume of essays whose title, *Pour une théorie du nouveau roman*,[25] indicates the main thrust: the effort to organize a decade's analyses into a coherent theory of literature as represented in the *nouveau roman*, with the inevitable result that corners are cut as the odd square peg is fitted into the even odder round hole. The volume adds little to his work on Simon but concentrates on the production of meaning through the ceaseless re-working of words.

Not until 1972 could we welcome the first complete volume devoted to Simon alone. The special issue of *Entretiens*[26] is, surprisingly enough, preoccupied with texts before 1960, but the novelist's answers to Ludovic Janvier's questions form a useful lead-in to the main body of the volume, whose outstanding pages are by Serge Doubrovsky.[27] His profound reading of *La Route des Flandres*, based on the premise that 'La genèse d'une écriture (et le principe ultime de son fonctionnement) doit être recherchée dans le mouvement, propre à chaque écrivain, par lequel il contourne l'impossibilité même d'écrire' (p. 52), ranks alongside 'Un Ordre dans la débâcle' and shows how meaning is produced by the patient exploration of metaphoric networks. The other leading contribution is C.-G. Bjurström's 'Dimensions du temps chez

Claude Simon', but the bibliography is woefully inadequate and inaccurate, although there is a fascinating iconography.

Lack of organization is a criticism that can scarcely be aimed at Stephen Heath, whose book on the *nouveau roman* also appeared that year.[28] Writers in English have either espoused Francophone, linguistics-based methodology wholeheartedly or shunned it altogether: Heath's book seems an uneasy attempt to reconcile cross-Channel differences, and indeed one reviewer dismissed it as 'a morass of pseudo-scientific semiotics'.[29] The nuggets of Heath's thought do have to be dug out of a fashionably unreadable prose, but he is strong on Simon's exposure of the fiction of identity and insistent on language as the locus of transformation. Basing his ideas on the use of metonymy and metaphor in *La Route des Flandres* especially, Heath pays so much attention to the trees that the wood is never clearly visible, but this is serious and often seductive work.

What might be seen as the first *annus mirabilis* of Simon criticism came about in 1973, when a whole series of important articles appeared, partly in response to the publication of *Triptyque*. They present in miniature a picture of the full range of writing about Simon. Alastair Duncan made a sustained investigation into the links between Simon and Faulkner,[30] comprehensive in its review of references and exhaustive in analysing themes and stylistic traits. Abandoning chronology for a moment, this piece could most usefully be read in conjunction with my own 'The novel as conjuration'[31] and the companion piece by Jacqueline de Labriolle, 'De Faulkner à Claude Simon' in the same volume (pp. 358-88).

That most Faulknerian of Simon texts, *La Route des Flandres*, attracted in 1973 an essay of subtlety and no little rigour dealing with a specific and often neglected problem. Dominique Lanceraux[32] gets to grips with Simon's use of punctuation, going on to show how the text can progress on the ruins of representational literature and construct a *textualité* that is the basis of modernist writing. Lanceraux followed up with an equally brilliant analysis of Simon's next novel,[33] and these two essays represent close textual readings and the elaboration of a theory at their most harmonious and stimulating.

Still in 1973, *Le Palace* gave rise to another essay that ranks amongst the finest on any Simon book. J. A. E. Loubère[34] looks at the apparently outmoded question of character, tracing Simon's views on this knotty problem through the early novels before homing in on the student-narrator of *Le Palace*, who aims at integrating his own experience with that of others in his pursuit of a 'fatality composed of uncertainties' (p. 55). Loubère has written a definitive piece on this recurrent Simonian concern, relating theme and structure in a broader discussion of the ties that bind fiction and history — questions to which any reader of Simon must at some time address himself. Exaggeratedly intellectual, perhaps, this essay pinpoints vital moments in the erosion of a realist literature and demonstrates the crucial relevance of *Le Palace* to Simon's output as a whole.

Two other texts to provoke stimulating articles in that year were *La Bataille de Pharsale* and *Les Corps conducteurs*. Roland Mortier's 'Discontinu et rupture dans *La Bataille de Pharsale*'[35] sees that novel as 'une des expressions les plus radicales d'une esthétique du discontinu' (p. cl), grounding its thesis in the work of Ricardou and building a tentative bridge from the novel to the plastic arts in its description of the text's 'totalité signifiante' (p. c4) and the Baroque figure of the spiral. Though short, it is an incisive reading of this infinitely complex book. Much more daunting is Jean-Claude Raillon's unremittingly brilliant dissection of *Les Corps conducteurs*.[36] Almost precious in its style, the essay highlights the notions of generation and 'nécessité scripturale' (p. g2) underlying the new physics of writing. With echoes of Mallarmé, Marx and Ricardou it may deter the Anglo-Saxon mind, but it is a major contribution to the discussion of writing as production and of what is meant by *la matérialité du texte*.

As for the novel published in 1973, *Triptyque*, Georges Raillard's review article[37] is among the best, with its preference for a chromatic rather than thematic approach to the book. It is clear that by this stage the bias is towards textual craftsmanship and towards criteria other than the traditionally novelistic, with a growing number of references to painting and a linguistics-based concern with formal analysis. Raillard himself was to figure in one of the more fertile discussions that marked the most important single event in the history of Simon criticism: the 1974 colloquium at Cerisy.[38]

Shaped by the Marxian work-ethic of the indefatigable Ricardou, the ten days at Cerisy sought to define and overthrow the *idéologie dominante* and to split intertextuality into two categories, the general and the restricted (p. 17), as stated in the keynote speech by Ricardou himself, that other J. R. of our unfortunate times. Be that as it may, the best contributions were those with most to say about individual texts. Pursuing her work on *La Bataille de Pharsale*, Françoise Van Rossum-Guyon elaborated a theory of 'La Mise en spectacle' (pp. 88-106), while

Lucien Dällenbach did parallel duty for the 'mise en abyme' (pp. 151-71) and Raillon performed a veritable economics of materialist writing with 'La Loi de conduction' (pp. 275-94). Once the layers of dogma are peeled away, many of the comments made at Cerisy renew our approach to Simon or at least suggest fruitful ways of re-reading his novels afresh. Several of the contributors were clearing their throats before publishing full-scale books, in fact.

Contemporaneous with Cerisy is the special number of the American journal *Sub-stance,*[39] with articles on Simon by Christine Makward ('Claude Simon: earth, death and eros', pp. 35-43) and Claud DuVerlie ('"Amor interruptus": the question of eroticism or, eroticism in question in the works of Claude Simon', pp. 21-33). The first explores symbolism and mythology with special reference to *La Route des Flandres* and its deployment of colour and archetype, opposing Death to Love as the Manichean principles at work in Simon's universe, the second takes a more specific aspect of the erotic and situates it at the centre of the Simonian 'cosmogony' (p. 30). Both are combative and inventive in a way that writing on this subject (in, for example, the *Entretiens* volume) has rarely been.

In the two years that followed we were given, at last, two books on Claude Simon. The first stands as the best single introductory work. *The Novels of Claude Simon*[40] is free of jargon, clearheaded in judgment, and admirably eclectic. Taken to task by some[41] for favouring composition at the expense of theme, Loubère nevertheless provides a lucid survey, never superficial and indeed frequently profound, and strongest on the novels up to 1967. More weighty still, though more restricted in scope, is Roubichou's painstaking analysis of *L'Herbe.*[42] Both in its own right and for its place in Simon's development, claims Roubichou, this is a vital and undervalued novel. It provides first evidence of the production of meaning, as opposed to its mere expression, and opens a Simon Text comparable to the Joycean Work in Progress. In a concise but suggestive phrase, he describes Simon's writing as a 'mise en scène — à la fois spectacle et expérience — d'un parcours de l'écriture' (p. 32) and demonstrates convincingly the accumulation of *micro-textes* and their part in a coherent structure based, once again, on the Baroque form of the spiral.

There is no doubt that Roubichou's book breaks down at times into rebarbative detail, and the same can be said of the issue of *Etudes littéraires*[43] where a lot of critical insight is lost in the ever-diminishing circles of self-congratulatory prose. But it has one of the most ingenious readings that this reviewer knows in Vidal's 'Le Palace, palais des mirages intestins ou l'auberge espagnole' (pp. 189-214). Under a sparkling surface of wit and verbal play, Vidal develops a cogent analysis of metaphor, relating it to historical realism before straying into an overheated discussion of recurrent *vocables* as they figure in a polyglot play of language defying the limitations of a non-materialist reading. The volume is otherwise distinguished by Pugh's suasive argument for intertextuality in 'Du *Tricheur* à *Triptyque,* et inversement' (pp. 137-60).

Reviews of *Leçon de choses* were bound to predominate in 1976, but Laure Hesbois[44] turned a Nathalie Sarraute question to good account in discussing Simon's refusal to hierarchize the voices in *L'Herbe:* the resultant structural instability, she insists, is redeemed by the unifying presence of the central character, Louise. Amongst the studies of *Leçon de choses,* two stand out, and both are in French — very much a sign of the critical times.

'Nul doute qu'aujourd'hui le lecteur n'aborde plus un "nouveau roman" comme il y a dix ans', asserts François Jost[45] before embarking on a study of the 'problème de la diégèse' as highlighted in Simon's latest novel. Jost leans heavily on Genette's notion of the 'récit motivé' in working out a scheme that accounts for 'effets de production' (p. 89) even if it strays down the occasional blind alley.[46] Like Jost, Colette Gaudin[47] is at pains to get round the 'difficulties' of modern reading: she provides a rapid survey of recent theory from Hamon to Ricardou while not disguising her own allegiance to Barthes and Greimas in particular. Postulating the *lisible* and the *visible* as polar opposites, she constructs a plausible model for a reading based in psychoanalysis and linguistics, but without abandoning the text in hand.

The remaining critical item of note from 1977 is an absorbing piece on *Histoire.* David Carroll[48] starts from Merleau-Ponty and works through Simon's own theoretical pronouncements to arrive at a definition of fiction and history in relation to each other. Sweeping at times, his essay is a model of combative criticism, taking issue with much of the novelist's own thinking about form while not omitting to read closely those visual representations in *Histoire* which are seen as proof of the inadequacy of both history and literature. Otherwise, 1977 is memorable for Dällenbach's book on the *mise en abyme*[49] and his description of the fictional text as 'une moire' (p. 197), a puzzle that needs patient work from both writer and reader of the book.[50]

Before moving on, there is another item from 1977 that repays attention even if it is not a critical study. There is, of course, no shortage of interviews with Claude Simon, from the brief nods in the direction of fashion made by journals like *L'Express* or *Le Nouvel Observateur* to more considered pieces in serious reviews. But if one were to single out any particular interview for throwing light on Simon's activity, it would be Alain Poirson's 'Un Homme traversé par le travail',[51] where informed questions are met with tough but unassuming answers and a real flavour of the man and his work is allowed to come through.

Claudia Hoffer Gosselin redeemed a rather drab 1978 with her essay on *La Bataille de Pharsale*,[52] which argues that the text contains a 'potentially infinite reinvention of meaning' (p. 23) and, taking up the work of Van Rossum-Guyon, denies the existence of a single authorial voice, or the possibility of literature's being a system of recuperation. The work of these few years has moved towards a reading of the non-hierarchized text, in which there is a radical flattening of perspective: in keeping with that drift, Gosselin says 'nothing in the text can be perceived as a centralizing element' (p. 31), a point which some might wish to dispute. But her extraordinarily wide definition of intertexuality makes it the instrument by which our reading of texts is transformed. In dismissing this as a drab year, I was not forgetting that Ricardou came up with *Nouveaux Problèmes du roman*[53] and in many respects went along with this notion of flattening: but his essay on Simon reads more and more like a statistician's notes and, in my contention, alienates the reader from the text under discussion.

And so to 1979, when the first — and so far the only — book in French on Claude Simon appeared. *Les Romans de Claude Simon*[54] is deliberately non-aligned: it tries to put composition at the centre of things and to offer a coherent reading, based on the idea of an *ensemble centré*, of an enormously varied and lengthening series of novels. Broadly speaking, it concentrates on the figure of the triptych, with particular reference to the novel of that title, *La Route des Flandres* and *La Bataille de Pharsale*. Its author, not willing or competent to place these texts in the context of linguistic theory, has chosen instead to contend that re-readings provide a mental grasp of spatial form in the novel, working against the forces of dispersal and independently of any realist assimilation of the text.[55]

There is a case for saying that the present decade marks a new departure in Simon studies, rather as the gap after *Le Palace* had done twenty years before. For one thing, the novelist has given us a text that seems to re-establish contact with his work of the sixties, making us reconsider our allegiance — or lack of it — to the critical schools developed since that time. But *Les Géorgiques* produced also a new burst of energy from Simon's readers and critics, whose first fruit was the special issue of *Critique*[56] combining essays on that novel with some wider-ranging retrospective studies. Of the former, the best is Dällenbach's '*Les Géorgiques* ou la totalisation accomplie' (pp. 1226-42). Pressing his claim to be considered the foremost writer on the *nouveau roman*, he points up the satirical tone of the book, seen as a polyphonic text surpassing even its Proustian antecedent and as a radical recombination of biography, fiction and history that forms a universe on its own. The more general essays are headed by Alastair Duncan's 'Claude Simon: la crise de la représentation' (pp. 1181-1200), an incisive statement of a problem that has marked Simon's work since it first came to the fore. Duncan's 1980 essay on 'La Description dans '*Leçon de choses*'[57] also focused on a specific problem and cleared the ground for the *Critique* piece. He examines the *déchaînement métaphorique* that liberates description from the tutelage of narrative in undermining realist ambitions, and goes on to trace the evolution of Simon's own stance, culminating in *La Route des Flandres*, where Georges, not reducible to the norms on which literary 'character' is built, is seen as 'une voix qui flotte' (*Critique*, p. 1191). From then on it is a question of the prison-house of language, within which description is the instrument of (self-)discovery. Duncan's work has a useful adjunct in the shape of Martin Van Buuren's 'L'Essence des choses: étude de la description dans l'œuvre de Claude Simon'.[58] The general quality of the *Critique* volume is high, with François Châtelet ('Une Vision de l'histoire', pp. 1218-25) and Jean Rousset ('La Guerre en peinture', pp. 1201-10) its other most stimulating contributors.

The enduring interest of the *nouveau roman* is shown in the fact that a special issue of *Romance Studies*[59] was given over to it in 1983. Based on the Glasgow conference of September 1982, it has two papers on Simon's latest novel as well as the provocative essay by Jean Duffy already referred to (see note 15). While my own contribution looks at Simon's return to the 'manner' of the sixties, Alastair Duncan makes us examine again the very nature of our role and function as readers.

This, it seems, is the new direction of recent years, and the most fruitful terrain for the immediate future: the development of theories of reading. The question is bound up with emerging ideas on the problem of intertextuality, and none has set out those arguments more forcefully

than Maria Minich Brewer.[60] Hailing 'this new age of textual enlightenment' (p. 489), Brewer surveys recent contributions to the theory of
reading and takes issue with an often neglected but rewarding essay by
Laurent Jenny.[61] The debate between their opposite stances offers rich
possibilities for the discussion of Simon's texts, as the present volume
begins to show. Patrick O'Kane analyses the theme of reading in Simon
using Don Quixote as antecedent for the defective reader and making a
spirited appeal for a more self-conscious practice of reading. This idea is
also taken up in two other essays that complete one half of this volume,
with Maxim Silverman's intelligent placing of Simon in the context of
theories on the practice of the text in the last two decades, and Jean
Duffy's determined correction of recent critical imbalance with her
study of Simon's own corrections of his shorter texts.

Clearly this is a path that must be followed: no other modern writer
has so often stressed the vagueness of the project with which each new
novel begins, and the close analysis of his manuscripts in relation to the
published texts would do much to account for the productive nature of
that *tâtonnement* which Simon has long claimed as his basic method.
Only then could the question of composition, the organization of what
has been produced, be examined in any definitive way. 'On n'a pas
assez étudié le tâtonnement en art', said Jérôme Lindon to me in 1978,
and his statement still holds good.

The Brewer article also has the merit of pinpointing a sorely
neglected aspect of Simon's work and personality, namely his highly
engaging sense of humour. If one disregards the arch and trivial games
of Robbe-Grillet, the *nouveau roman* and its critics have been singularly
joyless through the years, with the notable exceptions of Pinget and
Claude Simon. While it may seem outrageous to speak of humour in an
oeuvre so often described as doom-laden, there can be no doubt that
humour is an essential ingredient of texts like *Histoire, La Bataille de
Pharsale* and *Les Géorgiques*. The point is that this humour is often
either an effect of language itself, or of Simon's manipulation of the
reader's expectations, in a way which to my knowledge has never been
the subject of any serious analysis. This humour, as Dällenbach pointed
out in regard to Simon's latest novel, is more often in the satirical vein,
and a developed essay on parody, satire and irony in his work is long
overdue.

Our present collection also points the way to another area of
discussion. There is a clear need for revision of the relationship between
the text and the *hors texte* where Simon is concerned, as *Les Géorgiques*

so cogently reminds us. Celia Britton founds Simon's writing in family history, seeking in it a response to chaos on all levels. Using Lacanian concepts, she places history at the centre of her discussion, and the article must be read in conjunction with her earlier 'The imaginary origins of the text'[62] for a rounded picture of a deeply intelligent and fertile reading. Taking as starting-point his own reading of *Les Géorgiques*, Anthony Cheal Pugh questions the very possibility of historical fiction, while Michael Evans offers a sustained and highly revealing study of the Orpheus myth in the same novel. The collection is thus typical of Simon criticism at virtually every phase of its development: one half stays resolutely within the domain of the text, the other moves outside in a search for structures that account for the complexity of those texts seen against a broad philosophical or cultural backcloth. This is simply further evidence for the belief that Claude Simon is not only the most consistently productive modern novelist but also the most challenging in his relationship with the systems of thought and artistic expression that constitute our human experience.

There are two names I would like to mention before this rapid survey comes to a conclusion. One takes us back to Anthony Pugh's 1971 essay on the narrator and his double, for it ended on a reference to Maurice Blanchot. I do not understand why Blanchot's lucid and provocative writing about literature has not been the basis for more general inquiry, and I believe his work could be the starting-point for a very interesting discussion of the later Simon. One of his most telling statements is this:

> *L'œuvre demande cela, que l'homme qui l'écrit se sacrifie pour l'œuvre, devienne autre, devienne non pas un autre, non pas, du vivant qu'il était, l'écrivain avec ses devoirs, ses satisfactions et ses intérêts, mais plutôt personne, le lieu vide et animé où retentit l'appel de l'œuvre.*[63]

I know of no more succinct or curiously moving statement of the writer's position as Simon himself has expressed it, whether in the idea of 'un homme traversé par le travail' or in his often-quoted borrowing from Merleau-Ponty of the view that the writer calls into being a *superior* being even as he writes and only for the period during which he writes. Blanchot's ideas, it seems to me, range across the whole spectrum of contemporary critical thinking on the novel in general and Simon in particular: they deserve more systematic absorption and acknowledgement.

The other name is a familiar one indeed to anyone who has read what reviewers and critics have written on Simon, and that is Marcel Proust. How curious that a man seen as the corner-stone of the modern novel, especially by Simon himself, should have attracted so little attention in relation to the novels of the latter. As the preceding pages have shown, the problem of description is uppermost in Simon's mind: an analysis of Proust's descriptive writing could be the beginnings of an even more fertile examination of Simon's own ideas. Recent work on Proust[64] himself has indicated the riches still to be gleaned from such an approach, and I would maintain that Proust is an antecedent whose importance for Simon has been stated but never fully explained.

To finish with, a word on the title I have chosen for this highly personal review. It is not intended as a slight against colleagues whose work I admire and often envy, that much must be clear. I have merely taken up again the metaphor that subtends a great deal of Claude Simon's writing in and about the novel, that of the blind Orion feeling his way toward the light.[65] All one can do, when so much is being produced by and about the novelist, is suggest possible paths for his critics to follow: by virtue, I suspect, of age and long experience, I was invited to hazard some informed guesses. As this collection shows, there is no shortage of readers who can shed light on the work of this profound and admirable man.

REFERENCES

1.   'Le "Nouveau Roman"', *Esprit*, 26, nos. 263-4 (1958).
2.   'Midnight novelists and others', *Yale French Studies*, 24 (Winter 1960).
3.   *Critique*, no. 163 (décembre 1960), 1011-24; reprinted in his *Problèmes du nouveau roman* (Paris, Seuil, 1967), pp. 44-55.
4.   *Nouvelle Revue Française*, 9, no. 97 (janvier 1961), 95-109.
5.   *Médiations*, no. 4 (hiver 1961-62), 5-10; reprinted in *Entretiens*, no. 31 (1972), 41-6.
6.   *Critique*, no. 187 (décembre 1962), 1009-32.
7.   See the proceedings of that colloquium, *Claude Simon: colloque de Cerisy* (Paris, UGE, 1975), pp. 68ff.
8.   'Un Nouveau Roman? Recherches et tradition', *Revue des Lettres Modernes*, nos. 94-9 (1964), ed. J. H. Matthews.
9.   These are: B. T. Fitch, 'Participe présent et procédés narratifs chez Claude Simon', 199-216; Laurent LeSage, 'Claude Simon et l'Ecclésiaste', 217-23; Jean-

Luc Seylaz, 'Du *Vent* à *La Route des Flandres:* la conquête d'une forme romanesque', 225-40.

10. Paris, Minuit, 1964. The essay on Simon, 'Vertige et parole dans l'oeuvre de Claude Simon', is on pp. 89-110.

11. *Zeitschrift für französische Sprache und Literatur,* 75, Heft 4 (Dezember 1965), 309-52.

12. 'Perception and metaphor in the "new novel": notes on Robbe-Grillet, Claude Simon and Butor', *Tri-Quarterly,* no. 4 (Fall 1965), 153-82.

13. Tzvetan Todorov, *Théorie de la littérature* (Paris, Seuil, 1965).

14. When I first met Simon, the opening question came not from me but from him, and it was: 'Vous avez lu le livre de Todorov?'

15. This may be the point at which to indicate Jean Duffy's combative essay on Simon and the Russian Formalists, 'Art as defamiliarization in the theory and practice of Claude Simon', *Romance Studies,* no. 2 (Summer 1983), 108-22.

16. Paris, Seuil, 1968: Foucault, Barthes and Derrida are given pride of place amongst the fourteen contributors.

17. London, Oxford University Press, 1969: 'Claude Simon', pp. 43-103.

18. *Critique,* no. 224 (mars 1970), 226-56; reprinted in his *Pour une théorie du nouveau roman* (Paris, Seuil, 1971), pp. 118-58.

19. *Pour une théorie du nouveau roman,* pp. 200-10.

20. *Het Franse Boek,* 40 (1970), 91-100.

21. *Les Lettres nouvelles,* no. 4 (septembre-octobre 1972), 107-37.

22. 'Le Nouveau Roman est-il valéryen?', in *Entretiens sur Paul Valéry* (The Hague, Mouton, 1968), p. 77.

23. *20th Century Studies* (December 1971).

24. *Nouveau Roman: hier, aujourd'hui* (Paris, UGE, 1972), II, pp. 73-97.

25. See note 18.

26. See note 5.

27. 'Notes sur la genèse d'une écriture', pp. 51-64.

28. *The Nouveau Roman: A Study in the Practice of Writing* (London, Elek, 1972).

29. John Weightman, 'Pre-text in Frenglish', *The Observer,* 21 January 1973, p. 34.

30. 'Claude Simon and William Faulkner', *Forum for Modern Language Studies,* 9 (1973), 235-52.

31. *Revue de littérature comparée,* 53 (1979), 348-57.

32. 'Modalités de la narration dans *La Route des Flandres*', *Poétique,* no. 14 (1973), 235-49.

33. 'Modalités de la narration dans *Le Palace* de Claude Simon', *Littérature,* no. 16 (décembre 1974), 3-18.

34. 'Claude Simon's *Le Palace:* a paradigm of otherness', *Symposium,* 27 (1973), 46-63.

35. *Dégres,* I, no. 2 (avril 1973), c1-c6.

36. 'Eléments d'une physique littérale', *Degrés,* I, no. 4 (octobre 1973), g1-g29.

37. '*Triptyque:* le rouge et le noir', *Cahiers du Chemin,* 18 (15 avril 1973), 96-106.

38. See note 7.

39. No. 8 (Winter 1974).

40. London, Cornell UP, 1975.

41. See for example John Sturrock, 'Destructive tendencies', *TLS,* 3 October 1975, p. 1151.

42.   Gérard Roubichou, *Lecture de 'L'Herbe' de Claude Simon* (Lausanne, L'Age d'Homme, 1976).

43.   Volume 9, no. I (1976), ed. Jean-Pierre Vidal.

44.   'Qui dit ça? Identification des voix narratives dans *L'Herbe* de Claude Simon', *Revue du Pacifique*, 2 (1976), 144-59.

45.   'Les Aventures du lecteur', *Poétique*, no. 8 (1977), 77-89.

46.   Jost is taken to task by Michael Evans in 'Two uses of intertextuality: references to Impressionist painting and *Madame Bovary* in Claude Simon's *Leçon de choses'*, *Nottingham French Studies*, 19 (1980), 33-45.

47.   'Niveaux de lisibilité dans *Leçon de choses* de Claude Simon', *Romanic Review*, 68 (1977), 175-96.

48.   'Diachrony and synchrony in *Histoire'*, *Modern Language Notes*, 92 (1977), 797-824.

49.   *Le Récit spéculaire* (Paris, Seuil, 1977): there are sections on *L'Herbe* (pp. 171-3) and *Triptyque* (pp. 193-200).

50.   On the text as puzzle, see also François Jost, 'Claude Simon: topographies de la description et du texte', *Critique*, no. 330 (novembre 1974), 1032-40.

51.   *La Nouvelle Critique*, no. 105 ('Ecrire', juin-juillet 1977), 32-46.

52.   'Voices of the past in Claude Simon's *La Bataille de Pharsale'*, *New York Literary Forum*, 2, (1978: 'Intertextuality: New Perspectives in Criticism'), 23-33.

53.   Paris, Seuil, 1978: 'Le dispositif osiriaque', on *Triptyque*, pp. 197-243.

54.   Stuart Sykes, *Les Romans de Claude Simon* (Paris, Minuit, 1979).

55.   For a shorter version of that thesis see my 'Ternary form in three novels by Claude Simon', *Symposium*, 32 (1978), 25-40.

56.   'La Terre et la guerre dans l'oeuvre de Claude Simon', *Critique*, no. 414 (novembre 1981).

57.   *Littérature*, no. 38 (1980), 95-105.

58.   *Poétique*, no. 43 (1980), 324-33.

59.   'The Nouveau Roman', *Romance Studies*, no. 2 (Summer 1983).

60.   'An energetics of reading: the intertextual in Claude Simon', *Romanic Review*, 73 (1982), 489-504.

61.   'La Stratégie de la forme', *Poétique*, no. 27 (1976), 257-81.

62.   *Degré Second*, no. 5 (July 1981), 115-30.

63.   *Le Livre à venir* (Paris, Gallimard, Collection 'Idées', 1971), p. 316.

64.   See for example *Proust et le texte producteur*, ed. J. Erickson (Guelph, Ontario, 1980).

65.   It also provides, for example, the title of *Orion Blinded*, the useful collection of essays edited by Randi Birn and Karen Gould (Bucknell UP, Lewisburg, 1980). See especially J. A. E. Loubère's first contribution, 'Announcing the world: signs and images at work in the novels of Claude Simon' (pp. 117-32), where the idea of a *transformational dynamism* is explored in tracing the three great themes in Simon: battle, change, and time; and Claud DuVerlie's further analysis of Simon's preoccupation with the painterly in 'Pictures for writing: premises for a graphopictology' (pp. 200-18).

Select Bibliography

Jean H. Duffy

I should like to thank Alastair Duncan, Michael Sheringham, Mary Orr, Lawrie Ginn and Douglas W. Alden for drawing my attention to a number of the references contained in this bibliography.

Unless otherwise indicated, the place of publication is Paris.

1. WORKS by CLAUDE SIMON

Le Tricheur (Sagittaire, 1945; reissued by Minuit)
La Corde raide (Sagittaire, 1947; reissued by Minuit)
Gulliver (Calmann-Lévy, 1952)
Le Sacre du printemps (Calmann-Lévy, 1954; Livre de poche, 1975)
Le Vent (Minuit, 1957)
L'Herbe (Minuit, 1958)
La Route des Flandres (Minuit, 1960; UGE, 1963, with an essay by J. Ricardou; Minuit 'double', 1982, with an essay by L. Dällenbach)
Le Palace (Minuit, 1962; UGE, 1971; Methuen, 1972, edited and with an introduction by J. Sturrock)
Femmes (Maeght, 1966. Text by Claude Simon, 23 colour plates by Joan Miró. Reprinted, text only, in 'Claude Simon', *Entretiens*, no. 31, 1972, 169-78; and again as *La Chevelure de Bérénice*, Minuit, 1983.)
Histoire (Minuit, 1967; Folio, 1973)
La Bataille de Pharsale (Minuit, 1969)
Orion aveugle (Geneva, Skira, 'Les Sentiers de la création', 1970. Text by Claude Simon, accompanying illustrations of photographs, drawings, and paintings by Rauschenberg, Poussin, Dubuffet, Picasso and others.)
Les Corps conducteurs (Minuit, 1971)
Triptyque (Minuit, 1973)
Leçon de choses (Minuit, 1976)
Les Géorgiques (Minuit, 1981)

English translations in print:
Conducting Bodies (London, Calder, 1975; New York, Riverrun, 1980)
Triptych (London, Calder, 1977; New York, Riverrun, 1982)

The World About Us (Leçon de choses) (Princeton, N.J., Ontario Review, 1983)
Georgics (Forthcoming, New York, Riverrun)

2. SHORT TEXTS by Claude Simon

*A corrected and updated version of G. Roubichou's bibliographies in
'Lecture de "L'Herbe"' and in 'Claude Simon: colloque de Cerisy'.*

'Babel', *Les Lettres nouvelles*, no. 31 (oct. 1955), 391-413 [Not taken up]
'Le Cheval', *Les Lettres nouvelles*, no. 57 (févr. 1958), 169-89 and no. 58 (mars
1958), 379-94 [This text constitutes a stage in the evolution of the motif,
in *La Route des Flandres*, based on the adulterous intrigues in a Flanders
Village. Although Roubichou claims that it was taken up in *La Route des
Flandres*, it is very different in form from the corresponding passages in
the novel.]
'Le Candidat', *Arts*, 26 nov.-2 déc. 1958, 3 [Part of this text — in a substantially
modified and fragmented form — was taken up in *Histoire*, pp. 328, 331,
332, 353-4.]
'Cendre', *La Revue de Paris*, mars 1959, 79-81 [Not taken up]
'Mot à mot', *Les Lettres nouvelles*, 8 avril 1959, 6-10 [Not taken up]
'La Poursuite', *Tel Quel*, no. 1 (1960), 49-60 [Taken up in *La Route des
Flandres*, pp. 9-29, with numerous but minor alterations]
'Matériaux de construction', *Les Lettres nouvelles*, no. 9 (déc. 1960), 112-23
[The first section of this text has not been taken up; the second section
has been taken up, with a number of changes and omissions, in *Histoire*,
pp. 46-49, 155, 172, 149, 151; the third section has been taken up with a
few changes of detail and punctuation in *Le Palace*, pp. 41-44.]
'Comme du sang délayé, *Les Lettres françaises*, 1-7 déc. 1960, 1, 5 [Taken up in
part in *Histoire*, pp. 336-40, but with a number of changes in emphasis]
'Sous le kimono', *Les Lettres françaises*, 19-25 janv. 1961, 5 [Taken up in part in
La Bataille de Pharsale, pp. 49-52, but with a number of changes in
emphasis]
'Funérailles d'un révolutionnaire assassiné', *Médiations*, no. 4 (1961-2), 11-24
[Taken up with a few changes in punctuation in *Le Palace*, pp. 103-19
and 135-41]
'L'Attentat', *NRF*, 19 (1962), 431-52 [Taken up with minor alterations in *Le
Palace*, pp. 47-76]
'Inventaire', *Les Lettres nouvelles*, no. 22 (févr. 1962), 50-58 [Taken up in *Le
Palace*, pp. 9-20, with a few changes in punctuation and detail]
'Des Roches striées vert pâle parsemées de points noirs', *Les Lettres nouvelles*,
juin-août 1964, 53-68 [Taken up in *Histoire*, pp. 303-19, with changes in
punctuation and a few minor omissions and additions]
'La Statue', *Mercure de France*, 352 (1964), 393-409 [Taken up in *Histoire*, pp.
71-99 and 204, with a number of changes of emphasis]

'Correspondence', *Tel Quel*, no. 16 (1964), 18-32 [Taken up in part and intermittently in *Histoire*, pp. 14-37, 258, 388-402, with a number of changes in order and content]

'Propriétés des rectangles', *Tel Quel*, no. 44 (1971), 3-16 [Taken up in *Les Corps conducteurs*, pp. 130-62, with a number of changes in order and detail]

'Deux personnages', *Art press*, févr. 1973, 14-15 [Taken up with a few minor changes in *Les Géorgiques*, pp. 11-17]

'Essai de mise en ordre de notes prises au cours d'un voyage en Zeeland (1962) et complétées', *Minuit*, no. 3 (mars 1973), 1-18 [Not taken up but may contain some ideas which were to be developed in *Les Géorgiques*]

'Progression dans un paysage enneigé', *Etudes littéraires*, 9 (1976), 217-21 [Not taken up]

'Le Général', *Art press* (été 1977) [Taken up with a few minor alterations in *Les Géorgiques*, pp. 119-25]

'Le Régicide', *La Nouvelle Critique*, juin-juillet 1977, 45-46 [Not taken up]

'Les Géorgiques', *NRF*, 52 (sept. 1978), 1-27 [A combination of a passage taken up, with minor changes, on pp. 143-55, 157-66, 167-72 of *Les Géorgiques* and a number of truncated phrases presenting a fragmentary version of L.S.M.'s life as represented in *Les Géorgiques*]

3. BOOKS WHOLLY OR SUBSTANTIALLY ON CLAUDE SIMON

Bibliographies are indicated only when particularly comprehensive or helpful.

Apeldoorn, J. van, *Pratiques de la description* (Amsterdam, Rodopi, 1982) [On Simon, Balzac, Duras and Green]

Birn, R., and K. Gould, eds. *Orion Blinded: Essays on Claude Simon*, (Lewisburg, Bucknell UP, 1980) [Bibl. pp. 297-303]

Burden, J., *John Fowles. John Hawkes. Claude Simon. Problems of Self and Form in the Post-Modernist Novel. A Comparative Study* (Würzburg, Königshausen und Neumann, 1980)

Butler, C., *After the Wake. An Essay on the Contemporary Avant-garde* (London, OUP, 1980) [Chapter on *Triptyque*]

Calle-Gruber, M., *Itinerari di scrittura: nel laberinto del 'nouveau roman' (Rome, 1982)* [On Butor, Robbe-Grillet and Simon]

Carroll, D., *The Subject in Question: the Languages of Theory and the Strategies of Fiction* (Chicago UP, 1982)

Fletcher, J., *Claude Simon and Fiction Now* (London, Calder and Boyars, 1975)

Gould, K. L., *Claude Simon's Mythic Muse* (Columbia, S. C., French Literature Publications Company, 1979)

Hammermann, I., *Formen des Erzählens in der Prosa der Gegenwart: an Beispielen von Philippe Sollers, Robert Pinget und Claude Simon* (Stuttgart, Klett-Cotta, 1979)

Heath, S., *The Nouveau Roman: A Study in the Practice of Writing* (London, Elek, 1972)

Hollenbeck, J., *Eléments baroques dans les romans de Claude Simon* (La Penseé universelle, 1982) [Bibl. pp. 185-90]

Janvier, L., *Une Parole exigeante* (Minuit, 1964)

Jiménez-Fajardo, S., *Claude Simon* (Boston, Mass., Twayne, 1975)

Kadish, D. Y., *Practices of the New Novel in Claude Simon's 'L'Herbe' and 'La Route des Flandres'*, (Fredricton, N. B., York Press, 1979)

Kirpalani, C., *Approches de 'La Route des Flandres', roman de Claude Simon (1960)* (New Delhi, Vignette Arts, 1981) [Bibl. pp. 105-09]

Loubère, J. A. E., *The Novels of Claude Simon* (Ithaca and London, Cornell UP, 1975) [Bibl. pp. 255-61]

Pugh, A. C., *'Histoire' by Claude Simon* (London, Grant and Cutler, 1982)

Ricardou, J., *Problèmes du nouveau roman* (Seuil, 1967)

Ricardou, J., *Pour une théorie du nouveau roman* (Seuil, 1971)

Ricardou, J., ed., *Claude Simon: colloque de Cerisy* (UGE, 1975) [Bibl. pp. 432-43]

Ricardou, J., *Nouveaux problèmes du roman* (Seuil, 1978)

Rice, D., and P. Schofer, *Rhetorical Poetics: Theory and Practice of Figural and Symbolic Reading in Modern French Literature* (Madison, Wisconsin UP, 1983) [On Balzac, Baudelaire, Mallarmé and Simon]

Roubichou, G., *Lecture de 'L'Herbe'* (Lausanne, L'Age d'homme, 1976) [Bibl. pp. 323-34]

Storrs, N., *Liquid. A Source of Meaning and Structure in Claude Simon's 'La Bataille de Pharsale'* (New York, Peter Lang, 1983)

Sturrock, J., *The French New Novel* (London, OUP, 1969)

Sykes, S. W., *Les Romans de Claude Simon* (Minuit, 1979) [Bibl. pp. 190-94]

Wasmuth, A., *Subjektivität, Wahrnehmung und Zeitlichkeit als poetologische Aspekte bei Claude Simon. Untersuchungen zu den Romanen 'Le Vent', 'L'Herbe' und 'La Route des Flandres'* (Hamburger Romanistische Dissertationen, 1979)

Wehle, W., ed., *Nouveau Roman* (Darmstadt, Wissenschaftliche Buchgesellschaft, 1980)

Wilhelm, K., *Der Nouveau Roman: ein Experiment der Französischen Gegenwartsliteratur* (Berlin, Erich Schmidt, 1969)

4. SPECIAL NUMBERS OF PERIODICALS ON SIMON

'Claude Simon', *Entretiens,* no. 31 (1972)

'Claude Simon', *Etudes littéraires,* 9. no 1 (1976)

'La Terre et la guerre dans l'oeuvre de Claude Simon', *Critique,* 38, no. 414 (1981) [Bibl. pp. 1244-52]

'Claude Simon', *The Review of Contemporary Fiction* (Forthcoming, 1985)

5. GENERAL ARTICLES on Simon

*This section consists solely of items which have not been taken up in
any of the bibliographies mentioned above.*

Amprimoz, A. L., 'Triptyque: mort et résurrection du récit', *Chimères* (Summer
    1979), 30-40

Apeldoorn, J. van, 'Comme si . . . figure d'écriture', in *Ecriture de la religion,*
    écriture du roman, ed. C. Grivel (Lille UP, 1979), pp. 175-193

Apeldoorn, J. van, and C. Grivel, 'Claude Simon. Entretien avec Jo van
    Apeldoorn et Charles Grivel, 17 avril 1979', in ibid., pp. 87-107

Apeldoorn, J. van, 'Entre les lignes de l'écriture, la lignée', *Rapports,* 51 (1981),
    148-53

Apeldoorn, J. van, 'Balzac, à la lecture de Claude Simon, divertissement', in
    Balzac et les parents pauvres, ed. F. van Rossum-Guyon (SEDES, 1981),
    87-97

Bajomée, D., 'Blessures du temps: mythe et idéologie dans *Le Palace* de Claude
    Simon', *Cahiers internationaux du symbolisme,* nos. 42-44 (1981), 29-40

Brandt, J., 'History and art in Claude Simon's *Histoire'*, *Romanic Review,* 73
    (May 1982), 373-84

Brès, J., 'Problématique temporelle de *La Route des Flandres* de Claude Simon',
    in *Mélanges de littérature du Moyen Age au vingtième siècle offerts à*
    Mademoiselle Jeanne Lods par ses collègues, ses élèves et ses amis (Ecole
    Normale Supérieure de Jeunes Filles, 1978), pp. 653-64

Brewer, M., 'An energetics of reading: the intertextual in Claude Simon',
    Romanic Review, 73 (Nov. 1982), 489-504

Britton, C., 'The imaginary origins of the text in the novels of Claude Simon',
    Degré Second, no. 5 (July 1981), 115-30

Britton, C., 'Voices, absence and presence in the novels of Claude Simon',
    French Studies, 36 (1982), 445-54

Cali, A., 'Problèmes de la fragmentation textuelle à partir de "Propriétés des
    rectangles" de Claude Simon', in *Pratiques de lecture et d'écriture. Ollier.*
    Robbe-Grillet. Claude Simon (Nizet, 1980), pp. 63-105

Caminade, P., 'Claude Simon: lyrisme, musique du texte, érotisme .et
    pornographie', *Sud,* no. 27 (1978), 113-18

Carroll, D., 'Diachrony and synchrony in *Histoire'*, *Modern Language Notes,* 92
    (May 1977), 797-824

Carroll, D., 'For example: psychoanalysis and fiction or the conflict of the
    generation(s)', *Sub-stance,* no. 21 (1978), 49-67

Dällenbach, L., 'Le Tissu de la mémoire', in *La Route des Flandres* by Claude
    Simon (Minuit 'double', 1982), pp. 299-316

Dällenbach, L., 'La Lecture comme suture. Problèmes de la réception du texte
    fragmentaire: Balzac et Claude Simon', in *Problèmes actuels de la lecture*
    (Clancier-Guénaud, 1982), pp. 35-47

Duffy, J. H., 'Art as defamiliarisation in the theory and practice of Claude Simon', *Romance Studies*, no. 2 (1983), 108-23

Duffy, J. H., 'The scriptural and the pictorial in Claude Simon's *Orion aveugle*', *French Studies Bulletin*, no. 9 (Winter 1983-84), 8-10

Duisit, L., 'La Fonction novatrice: Claude Simon — *La Route des Flandres*', in *Satire, parodie, calembour. Esquisse d'une théorie des modes dévalués* (Sarratoga, Cal., Stanford French and Italian Studies, no. 11, 1978), pp. 121-8

Duverlie, C., 'Claude Simon: *Leçon de choses*', *French Review*, 50, (1977), 815-6

Evans, M. J., 'Intertextual tryptich. Reading across *La Bataille de Pharsale, La Jalousie* and *A la recherche du temps perdu*', *Modern Language Review*, 76 (Oct. 1981), 839-47

Frette, X., 'Le Temps dans *La Route des Flandres* de Claude Simon', *Franzis Dili ve Edebyati Bölümü Dergisi*, no. 8 (Winter 1981), 116-29

Gay-Crosier, R., '*Orion aveugle* ou les configurations de serpent: la palette du verbe', *French Forum*, 2 (1977), 168-73

Gregorio, L. A., Prométhée et la croix: mythe et métatexte dans *Les Corps conducteurs*', *Romance Notes*, 23 (1982), 3-9

Gruaz, C., 'La Ponctuation, c'est l'homme . . . Emploi des signes de ponctuation dans cinq romans contemporains', *Langue française*, no. 45 (févr. 1980), 113-24

Hollenbeck, J., 'Claude Simon and the Baroque', *South Atlantic Bulletin*, 44 (1979), 31-42

Ianelli, L. L., 'Claude Simon et *La Route des Flandres*', *Romanica*, 15 (1978-79), 109-11

Kelly, L. H., 'Spatial composition and formal harmonies in Claude Simon's *Histoire*', *Modern Language Studies*, 9, 73-83

Kreiter, J., 'Perception et réflexion dans *La Route des Flandres*: signes et sémantique', *Romanic Review*, 72 (Nov. 1981), 489-94

Krysinski, W., 'Le "Littéraire" et le "paralittéraire". Fonctionnement de la citation et de l'objet chez John Dos Passos et Claude Simon', in *Carrefours de signes: essais sur le roman moderne* (The Hague, Mouton, 1981), pp. 295-311

Labriolle, J. de, 'De Faulkner à Claude Simon', *Revue de littérature comparée*, 53 (1979), 358-88

Leonard, D. R., 'Simon's *L'Herbe*: beyond sound and fury', *The French-American Review*, 1 (1976-77), 13-30

Léonard, M., 'Photographie et littérature: Zola, Breton, Simon', *Etudes françaises*, 18, no. 3 (1983), 93-108

Loubère, J. A. E., 'Views through the screen: in-site in Claude Simon', *Yale French Studies*, no. 57 (1979), 36-47

Park, R., 'Pour une nouvelle lecture de *La Bataille de Pharsale* de Claude Simon', in *Ecrivains de la modernité*, ed. B. T. Fitch, *Revue des lettres modernes*, nos. 605-10 (1981), 153-72

Park-Leduc, R., 'L'Expression métaphorique du complexe de castration dans *La Bataille de Pharsale* de Claude Simon', in *Psychanalyse et langage littéraire: théorie et pratique* by J. Le Galliot and others (Nathan, 1977), pp. 68-70

Paulhan, C., 'Claude Simon. "J'ai essayé la peinture, la révolution, puis l'écriture"', *Nouvelles*, 15-21 mars 1984, 42-45 [Interview]

Pellegrin, J., 'Les Ineffables', *Poétique*, no. 37 (1979), 1-9 [On Beckett, Lacan, Rimbaud, Claude Simon]

Pugh, A. C., 'Histoire d'une lecture — lecture d'*Histoire* ou comment lire un roman "circulaire"', in *Le Lecteur et la lecture dans l'œuvre*, Actes du colloque de Clermont-Ferrand, 1981 (Clermont-Ferrand UP, 1982), pp. 177-88

Rousset, J., '*Histoire* de Claude Simon: le jeu des cartes postales', *Versants*, no. 1 (1981), 121-33

Rousset, J., '*Histoire* de Claude Simon: les cartes postales', *Studi di Letteratura Francese*, 8 (1982), 28-33

Sarkonak, R., 'Dans l'entrelacs d'*Histoire*— construction d'un réseau textuel chez Claude Simon', in *Ecrivains de la modernité*, ed. B. T. Fitch, *Revue des lettres modernes*, nos. 605-10 (1981), 115-51

Scheller, W., '"Geschichte machen, heisst: sie ertragen." Claude Simon und der *Nouveau Roman*', *Frankfurter Hefte*, 37, no. 3 (1979), 58-66

Sherzer, D., 'Serial constructs in the *nouveau roman*', *Poetics Today*, 1, no. 3 (1980), 87-106

Simon, C., 'La Voie royale du roman', *Le Nouvel Observateur*, 6 fèvr. 1982, 74

Sims, R. L., 'Simon's *The Flanders Road*', *Explicator*, 37 (Spring 1979), 15-17

Sims, R. L., 'Myth and history — primordial memory in Claude Simon's *La Route des Flandres*', *Nottingham French Studies*, 17 (1979), 74-86

Sims, R. L. 'Claude Simon's *bricolage* technique in *La Route des Flandres, Le Palace* and *Histoire*', *Degré Second*, no. 7 (July 1983), 81-108

Sims, R. L., 'War and myth in the Twentieth Century: Drieu la Rochelle, Céline and Claude Simon', *Neophilologus*, 68 (1984), 179-92

Sykes, S., 'The novel as conjuration: *Absalom, Absalom!* and *La Route des Flandres*', *Revue de littérature comparée*, 53 (1979), 348-57

Sykes, S., '"Tintin faisant la révolution"? Novel attitudes to the Spanish Civil War', *Romance Studies*, no. 3 (Winter 1983-84), 122-34

6. REVIEWS, INTERVIEWS AND ARTICLES ON *LES GÉORGIQUES*

Anex, G., 'A bride abattue', *Journal de Genève*, 5 sept. 1981, 13, 20 [Review]

Aunette, J. P., 'La Respiration Simon', *Le Point*, 19 oct. 1981, 134-5 [Review]

Bjurström, C. G., 'Som en väldig symfoni', *Dagens Nyheter*, 17 Sept. 1981, 4 [Review]

Bosquet, A., 'Claude Simon. Des fragments de certitude', *Le Quotidien de Paris*, 22 sept. 1981, 36 [Review]

Clavel, A., 'Le Samouraï du nouveau roman', *Les Nouvelles littéraires*, 10 sept. 1981, 38-9 [Review]

Dulac, P., 'Claude Simon. *Les Géorgiques*' *NRF*, no. 347 (déc. 1981), 111-14

Duncan, A. B., 'Claude Simon's *Les Géorgiques:* an intertextual adventure', *Romance Studies*, no. 2 (Summer 1983), 90-107

Eribon, D., 'Fragments de Claude Simon', *Libération*, 29-30 août 1981, 20-22 [Interview]

Ezine, J.-L., 'Un Air de famille', *Les Nouvelles littéraires*, 10 sept. 1981, 39

Fydal, F., 'Le Temps de l'écriture. *Les Géorgiques* évidemment', *Franc-Tireur*, no. 1 (nov.-déc. 1981), 19 [Review]

Gallaz, C., 'Claude Simon. La guerre, la terre, l'écriture et la menuiserie', *Tribune*, 22 nov. 1981 [Interview]

Garcin, J., 'A la tribune officielle', *Les Nouvelles littéraires*, 10 sept. 1981, 39

Guissard, L., 'La Composition de l'histoire', *La Croix*, 18 sept. 1981, 6 [Review]

Haroche, C., 'Claude Simon, romancier', *L'Humanité*, 26 oct. 1981, 15, [Interview]

Holter, K., 'Revolusjon og landbruk', *Dagbladet*, 2 januar 1982, 4 [Review]

Marissel, A., 'Romanciers français. Le plus grand', *Réforme*, 16 janv. 1982, 9

Marre, J.-C., 'Les Géorgiques de Claude Simon', *L'Indépendant*, 18 sept. 1981

Mertens, P., 'Claude Simon. *Les Géorgiques*. Description fragmentaire d'un désastre', *Le Soir*, 20 oct. 1981

Nuridsany, M., 'Claude Simon: une maturité rayonnante', *Le Figaro*, 4 sept. 1981, 16 [Review]

Piatier, J., 'Claude Simon ouvre *Les Géorgiques*', *Le Monde*, 4 sept. 1981, 11, 13 [Interview]

Piater, J., 'Les Géorgiques de Claude Simon: la terre, les hommes, le feu, le sang', *Le Monde*, 4 sept. 1981, 1, 11, 13.

Poirson, A., 'Avec Claude Simon sur des sables mouvants', *Révolution*, 22 janv. 1982, 35-39 [Interview]

Prévost, C., 'La Confiance dans les mots', *Révolution*, 11 sept. 1981, 44-46 [Review]

Raillard, G., 'Claude Simon, le temps, la mort', *La Quinzaine littéraire*, 16-29 sept. 1981, 5

Rinaldi, A., 'Claude Simon: un catalogue cousu de fil blanc', *L'Express*, 18-24 sept. 1981, 72-73

Roques, J., 'Lacombe Saint-Michel de Saint-Michel-de-Vax, personnage central des *Géorgiques* de Claude Simon', *Revue du Tarn*, no. 103 (automne 1981), 436-38

Roudaut, J., 'Les Travaux de la terre', *Magazine littéraire*, no. 178 (nov. 1981), 36-37

Rudbeck, C., 'Claude Simon och betydelsens Knutar', *Svenska Dagbladet*, 1 Sept. 1981

Salvaing, F., *'Les Géorgiques* chef-d'œuvre', *Humanité dimanche*, 11 sept. 1981, 19

Schmid, G., 'Georgicon über Simon oder Versuch, die (Post-)Moderne besser zu verstehen', *Manuskripte*, 80 (1983), 69-80

Stow, R., 'Of O. and the General's stock', *TLS*, 4 Dec. 1981, 1412

Sykes, S., *'Les Géorgiques:* "une reconversion totale"?', *Romance Studies*, no 2 (Summer 1983), 80-89

Weyergans, F., 'Un Grand-père déphasé', *Le Matin des livres*, 2 oct. 1981, 19

Wurmser, A., 'Le Guerrier des quatre saisons', *L'Humanité*, 5 oct. 1981, 12

Zeltner, G., '". . . avec une indécourageable persévérance". Ein neuer Roman von Claude Simon', *Neue Zürcher Zeitung*, 24 Sept. 1981, 37 [Review]

7. SUPPLEMENT

Birn, R., 'From sign to saga: dynamic description in two texts by Claude Simon', *Australian Journal of French Studies*, 21 (1984), 148-60

Britton, C., 'Diversity of discourse in Claude Simon's *Les Géorgiques*', *French Studies*, 38 (1984), 423-42

Duffy, J. H., *'Les Géorgiques* by Claude Simon: a work of synthesis and renewal', *Australian Journal of French Studies*, 21 (1984), 161-79

Pugh, A. C., 'Defeat, May 1940: Claude Simon, Marc Bloch and the writing of disaster', *Forum for Modern Language Studies*, 21 (1985), 59-70

Reitsma—la Brujeere, C., 'Récit et métarécit, texte et intertexte dans *Les Géorgiques* de Claude Simon', *French Forum*, 9 (1984), 225-35

Notes on Contributors

Celia Britton.
Lecturer in French, Reading University, PhD. on Nathalie Sarraute. Has published articles on Sarraute and Simon, and has also written on Butor and Robbe-Grillet.

Alastair B. Duncan.
Lecturer in French, Stirling University, PhD. on Simon. Has published a number of articles on Simon, and has also written on Robbe-Grillet and Mauriac.

Jean H. Duffy.
Lecturer in French, Sheffield University. D.Phil., 'Problems of perception and representation in the novels of Claude Simon', Oxford, 1981. Has published articles on Simon and Monique Wittig.

Michael Evans.
PhD., 'A Poetics of Claude Simon's novels from *La Route des Flandres* to *Leçon de choses'*, Warwick, 1978. Has published articles on Simon and Borges.

John Fletcher.
Professor of Comparative Literature, University of East Anglia. Publications include *Claude Simon and Fiction Now*, 1975. Currently working on a translation of *Les Géorgiques*.

Patrick O'Kane
Postgraduate student at the University of Liverpool. Preparing PhD. on the novels of Simon.

Mary Orr.
M.A., Saint Andrews. Preparing PhD., Cambridge, on the novels of Simon.

Anthony Cheal Pugh.
Lecturer in French, Durham University, PhD. on Simon. Articles on Simon and Robert Pinget. His monograph on Simon's *Histoire* was published by Grant and Cutler in 1982.

Maxim Silverman.
Lecturer in French, New University of Ulster. PhD., 'Developments in narrative techniques and practice of writing in the later novels of Claude Simon', Kent, 1981.

Stuart Sykes.
Formerly Senior Lecturer in French, Liverpool University. Author of *Les Romans de Claude Simon*, Minuit, 1979.